Treasures from the Tower of London

Treasures from the Tower of London

Patrons of the exhibition

An exhibition of Arms and Armour

Treasures from the Tower of London

Catalogue compiled by A.V.B. Norman and G.M. Wilson

1982
Sainsbury Centre for Visual Arts, University of East Anglia, Norwich
8 June–29 August 1982

Cincinnati Art Museum, Cincinnati, Ohio
9 October 1982–9 January 1983

Royal Ontario Museum, Toronto
19 March–19 June 1983

Copyright © 1982 Sainsbury Centre for Visual Arts, University of East Anglia

ISBN 0 946009 00 7 (casebound)
ISBN 0 946009 01 5 (paperback)

Produced for the Sainsbury Centre for Visual Arts by
Lund Humphries Publishers Ltd London

Designed by Mafalda Spencer
Colour photographs by Chris Ridley

Made and printed in Great Britain by
Lund Humphries, Bradford

Contents

Foreword   by General Sir Peter Hunt

Introduction

Page 1   The History of the Armouries   by Alan Borg

5   Colour Plates

21   The History of Arms and Armour

35   Catalogue

121   Select Reading List

125   Glossary

Foreword

The Tower of London, founded by William the Conqueror over 900 years ago, must always have contained an armoury, partly for the use of the successive sovereigns themselves, and partly to equip their household guards and later their armies. Over the centuries great quantities of arms and armour have been issued from the Tower Armouries, at first for use on campaign and on the tournament field, and, since the seventeenth century, also for the decoration of the state rooms of royal palaces and castles. The role of the Armouries as a museum, as distinct from an arsenal, can be traced back to the seventeenth century, but it is only now for the first time that a great loan exhibition of Armouries treasures has been allowed to leave the walls of the Tower.

Although some of the objects being lent have been chosen for their association with the history of the Armouries, the principal purpose of the exhibition – and I believe this to be important – is to show ancient arms and armour as works of art, in the context of modern museums of the fine and decorative arts, in order to dispel once and for all the idea that they are quaint and slightly comical relics from a barbaric past. They will be seen as the triumphs of functional design and of superb craftsmanship which they actually are.

We are all particularly grateful for the kindness and generosity of the sponsors who have made this exhibition possible; the Norwich Union Insurance Group who are sponsoring it at the Sainsbury Centre for Visual Arts, Norwich, and the Central Trust Company who are sponsoring it at the Cincinnati Art Museum, Cincinnati, Ohio.

General Sir Peter Hunt GCB, DSO, OBE
Constable of HM Tower of London

Introduction

That arms and armour may be viewed and understood as an art form is the principal purpose of this exhibition and its accompanying catalogue. *Treasures from the Tower of London* is an exhibition of *works of art*, triumphs of functional design and superb craftsmanship. The exhibition, shown in a museum context, illustrates the artistic excellence that earned pre-eminent rank for arms and armour designers, armourers, and craftsmen among their artist contemporaries.

The concept for this unprecedented exhibition of masterpieces was first discussed in the summer of 1976, at a meeting arranged through the kindness of Mr Ronald W. Lightbown, between Mr A.V.B. Norman (then on the staff of the Wallace Collection, London) and Mr Millard F. Rogers, Jr, Director of the Cincinnati Art Museum, in the London home of Mr and Mrs Lightbown. By April 1977, specific ideas for an exhibition of arms and armour were shared by Mr Norman (who had recently been appointed Master of the Armouries, H.M. Tower of London), Dr Alan Borg (now Keeper of the Sainsbury Centre for Visual Arts, Norwich, England, but then Keeper of Blades, Tower of London), and Mr Rogers. Enthusiasm never waned for an exhibition of this importance, and complex planning and organisation proceeded until the show was realised in 1982–3. In 1981, the itinerary was enlarged to include the Royal Ontario Museum, Toronto, providing an international trio of exhibition sites in England, the United States, and Canada.

In the 900-year history of the Tower of London, this is the first exhibition of its treasures of arms and armour ever lent beyond its walls. We are especially grateful to the Master of the Armouries for his patient attention to our proposals for this exhibition and for the continuing support and involvement he has given to every facet of its planning and fulfilment.

We acknowledge with deep gratitude those individuals and institutions that have assisted and supported this exhibition, its catalogue, and its attendant programs at the exhibiting museums in England, the United States of America, and Canada, including The Department of the Environment, particularly Sir Hector Munro, MP, and his successor Mr Neil Macfarlane, MP, as Ministers responsible for the Armouries, General Sir Peter Hunt, Constable of the Tower of London; Major General Giles Mills, Resident Governor of the Tower of London; Norwich Union Insurance Group and its Chairman, Mr Michael Falcon; Central Trust Company, Cincinnati and its Chairman, Mr Oliver W. Birckhead, Jr; The National Endowment for the Arts, Washington, DC; the staff of the Armouries, Tower of London, especially Mr Norman, Mr Guy M. Wilson, Mr I.D.D. Eaves, and Mr Peter Hammond.

Alan Borg, Keeper
Sainsbury Centre for Visual Arts
University of East Anglia
Norwich

James E. Cruise, Director
Royal Ontario Museum
Toronto, Canada

Millard F. Rogers, Jr, Director
Cincinnati Art Museum
Cincinnati, Ohio

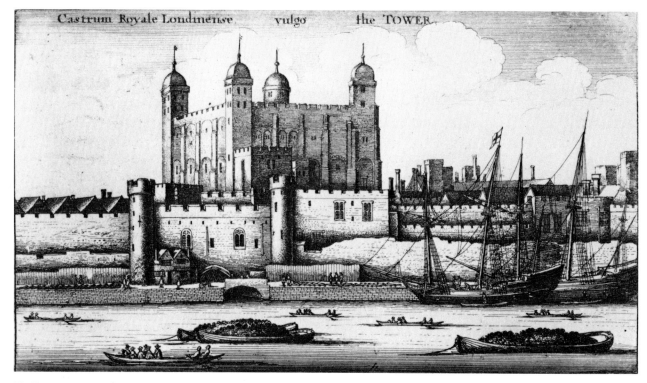

The Tower of London from the river, engraved by Wenzel Holler 1640.

The History of the Armouries

The Armouries in the Tower of London contain many remarkable treasures, but it is not always realised that the growth and evolution of the Armouries, from national arsenal to national museum, is itself a fascinating piece of history. The Armouries is the oldest museum in Britain, and the antiquity of the institution is delightfully illustrated by the fact that the administrative headquarters, as well as some of the galleries, are housed in a building called, apparently perversely since it dates from the 1660s, the New Armouries. Thus we are immediately aware that we are in the presence of an ancient organisation, since if the seventeenth century is to be considered new, what is to be called old? The New Armouries provides another clue as to the uniqueness of the institution, for the Tower contains the only great national armoury still to be housed entirely in its original buildings.

It is well known that William the Conqueror founded the Tower of London after his victory at Hastings in 1066. The first temporary stronghold was sited in the corner of the existing Roman wall of London, just to the south of the present White Tower. It was probably built only of earth and wood, but once constructed it no doubt served in part as a repository for arms. In the same way the great stone keep known as the White Tower, begun by the Conqueror around 1078 and completed before 1100, in the reign of William II, would certainly have been used as a store for arms from the beginning. In times of peace it was unnecessary and often politically unwise for the King to have too obvious or too great an armed presence in his capital city; equally, London was the key to the Kingdom, and the London mob was a volatile and dangerous body, and so it was only prudent to keep a sufficient store of arms and a suitable body of trained men in the greatest of the city fortresses. However, we can only guess at the nature, size and location of these early stores and it is not until the thirteenth century that the first evidence survives for arms held in the Tower, in the form of lists drawn up by storekeepers.

The primary purpose of any store is to provide a source of supply in time of need, and clearly the Armouries within the Tower have fulfilled this role for much of their history. In the Middle Ages matters of military supply were controlled from within the Tower by the Keeper of the Privy Wardrobe, although during the fifteenth century these duties were taken over by the Master of the Ordnance and the Master of the Armouries, whose offices were also in the Tower. In 1670 the Master of the Ordnance finally absorbed the office and duties of the Master of the Armouries. The title was only revived in 1935. The Board of Ordnance remained responsible for military supplies to both the army and the navy until it was abolished and replaced by the War Office in 1855. It was a result of this long and close involvement with military supplies that made the Armouries such a superbly documented collection; clerks and storekeepers were as careful in the past as most of their kind are today, and scrupulous lists were kept of what was issued from the Tower and what returned. Indeed, it was this clerical mentality which was partly responsible for the growth of the collection, for the insistence upon the return of issue meant that inevitably stocks of obsolete arms began to build up. This stock of obsolete equipment probably grew faster as the armed forces increased in size and became less directly the King's personal defence force. Old and out-of-date arms were often returned to the Tower, while new stock was more likely to be issued from regional depots, close to the points of manufacture.

Nevertheless, the earliest recorded visitors to the Armouries, from the fifteenth century, were foreign ambassadors who were clearly taken there to

View of the display of arms and armour, known as 'the Line of Kings', in the early years of the nineteenth century, by Thomas Rowlandson (1756–1827). (I. 45)

be impressed in much the same way as visiting dignitaries might be taken to an air base or a naval station today. Such early visitors were not seeing a museum, but an active supply depot and many were greatly impressed, especially by the number of cannon they saw. After touring the Armouries a fifteenth-century visitor would almost certainly be shown the first real tourist attraction in the Tower, the Royal Menagerie, with its collection of extraordinary beasts. The Menagerie was to remain in the Tower until the early nineteenth century, when it was transferred to Regent's Park and formed the basis of the modern London Zoo.

It is often said that Henry VIII was the last medieval king, and that the sixteenth century marks the real transition from the medieval to the modern world. Certainly for the Tower and its Armouries this was a crucial century. On the death of Henry VIII in 1547 a great inventory of his possessions, including his arms and armour was drawn up. Many of the items still in the collection can be found in this inventory, including a number shown in this exhibition. A notable example is Henry VIII's own breech-loading gun (60). Many of Henry's personal and guard arms which are included in this exhibition are listed in this inventory, as well as some older items which we can still identify. Thus the huge fifteenth-century processional sword may well be one of the two 'grete slaghe swordes' listed in 1547 (*see* 15).

The arms and armour listed in the 1547 inventory was not all at the Tower, but spread among Henry's palaces, particularly at Westminster and at Greenwich. However, there seems to have been a conscious policy in the second half of the sixteenth century to bring the remains of Henry's arsenal together at the Tower. Henry was already acquiring the semi-legendary status that he enjoys today and visitors to the Tower in the reign of Elizabeth I stared at her father's great armours and at his extraordinary experimental devices, often involving the still comparatively new small 'hand-guns' (e.g. the pistol shield in this exhibition, 11), just as they still do in the reign of Elizabeth II.

Although the Armouries in the Tower were often opened as a showplace in the late sixteenth and early seventeenth centuries, it was not until after the Civil War that these openings took on a formal and regular pattern, allowing the Armouries to be seen as a museum in the modern sense. In 1660 the restored Stuart monarchy was anxious to produce propaganda for its cause, and saw in the Armouries an ideal vehicle. What could better demonstrate the legitimacy of the monarchy than a Line of Kings, from the Conqueror to Charles II, represented by their personal armours from the Tower stores? Wooden dummies of men and horses were provided by some of the best sculptors of the day, including Grinling Gibbons and John Nost, and these were dressed in the aforementioned 'personal' armours. In fact, only the figures of Henry VIII and Charles I were shown in what were these Kings' own armours, and the other figures were arrayed in any ancient armour from the stores. Thus the very fine armour of Robert Dudley, Earl of Leicester, which is in this exhibition (3) was for many years shown in the Tower as the armour of King James I. The Line of Kings survived and was added to until, in 1826, one of the great early armour scholars, Sir Samuel Meyrick, set about removing the worst historical errors. Meyrick also poured scorn on another of the early Tower displays the Spanish Armoury, which was set up around 1688, shortly after the Line of Kings was first established and with a similar propaganda purpose. The display contained what were claimed to be weapons and instruments of torture captured from the Spanish Armada in 1588, but, like the Line, it had almost no historical foundation. Nevertheless, these two displays, together with the Grand Storehouse of modern small arms, cannon and captured trophies formed the basis of the Armouries as a showpiece for over two and a half centuries. Because it was essentially a showplace there was little real concern for the objects themselves, and many fine armours were scoured clean with a mixture of brick dust and oil, thus destroying much original decoration and surface colouring. The historical inaccuracies got worse as time went on, culminating in the erection of a tableau in 1779 showing Queen Elizabeth on horseback, accompanied by her page, addressing the troops at Tilbury. Needless to say, the Queen was shown in her armour, which included a suitably globose breastplate!

The position began to improve from 1826, when Meyrick reorganised the Line, and further changes were forced upon the Armouries in 1841, when the Grand Storehouse was destroyed by fire. By great good fortune, the Armouries were served during this period by two outstanding men, Robert Porrett and John Hewitt. Between them, they undertook major rearrangements of the collection, conducted serious historical research and most miraculous of all, persuaded the Government to allow them to purchase some of the remarkable objects which were available to collectors of the day. In this way the Tower acquired in the saleroom objects which have subsequently been identified as coming from the great armoury of Emperor Charles V. Other purchases in the nineteenth century brought a large number of extremely fine pieces into the collections, and it is heartening to know that this policy of acquisition continues in the present day. Among the works shown here there are a number, veritable Treasures of the Tower, which have been acquired within the last ten years. Such are the Monlong pistols (71), arguably the finest extant pistols to have been made in the British Isles, which were acquired for the Tower in 1975, although a public appeal was necessary to help raise the purchasing price.

Today, the Tower of London Armouries is an efficient and expanding museum – a point which is perhaps best made by someone who, like the present writer, is a former but not current member of the staff! An indication of this is provided by this exhibition, which in itself forms a new chapter in the history of the Armouries. Never before has such an assemblage of treasure from the Armouries been brought together in a cohesive exhibition, which will be seen in very different settings from the Tower of London itself.

It may not be inappropriate to end this brief introduction to the Armouries on a personal note. I had the misfortune to be present on 17 July 1974, when a terrorist bomb exploded in the White Tower, killing one person and injuring 40 others. When the horror and the ambulancemen had gone, my abiding memory is of members of the Armouries staff checking, counting, repairing, cleaning and re-displaying hundreds of historic pieces. It was as if this was just another crisis in the history of the Tower Armouries, and like all previous crises it would be overcome. There is, indeed, something to be said for being the oldest museum in Great Britain, and a storehouse which really does go back to William the Conqueror.

Alan Borg

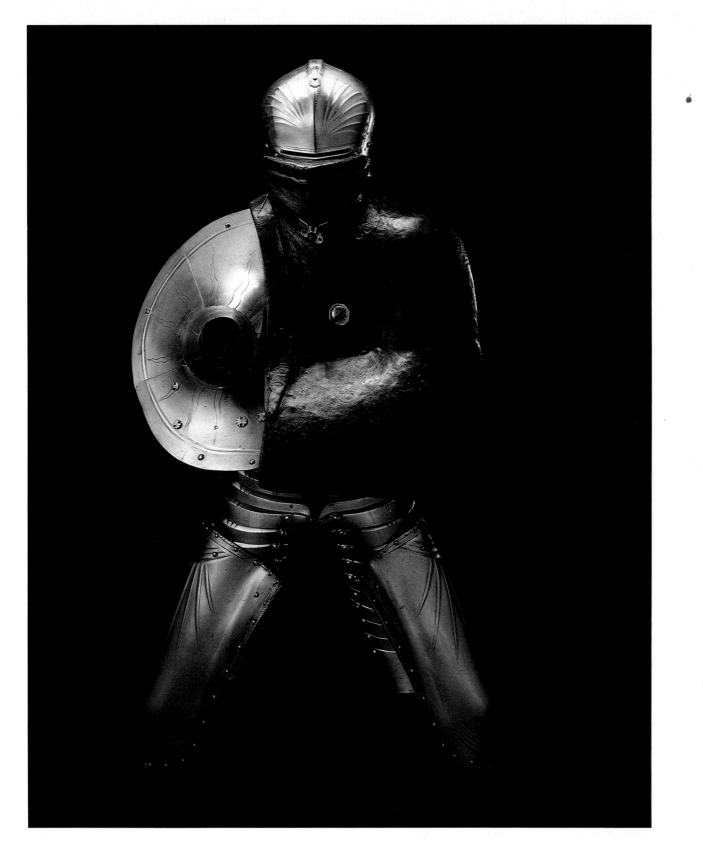

Plate 1   Tournament armour of the Emperor Maximilian I. German, about 1500 (1)

Plate II Armour for combat on foot of King Henry VIII, English, about 1520 (2)

Plate III   Armour for the tilt of Robert Dudley, Earl of Leicester, English, about 1575 (3)

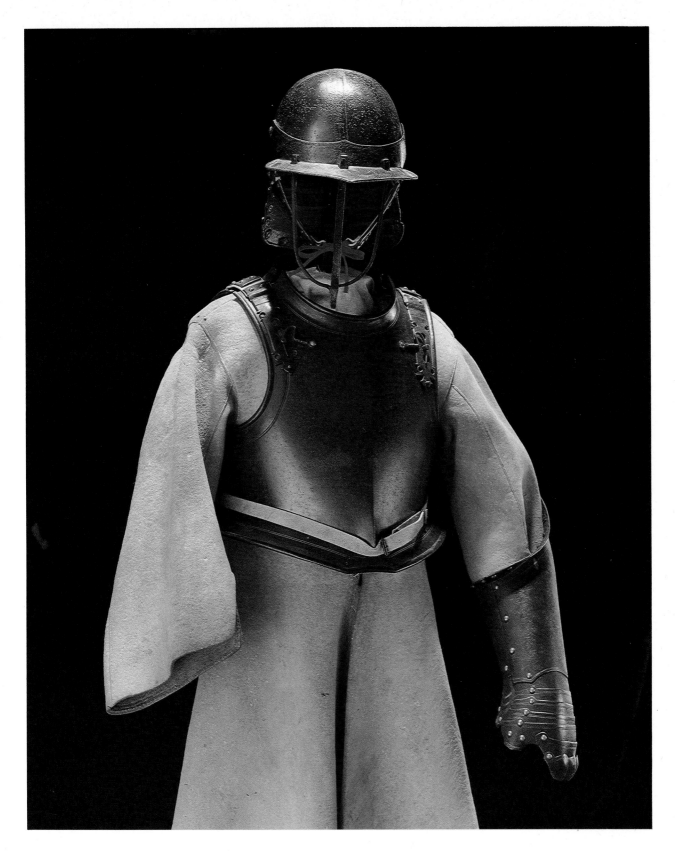

Plate V   Armour for Light Cavalry, British, about 1650 (6)

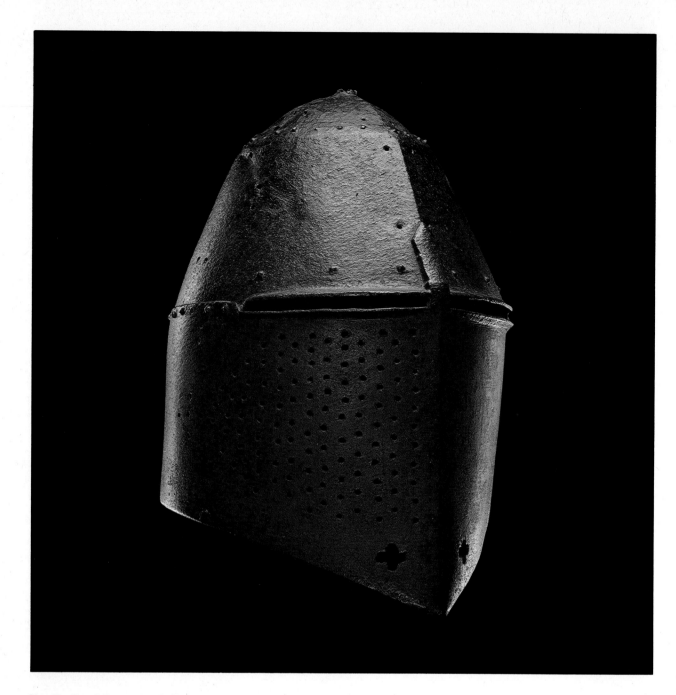

Plate VI   Great helm, possibly English, third quarter of the fourteenth century (7)

Plate VII   Parade helmet, probably Augsburg, about 1600 (10)

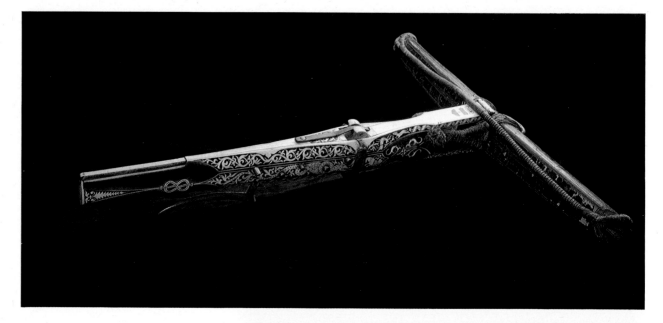

Plate VIII
Sporting crossbow, South German, early
sixteenth century (95)

Plate IX
Shield fitted with a lantern, Italian, about 1550
(12)

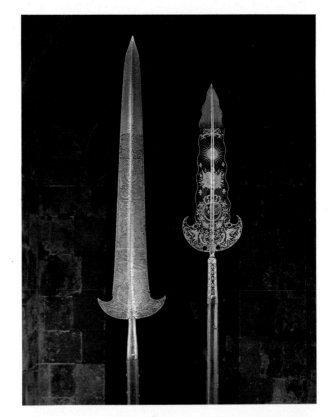

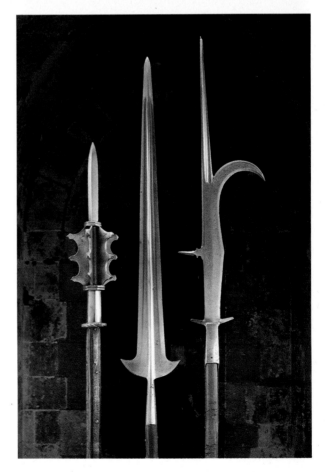

Plate X
Bronze cannon, probably Flemish, dated
1535 (92)

Plate XI (top right)
Partizans, left of Lyons, about 1650; right of
the French Royal Guard, about 1670 (58, 59)
Plate XII (below right)
left to right, Holy-water sprinkler, English;
Partizan, Italian; Bill, Italian: early sixteenth
century (54,47,53)

Plate XIII
Parts of a sporting garniture made at Tula in
Russia, about 1750 (73, 75)

Plate XIV
Powder-flask, Italian, late sixteenth century
(89)

14

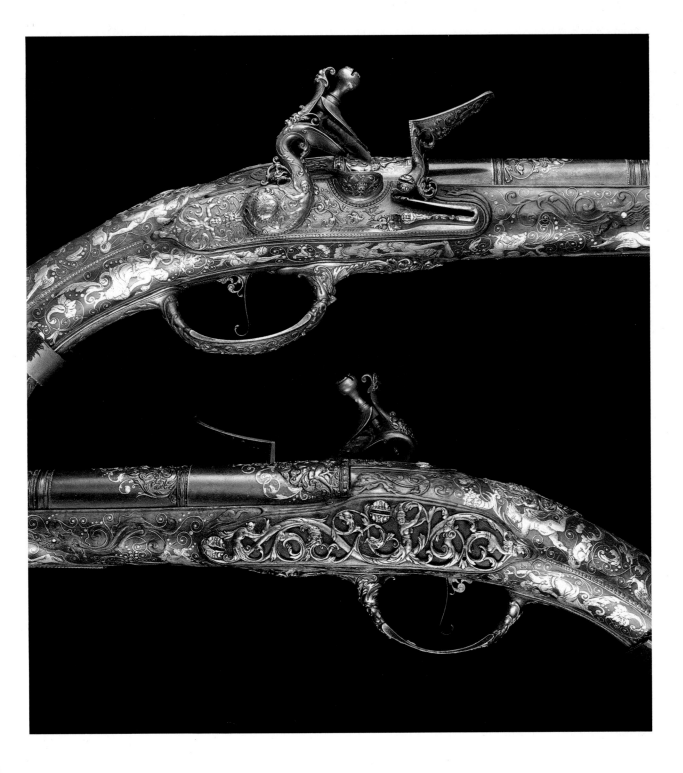

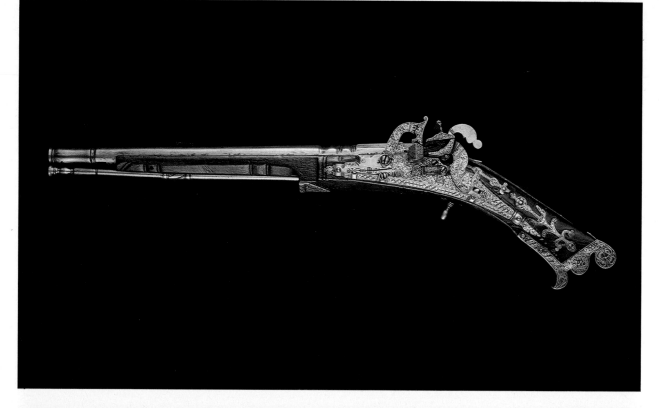

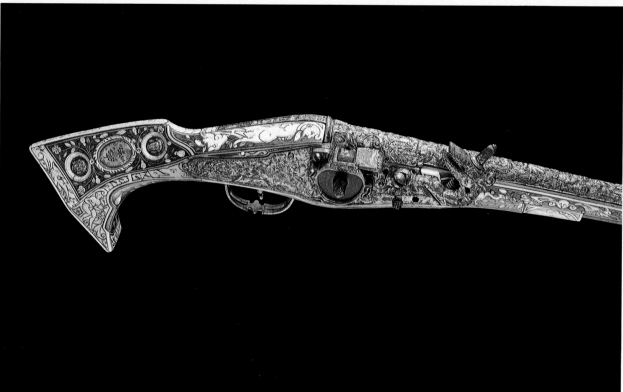

Plate XVI (above)
Snaphance pistol, Lowland Scottish, dated 1619 (64)
Plate XVII (below)
Wheel-lock pistol, probably French, about 1590 (61)

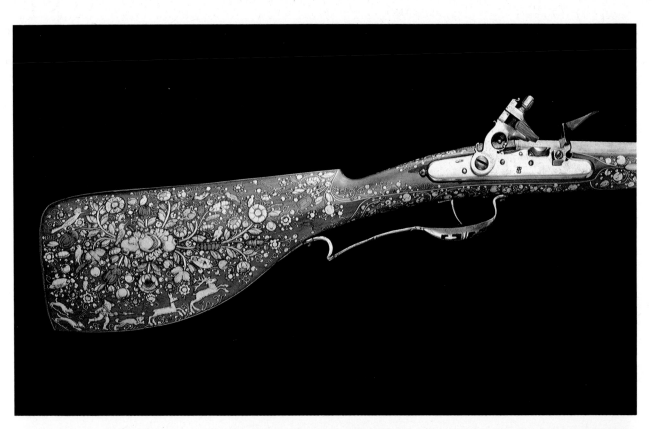

Plate XVIII (above)
Flintlock sporting gun, German (Alsace), dated 1646 (65)

Plate XIX (below)
Flintlock pistol, North African, second half of the eighteenth century (111)

17

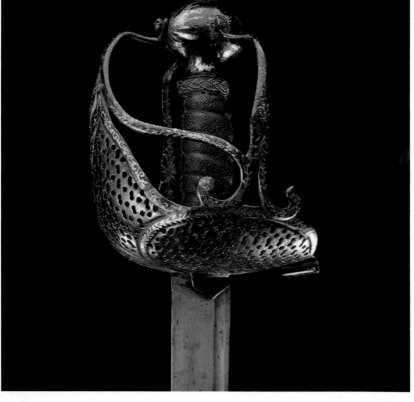

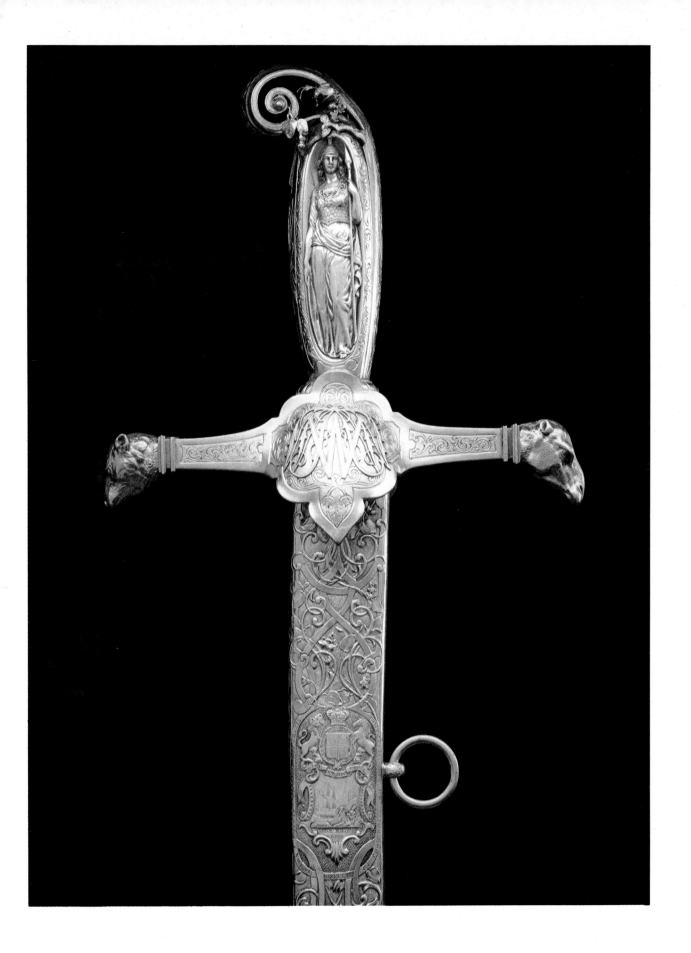

Plate XXIII
Presentation sword of Vice Admiral Lord Collingwood, London 1806/7 (37)

The History of Arms and Armour

1. Armour

The story of the development of armour is the un-ending contest between, on the one hand, the armourer seeking to improve his client's defences, and, on the other, the weapon-smith trying to devise new and better instruments for penetrating these defences.

From very early times there appear to have been body-armours made of hides or of quilted fabric. In the fifth century B.C., a form of exceptionally flexible armour, called mail, came into use. It was made of very large numbers of small iron or steel rings each linked through four of its neighbours. Worn over a quilted undergarment to prevent the rings from chafing the skin, it made a useful defence against sword cuts and arrows. However, it was less effective against the heavy blows of axes and maces, while the point of an arrow or spear might enter by bursting a ring apart. For this reason, from the thirteenth century onwards, experiments began to be made to reinforce mail with rigid plates either of hardened leather or of metal, both of which had long been used for helmets and, in antiquity, for armour generally.

At first only body-armour was used, either over or under the mail shirt. Later the especially vulnerable joints of the shoulder, knee and elbow were protected by saucer-like plates, the thighs were enclosed in quilted tubes, and the head and face were encased in a helm of steel or specially stiffened leather. These plates were designed to spread the force of a blow in order to minimise its bruising effect, and to prevent the bones from being broken, as well as to prevent the penetration of a weapon point. The impossibility of identifying a man with his head entirely concealed by his helm led to the development of a system of devices to aid in identification, known as Heraldry. The devices were painted on the side of the knight's helm or on a fan fixed to the top of it. Eventually these devices, which also appeared on the gown worn over the armour, on the shield, and on the cloth couverture of the horse, became hereditary, passing on the death of their original wearer to his son and, occasionally, if he had no male heir, to his son-in-law.

By about 1400 the mail was almost completely covered or replaced by plates. Vertically-hinged metal tubes protected the limbs, linked at the joints by narrow plates overlapping like the tail of a lobster, so that when the joints were flexed no unguarded opening would be exposed to an opponent's weapon. Wherever it was found impossible to use plates, for instance at the armhole, mail continued to be used. During the fourteenth century plate began to be used more scientifically. It was no longer employed simply as a rigid defence. By placing plates at angles a weapon could be deflected away from a vital spot. The basinet (8) is a good example; its rounded skull is designed to turn away a blow from the top of the head. Its pointed visor is intended to deflect a blow directed at the face. The positioning of the vision slits along the crests of ridges means that only a direct hit could enter the visor.

Very little medieval armour has survived, although its appearance is recorded in contemporary paintings and sculpture. For instance, Sir Richard Pembridge, the owner of another surviving helm almost exactly like No.7 is represented in stone on his tomb in Hereford Cathedral in a complete armour. A visored basinet like No.8 is worn by the effigy of Albert von

Engraving of the effigy of Sir Richard
Pembridge (died 1375) in Hereford Cathedral,
from T. & G. Hollis. *The Monumental Effigies of
Great Britain* (London 1840–2).

Limpurg, (died 1374), at Burg Komburg, Württemberg. The bronze effigy of Richard Beauchamp, Earl of Warwick, in St Mary's Church, Warwick, cast c. 453, is not only a great work of art but illustrates an armour from Lombardy as subtle in its forms and beautiful in its lines as any sculpture of its age.

By the sixteenth century, the period to which most surviving armour belongs, a complete armour for use in battle weighed only some fifty pounds and this was carefully distributed all over the wearer. The wearer could mount his horse quite normally from the ground or, at the most, from a mounting-block. The plates were designed to allow their wearer complete freedom of movement. The joints of foot-armour, for instance, are far more flexible than any human foot.

By the fifteenth century the tournament, originally a dangerous training exercise between companies of knights practising for real warfare, had become an organised sport with an elaborate series of rules. The combats themselves were only part of the pageantry accompanying the enactment of some complicated allegory, which might last many days, involving knights-errant, magicians, beautiful ladies, dragons, giants, wildmen of the woods, and dwarfs. As well as being designed to entertain the court and the common people, tournaments were an opportunity to display personal bravery, not in some distant land but before the admiring eyes of the ladies, and to show off conspicuous wealth and magnificent generosity. Sometimes interests of policy were involved as at the Field of Cloth of Gold in 1520, when Henry VIII of England met Francis I of France, and, as a result, a treaty of friendship between the two traditional enemies was signed.

The armour No. 1 was designed for tournament use in a combat between two horsemen armed with relatively sharp lances. In this case the owner was one of the foremost devisers of elaborate tournaments, the Emperor Maximilian I. No. 2 is an armour specially designed for a combat on foot between two similarly equipped opponents each armed with a pollaxe (46) in a ring called the barriers. Normally the rules stipulate how many blows might be exchanged, after which the contestants would be separated by the judges.

While the main purpose of armour was, of course, defensive, its secondary purpose was the aggrandisement of the owner. The possession of a splendid series of matching armours from one of the premier workshops of, for instance, Augsburg or Landshut, decorated with elaborate designs etched and brightly gilt against a deep blue or mirror-bright ground, was proof for all to see that the Emperor was really infinitely richer and more powerful than even the wealthiest of his subjects. Occasionally the designs were prepared by such artists as Hans Holbein the Younger, who worked for Henry VIII. Drawings by Albrecht Dürer for a silver armour to be made for Maximilian I still survive. The owner of such an armour would require it to be just as much a work of art as any other of the treasures with which he would surround himself, furniture, plate, or jewels. In a few cases the original owner of such grand armours can be identified by his devices incorporated into the decoration (3) or by means of a portrait showing the armour in wear (5).

During the late sixteenth century complete armour fell out of use because, as firearms became more effective and their users better trained, mobility was found to be a more efficient defence than additional or heavier plates. A lightly armed horseman could close with musketeers more rapidly than the heavily armoured cavalryman and was therefore under fire for a shorter time. Body-armour and an open helmet, however, survived for the pikemen of infantry regiments for most of the seventeenth century. They continued to be used by some heavy cavalry until the Franco-Prussian War (1870–71), by which time experiments had already begun in the United States to devise body-armours proof against modern firearms.

2. Swords

The sword has been man's principal weapon for much of his more recent history, at first with a blade of bronze and latterly with a blade of iron or steel. In the Middle Ages it achieved great symbolic significance; while retaining something of the magic of the dark-age smith Weland, it became the badge of

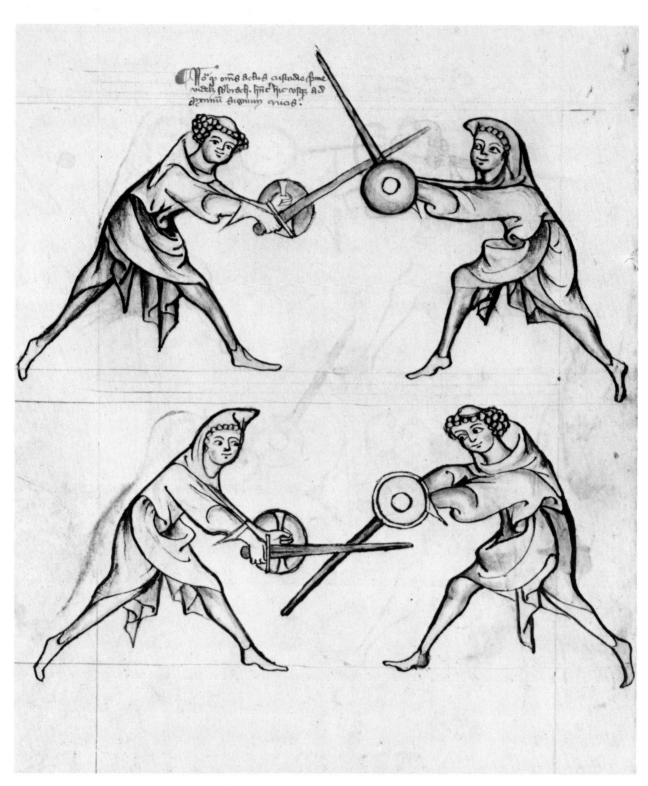

Page from a manuscript fencing manual, South German about 1300, showing the use of sword and buckler. (Ms I. 33).

the Christian knight. It was girt on the side of the young knight during the ceremony of his initiation, carried before Kings and Princes as a symbol of justice, and finally hung up over its owner's tomb with his helm and coat of arms. The early medieval sword, the blade made of a combination of iron and steel, was at first designed almost entirely for cutting and has a round point unsuited for thrusting. The more widespread use of mail armour as time went on, and perhaps some technical improvements by the blade-smith, led to the introduction of dual-purpose blades capable of delivering a lethal thrust as well as of cutting. A simple cross-guard (quillons) in front of the hand prevented an opponent's weapon from sliding down the blade onto the fingers. The solid plate defences of the fourteenth century led to the introduction of swords with narrow stiff blades, very sharply pointed to seek out the vulnerable joints of an armour and even to pierce its plates. The grip was lengthened to increase the counterbalancing effect of the pommel and thus prevent the point from drooping when a thrust was being delivered (*see*.14).

During the second half of the fifteenth century, in order to protect the usually unarmoured hand of the infantryman, the simple cross-guard (quillons) and the occasional small hook-like defence for the forefinger (*see* 13) were augmented by a variety of additional guards. These increased in complexity throughout the sixteenth and early seventeenth centuries as the disappearance of trial by combat in full armour led to the nobility settling their private quarrels by the duel with swords between unarmoured opponents. Since they were worn in civilian dress they were known as 'rapiers', from the Spanish '*espada ropera*', meaning a robe sword. Originally, these developed hilts were mounted on wide infantry blades designed for cutting. Italian fencing masters, however, taught that the thrust was more lethal than the cut, and duelling swords therefore began to be made with longer, narrower, and stiffer blades. A special dagger held in the left hand and, from about 1550 made to match the hilt of the sword, was used for parrying (*see* 42). This could also be done with the hilt of the sword. The use of a round target such as No. 12 was also taught in the fencing schools.

The open bars of the sixteenth-century hilt gave little protection against the thrust, and from the last years of the century hilts tended to have plates inserted in front to foil a point. In the early seventeenth century these grew into saucer-like plates on either side of the hand and, in Spain and Italy, into a cup-like guard through the centre of which the blade projected (*see* 25).

Under Louis XIV (1643–1715), the court of France set the fashions for all Europe. French fencing masters taught that speed was the essence of swordplay, and they advocated a light, short-bladed sword. Since parrying was to be done only with the part of the blade nearer to the hilt (the forte), there was no need for either complicated guards for the hand or a dagger (*see* 24). These survived only in areas under Spanish influence, including Mexico.

The small-swords which developed from this French weapon gradually became more pieces of costume jewelry than arms, the fashion of the decoration of their hilts changing almost annually (24, 30 & 36–8). The wearing of a sword, except in uniform or court-dress, went out of fashion entirely in Britain in the 1780s, and only a little later on the Continent.

Swords mounted in goldsmith's work and set with precious stones occur in medieval inventories, but few survive today. The mounts of Renaissance swords were sometimes designed by great artists; for instance, drawings survive by Hans Holbein the Younger, court painter to Henry VIII, for the mounts of swords and daggers to be carried out, presumably in precious metal and stones, and probably enamelling. The small-swords given away at the wedding of Louis XV in 1725 were designed by the great French architect, goldsmith, and designer, Juste-Aurèle Meissonier. The presentation sabre given to General Sir William Fenwick Williams in 1856 (39) was designed and made by Antoine Vechte, one of the greatest goldsmith-designers of the nineteenth century.

During the seventeenth and eighteenth centuries military swords continued to have heavier blades principally designed for cutting, while their hilts

Soldiers preparing to shoot fire-arrows into a besieged castle from both crossbows and hand-guns, from a South German manual on the use of gunpowder, about 1450. (Ms I. 34).

usually enclosed and protected the hand in a cage of bars (22, 26, 27, 29 & 32). In battle the niceties of the fencing school were inappropriate. For full-dress uniform, however, lighter swords were fashionable, some with hilts akin to that of the small-sword (33 & 35), others had hilts more like those of fighting swords (34). Latterly the officer's sword was intended only for defending his head, saluting, and directing his men. The sword went out of use by infantrymen, except officers, in the early nineteenth century but remained one of the main arms for cavalry until the First World War.

3. Staff Weapons

The principal weapons of the infantry in the Middle Ages and the Renaissance derive from the humble agricultural implements of the peasantry, such as the hedging bill (52 & 53) set on a long staff, originally the weapons of the poorest ranks of the levies. Some of these were later adopted for the use of royal guards and by knights when fighting on foot, once plate armour had rendered the sword less effective. By the sixteenth century the body-guards of princes and nobles, on state occasions, carried decorated versions of these weapons. The Yeoman Warders of the Tower of London, in full dress, still carry partizans decorated with the Royal Arms in blue and gold.

4. Missile Weapons

a) Bows
The principal missile weapons of the Middle Ages were the longbow and the crossbow. Of the equipment of the medieval archer nothing remains except a few excavated arrow heads and wrist-guards (bracers). Many sixteenth-century bows and arrows, however, are now being recovered from the wreck of the *Mary Rose*, one of the warships of Henry VIII, which sank while in action before his very eyes in 1545, and two recovered from this wreck in 1840 are in the Armouries (94).

The crossbow is more durable than the longbow and, because, as a hunting weapon of the nobility, it was frequently heavily decorated, many still survive (95). The bow or lath was mounted horizontally across the end of a wooden stock or tiller, which contained the catch or lock intended to hold the string in the drawn or spanned position. The great advantage of the crossbow over the longbow is that it can be carried spanned ready to shoot. Holding a bent longbow for any length of time would be impossible even for the strongest archer.

Early crossbows had laths of wood and were spanned simply by the strength of the arm. By the thirteenth century, if not earlier, the tiller was fitted with a stirrup on its fore-end. To span the bow, a hook hanging from the archer's waist-belt was placed over the bow-string. One foot was put into the stirrup and the leg straightened until the bowstring engaged on the catch. This could be released by means of a long lever lying close under the rear end of the tiller, allowing the bow-string to snap forward. The arrow or bolt was laid along the top of the tiller held in position by a cow-horn spring.

During the late twelfth century composite bows began to replace plain wooden ones. Made, like a sandwich, of wood with sinews at the front and cow- or goat-horn at the back glued together and covered with parchment, they were much stronger and springier than wooden bows. By the fifteenth century these again were being replaced by still stronger steel bows. The greater strength of these bows, both composite and steel, made mechanical devices necessary to span them, the most common of which were the windlass and pulleys, and the rack and pinion. Lighter bows were spanned by a bending lever called by modern collectors a 'goat's-foot lever'.

The missile of the crossbow was normally a short, stout arrow, called a bolt, usually with wooden or leather flights, sometimes arranged spirally to steady the bolt on its flight by making it rotate. Bows with pouches at the centre of their strings were used with either pellets or stones to shoot smaller game. The crossbow remained popular in some regions until the nineteenth century for shooting small game, and is still used today in Belgium and in Switzerland for target shooting.

View of the riverside Wharf of the Tower of London, showing Traitors' Gate and the old War Office storehouses, from *The Graphic* (London),
15 August 1885.

Since they were frequently playthings of the very rich, crossbows are often lavishly decorated. Their laths if of steel are sometimes etched, and their tillers inlaid with ivory, white stag's horn, mother of pearl, and sometimes even precious metals, with designs, for instance, of foliage, monsters, allegorical scenes, and, appropriately, hunting scenes.

b) Guns

Simple hand-guns first appeared in the second quarter of the fourteenth century, in the form of short tubes of brass or iron closed at one end. Near the closed end, the breech was pierced by a small hole through which the charge could be fired with a piece of burning slow-match or tinder. This barrel could be fixed to the end of a wooden staff and aimed rather approximately by tucking it under the arm, or by supporting it on a rest. In either case the rear end of the staff could be stuck into the ground to take the recoil.

Early in the next century, the first gun-lock appeared, the matchlock, giving the gunner's right hand more freedom while he took aim. A simple Z-shaped lever was pivoted at its centre on the side of the staff or stock. By pulling up the rear of the lower arm of the Z a piece of burning cord held at the forward end of the upper arm could be brought down onto the touch-hole. A movable cover now began to be used to protect the powder lying in the touch-hole from wind and rain, until just before the moment of firing. A much improved version of this device survived on military weapons until about 1700. It was inexpensive and easy to repair in an age when few had any experience at all of even the simplest of mechanical devices. It survived in the Orient until the middle of the nineteenth century (107).

By the end of the fifteenth century the simple straight shaft on which guns were mounted had developed into a shaped stock capable of being held to the cheek for sighting.

Early in the sixteenth century a type of lock, called a wheel-lock, was developed, based possibly on a mechanical tinder-lighter. The spark for the ignition was caused by a piece of iron pyrites scraping against the serrated edge of a rapidly rotating wheel made of steel. The wheel was set on the face of the lock-plate with its axle at right angles to the plate, and with its top edge projecting through the bottom of the powder-pan which lay alongside the touch-hole. A powerful V-spring lay along the lock-plate, usually on the inner face, with its upper end fixed, and its lower end attached to the axle of the wheel by a short length of chain similar to modern bicycle chains. A key, called a spanner, placed over the outer end of the axle and turned about three-quarters of a turn wound the chain around the axle, thus compressing the V-spring. The wheel was then locked automatically, by means of a sear, until the moment came to fire. A little fine powder was poured into the pan on top of the wheel, and covered by a sliding pan-cover. The pyrites held in a pair of jaws at the end of a long arm pivoted near the forward end of the lock-plate was lowered onto the top of the pan-cover. Pulling the trigger released the wheel. As it began to revolve the pan-cover was opened automatically allowing the pyrites to fall onto the sharp edges of the moving wheel. The resultant sparks ignited the powder in the pan and then, via the touch-hole, the charge in the breech. Locks of this sort, expensive, easily broken or disordered, and requiring an expert gunsmith to repair them, are usually found on the sporting guns of the aristocracy, as well as on the pistols of cavalry on which a matchlock would have been intolerably unhandy. A gun of this sort lavishly decorated in all its parts, and with a complicated mechanical lock containing perhaps some newly invented gadget, was an ideal medium to display the conspicuous consumption and the interest in art, allegory, and science so necessary for the Renaissance prince (61).

In the sixteenth century the manufacture of guns was usually the result of co-operation between members of quite different craft guilds. A member of the blacksmiths, would make the barrel, and a locksmith the lock while a member of one of the woodworkers' guilds would provide the stock. For guns of high quality intended for the gunrooms of the aristocracy the assistance of a goldsmith might be required to enrich the barrel and lock, and to provide decorated mounts. The decoration of the woodwork might be left to the man who made the stock. Alternatively, a specialist inlayer of furniture might be

The display of arms and armour on the top floor of the White Tower at the end of the nineteenth century, from *The Graphic* (London), 15 August 1885.

called in, who might use engraved pattern books as his source or even, occasionally, specially commissioned designs (69). One or more of these craftsmen might sign their work or at least stamp it with a punch bearing their trade-mark. By the following century gunmakers' guilds had appeared in many towns, and they normally held a monopoly locally in the manufacture and sale of all guns and gun-parts. Nevertheless, for any exceptionally lavish order specialist designers and decorators would still have to be called in; for instance, a professional engraver who would be equally at home working either on watch-cases or on table-silver as on gun-locks, or a professional chiseller who might normally decorate cane-handles, sword-hilts, or snuff-boxes. A few centres also had a brisk trade in the export of gun-parts; Brescia, for instance, exported parts particularly in the seventeenth century, as did Spain in the eighteenth. Gunmakers mounted these in stocks of their own local fashion.

Most early firearms were loaded from the muzzle, the powder and lead ball being pushed down from the fore-end and then held in place by a firmly fitting wad. This was a particularly lengthy process in the case of rifles, invented early in the sixteenth century, since the bullet had to be forced down the barrel against the grip of the rifling. In order to speed up loading, experiments were made with breech-loading: No.60 is one of the only two survivors of the large group of breech-loading guns owned by Henry VIII. No.11, a gun-shield of one of Henry's guards, is also a breech-loader. In these cases probably a number of pre-loaded cartridges would be carried. The insuperable disadvantage of all these early breech-loaders was the impossibility of making a gas-tight breech which meant that part of the force of the discharge was lost. In addition, after only a few rounds had been fired, excessive fouling might prevent the breech from closing.

Sometime during the first half of the sixteenth century a new ignition system was invented, simpler and therefore less expensive, and stronger and therefore less vulnerable to damage by mishandling. It was based on the flint and steel struck together used domestically to light fires. The steel was on an arm pivoted on the face of the lock-plate, and could be lowered over the top of the pan to form a vertical wall above the powder. The chisel-edged flint was held in the jaws of an arm, called the cock, pivoted on the side of the lock-plate. The cock was pulled back against the force of a strong V-spring and was automatically locked in position. When the trigger was pressed the cock was released and snapped forward striking the flint against the steel with a glancing blow which threw it forwards and sent a shower of sparks into the powder in the pan. In a few cases the pan-cover had to be opened by hand, but it usually opened automatically as on the wheel-lock. This system, known as the 'snaphance', is found on most early British and Dutch firearms, but was soon superseded by the flintlock described below. The snaphance lock retained its popularity in many Mediterranean countries for much longer, and survived in North Africa well into the nineteenth century.

Early in the seventeenth century this relatively simple lock was improved, apparently by French gunmakers, both in its internal mechanism, and by making the steel project from the rear edge of a pivoted pan-cover so that the pan was opened when the steel flew up on being struck by the flint. This new system, called the 'flintlock' by modern students, to distinguish it from the snaphance system, remained the principal form of ignition both for sporting and military firearms (see 65–6, 68–74, 77, 79–81, 83, 97–102, 111) until the first quarter of the nineteenth century, being gradually improved both in safety and in efficiency as the years passed. At the very height of its perfection it was superseded by the percussion-lock pioneered by the Reverend A.J. Forsyth, Minister of Belhelvie in Aberdeenshire, who for a time had his workshop within the walls of the Tower of London. The system at its simplest consisted of the detonation by means of a small hammer of a priming charge consisting of a small quantity of a fulminate in close proximity to the main charge in the breech. After very many experiments the detonating compound was placed in the base of a cartridge and the modern centre-fire and rim-fire cartridges were born.

Gun-stocks of the sixteenth century tended to be rather clumsy. In the majority either the butt rested along the right cheek for aiming, while the strength of the arms only took the force of the recoil (*see* 60), or, alternatively, it curved down to rest on the right breast (*see* 61). The French gunmakers developed a lighter and much more convenient form of stock which rested against the shoulder. This relieved the strain on the arms allowing the gun to be manoeuvered more easily and thus making it possible for the first time to shoot birds on the wing. France's dominant position in the fashionable world of the day ensured that this form of stock would be adopted all over Europe. The modern gun-stock developed directly from it. No.69, a gun made by Bertrand Piraube of Paris about 1785, no doubt in reality the result of the co-operation between the Royal Gunmaker and the best available designer, perhaps Jean Bérain himself (1637–1711), a silversmith, engraver, woodcarver, and steel-chiseller, can be compared with No.84 made by Lepage-Moutier of Paris and exhibited in London at the Great Exhibition in 1862. Both are examples of the work of the foremost artist-craftsmen of their day.

After about 1780 the simplicity and restraint of English design began to affect fashions all over Europe. The gunmakers of London then reached the zenith of their powers producing weapons noted for their extreme efficiency and characterised by the simplicity of their decoration and the elegance of their lines and proportions. The criteria of excellence were balance in the hand and efficiency in action, as shown, for instance, in the set of pistols by H.W. Mortimer (79).

A.V.B. Norman

King Phillip I of Castille, and 'old' King Henry VII of England, from the fictionalised autobiography of the Emperor Maximilian. *Der Weisskunig*, of about 1517.

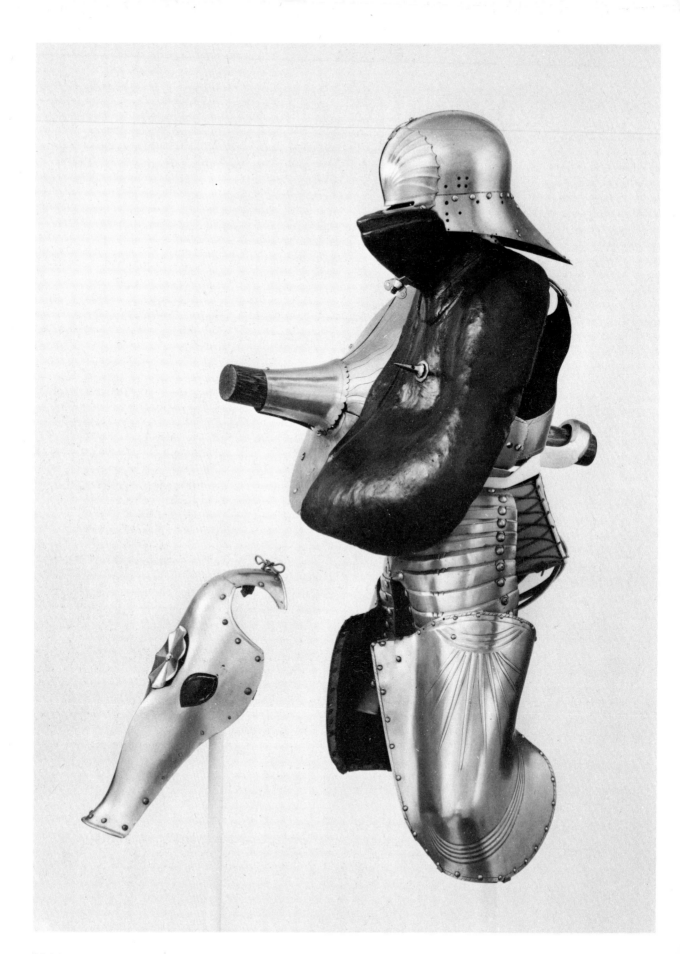

Catalogue

Note:
The scale of the photographs varies

1 (pl. I)

Tournament armour (*Rennzeug*) of the Emperor Maximilian I

German, the sallet probably Augsburg, late fifteenth century, the remainder
about 1500. The shaffron, vamplate, and 'sockets', although of similar date,
probably came from different armours in the Imperial Armoury.

The Emperor Maximilian I (1459–1519), from whose armoury these pieces
originally came, was the son of the Emperor Frederick III. His own marriage
to Mary, the heiress of Burgundy, and that of his son Philip to Joanna of Castile
and Aragon brought great territorial possessions to the Habsburg family and
linked Spain with the Holy Roman Empire under his grandson Charles V. He
succeeded as Emperor in 1493. He did much to improve the machinery of law
enforcement after the baronial wars of his father's day. He raised a standing
army of *Landsknechte*, and improved the Imperial artillery. He was the ally of
Henry VIII in the war with France in 1513 and made him several gifts of
armour parts of which are still in the Tower. He spent much of his time
devising elaborate court ceremonies, including tournaments, intended to
evoke a long-past and heroic age. This armour, intended for use in a friendly
combat between two riders, normally in the open field, armed with relatively
sharp lances (45), derives from the sort of equipment used by light cavalry in
the German lands. The saddle was without a rear cantle since the aim was to
unhorse one's opponent. A well-aimed blow striking the brow or the
vamplate caused the loose plates to fly off giving the illusion of broken
armour flying in the air in the way described by the chivalric poets.

Provenance: the Imperial Armoury, Vienna; the collection of William Randolph Hearst; purchased
by the Armouries in 1952 with the help of a grant from the National Art-Collections Fund and the
Pilgrim Trust.

Long-tailed sallet pierced with a single sight above which are two fluted plates lightly held in place
by a bolt at each side and a spring on top. A row of small holes around the lower edge indicate that
this helmet originally had an applied decorated border. Chin-defence (bevor), bolted to the
breastplate, with a protruding bolt at the centre for the attachment of the leather-covered
grandguard which protects almost the whole of the upper part of the body. A bolt with a pointed
head, pierced for a tommy-bar, secures the grandguard to the breastplate, which in turn is bolted
to a saltire-shaped backplate by means of hinged shoulder-straps of steel and hinged locks at the
sides. The very asymmetrical breastplate is heavily boxed at its lower right corner for the lance-
rest and the queue which together support the lance. To the lower edge of the breastplate is bolted
a waist-plate, and six heavy skirt lames supporting a pair of heavy knee-length articulated thigh-
defences (tassets). The back and breast each has riveted to its lower edge a plate supporting both a
leather corset to strengthen the wearer's hips and straps to pass between his legs.
The large hand-guard (vamplate) for the lance is composed of an inner plate with three outer plates
attached to it by bolts. The upper two of these fly off if struck by an opponent's lance. The
decoration of these plates consists of flames radiating from the lance-socket.
A pair of shield-like 'sockets' (*Dilgen*) decorated with a spray of embossed flutes, hung loosely
over the saddle one on each side to protect the thighs.
Head defence for the horses (shaffron), the eye-holes embossed but not pierced to prevent the
animal from swerving during the charge.
A combination-tool (not illustrated) accompanying the armour combines turn-screw, spanner, and
tommy-bar.

Weight: armour, 65 lb 14 oz (29.88 kg)   vamplate, 12 lb (5.44 kg)   'sockets': right 7 lb 3 oz (3.26 kg)
left 8 lb 4 oz (3.74 kg).

Literature: C.R. Beard 'Armours from St Donat's Castle in the collection of William Randolph
Hearst, I', *Connoisseur*, CIII, 1939, pp. 3–9, fig. XI; A.R. Dufty and A.N. Kennard, 'Arms and armour
from the Hearst collection acquired for the Tower of London Armouries', *Connoisseur*, CXXXI,
1953, pp. 23–30, figs I and II; Dufty & Reid, *European armour in the Tower of London*, HMSO 1968,
pls VIII, IX, CXXXIII, and CXLV.
(II 167)

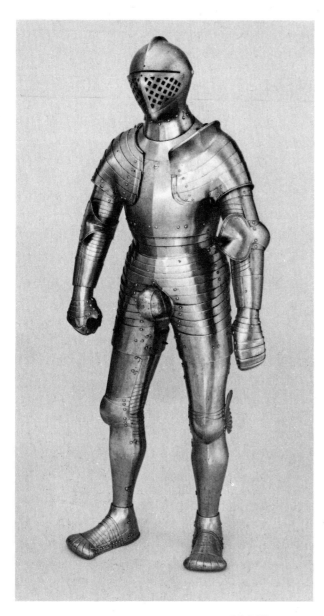
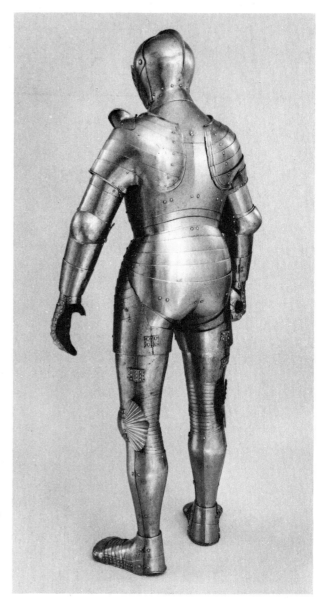

2 (pl. II)

Armour for combat on foot of King Henry VIII
English, made in the Royal Workshop at Greenwich, about 1520, under the
Master Armourer Martin van Royne.

This is one of four surviving armours of this type made for friendly combat on
foot in the barriers with axes. All the parts are locked together and yet are so
articulated that the movement of the wearer is not impeded except by the
weight of the steel. In 1515 Henry, in emulation of his foreign rivals, had
established an armour workshop at his Palace of Greenwich, staffed by
Germans and Flemings. This is one of the earliest surviving examples of
their work. It was originally black and 'rough from the hammer', as it is
described in an inventory of the Tower Armouries taken in 1683. The present
bright surface is due to regular cleaning for the last 300 years.
Although it is not identifiable in Tower inventories before that of 1611 this
armour undoubtedly formed part of the old Royal Armoury and must have
belonged to Henry VIII himself (1509–47) the founder of the present Tower
Armouries. The young King was a great sportsman, a first-rate archer, a
wrestler, and adept at all the different combats making up a tournament,
whether on horse or on foot. Some idea of the King's magnificent physique
can be gained from this armour. Martin van Royne was appointed Master of
the Royal Workshop at Greenwich when it was first set up in 1515. 'Old
Martyn' was still employed there in 1540, although by 1536 he seems to have
been superseded as Master Armourer by Erasmus Kyrkener, previously his
leading armourer.

Complete armour cap-à-pie of bright steel, consisting of a close-helmet rotating on the gorget which is bolted to the back and front of the cuirass; a one-piece visor, now lacking the brow-reinforce, pierced with two horizontal sights and on each side with a trellis of angular holes for ventilation; a pair of symmetrical shoulder-guards (pauldrons), that on the right lacking its removable standing-guard (haute piece); a pair of articulated guards of narrow lames for the armpits hooked into the cuirass; a pair of symmetrical arms with narrow horizontal lames protecting the inside of the elbow-joint; a pair of mitten gauntlets, originally made to lock round the haft of a weapon; a cuirass hinged on the left and with locking devices on the right, articulated to a breech of plate completely enclosing the hips and completed by a large cod-piece in front; a pair of leg harness completely encircling the legs locking inside the breech at the top and inside the broad-toed plate shoes (sabatons) at the lower end. These last are embossed to resemble the contemporary broad-toed shoe.

Dimensions: Height, 6 ft 2 in (187.9 cm)   Weight, 94 lb (42.64 kg).

Literature: F. Grose, *Treatise on ancient armour and weapons*, London 1786, pls 19 & 20; J.R. Planché, *Some accounts of the armour and weapons exhibited . . . at Manchester in 1857*, London 1857, pp. 21–2; Viscount Dillon, 'A suit of armour in the Tower of London', *Archaeological Journal*, LXIX, 1912, pp. 74–87; Sir Guy Laking, *A Record of European armour and arms through seven centuries*, III, London 1920, pp. 223–5, figs 1018–19; Dufty & Reid, *European armour in the Tower of London*, pls XII, XIII & LXXXVII; C. Blair, 'New light on four Almain armours, I' *Country Life*, December 1959, pp. 17–20, fig. 9; H.R. Robinson, *Armours of Henry VIII*, HMSO 1977, pp. 16–17.

Exhibited: Manchester Art Treasures, 1857; Armour made in the Royal Workshop at Greenwich, London 1951, No. 1.
(II 6)

3 (pl. III)
Armour for the tilt of Robert Dudley, Earl of Leicester
English, made in the Royal Workshop at Greenwich, probably about 1575, under the Master Armourer John Kelte.

The initials R.D. found on various parts of this armour are those of its owner Robert Dudley, Earl of Leicester (1532?–88), Master of the Horse and favourite of Queen Elizabeth I of England. He was the fifth son of John Dudley, 5th Duke of Northumberland and Earl of Warwick, who was Master of the Armouries from 1533 to 1544. He received the Order of the Garter in 1559 and the Order of St Michael in 1566. He commanded the English Army in the Low Countries from 1585 to 1587, and the great muster at Tilbury against the coming of 'the Invincible Armada' in 1588. It is possible that this splendid armour was made for the entertainment given by Lord Leicester at Kenilworth in 1575 for the visit of the Queen.

After the death of the only surviving legitimate son of Henry VIII, Edward VI, the succession passed to his sisters, first Mary and then Elizabeth, which meant that there was no demand for royal armours. However, the craftsmen at Greenwich continued to make fine armours both as diplomatic gifts and for members of the Court who were permitted to buy a warrant to have an armour made by them. Some of these can be recognised in sixteenth-century portraits, for instance an earlier armour of Robert Dudley was recorded in a drawing of him by Federigo Zuccaro, made in 1575. Others are recorded in the original album of designs used by the Greenwich armourers, now in the Victoria and Albert Museum, from which the drawings of this armour are unfortunately missing. The album also indicates what pieces one can expect to find included in a Greenwich garniture. In the case of the Leicester armour, which at present has only pieces for the tilt, there would probably also have been at least a field visor, and possibly a wrapper for the face, a left field-gauntlet, a light field breastplate, and perhaps an open-faced helmet for use as a light horseman.

In the tilt, a form of friendly duel between horsemen armed with lances, the contestants rode at each other along opposite sides of a barrier (the tilt) passing left side to left side. Additional reinforces were therefore fitted to the left side of the armour, each overlapping the one behind it, to deny lodgement for the point of the lance.

John Kelte, first recorded as a hammerman in the Greenwich workshop in November 1552, had been apprenticed to John Lindsay, who was twice Master of the Worshipful Company of Armourers of London. Himself a Freeman of the Company, he succeeded Erasmus Kyrkener as Master Workman at Greenwich in 1567, as the first Englishman to hold this office. He resigned in 1576.

Provenance: this armour is recorded as being mounted on a wooden horse 'In the greene Gallerie' at Greenwich Palace in 1611, and is first recorded at the Tower in 1660.

Complete armour cap-à-pie consisting of a close-helmet designed to rotate on the gorget, and fitted with a two-piece visor, the right side of the lower visor pierced with numerous circular breaths and fitted with hooks to prevent the parts from opening accidentally; a pair of asymmetrical shoulder-defences (pauldrons) and arms, the left elbow fitted with a pin for a reinforce; a right field-gauntlet with lobated edge to the cuff and separately laminated fingers, the left hand protected by the heavy tilt-gauntlet (main-de-fer), with a deep cuff and two lames to guard all the fingers (both thumbs are recent replacements made in the Armouries workshops); a cuirass with four staples for the missing lance-rest, closed by hinged steel shoulder-straps and a lock on each side; hinged to the skirt-plate are two large laminated hip-defences (tassets); a pair of complete leg-harness, with short single-lame thigh-defences (cuisses), the greaves laminated at the ankle and with holes for the missing spurs.

The armour, which was formerly blued or russet, is decorated with broad, slightly sunk bands, etched and formerly fire-gilt with narrow strapwork enclosing allegorical figures, masks, and trophies. The badges of the bear and ragged staff of Warwick occur in six places, in three of them with the badge and collar of the Order of the Garter and in three with the badge and collar of the French royal order of Saint Michael. The areas between these bands are crossed diagonally by sunken ragged staves charged with crescents, alternating with scrolled leaves. At the centre of the upper part of the breastplate is the badge of the Order of the Garter represented as if hung on a neck-chain and flanked by the initials RD.

Dimensions: Height, 70 in (177.8 cm)   Weight, 72 lb (32.66 kg).

Also exhibited are the two reinforces for the tilt en suite with the armour, the large passguard for the left elbow and the grandguard for the left shoulder and the front of the face; and the defence for the horse's head, the shaffron, which is decorated with the bear and ragged staff of Warwick Weight: grandguard, 12 lb 4 oz (5.56 kg)   passguard, 4 lb 1 oz (1.84 kg) shaffron, 5 lb 3 oz (2.35 kg).

Literature: Laking, *Record*, IV, pp. 19–23, fig. 1102; Dufty & Reid, *European armour in the Tower of London*, pls XLIV, XLV, and XCIV.

Exhibited: Armour made in the Royal Workshops at Greenwich, London 1951, No. 11; The Elizabethan Image, London 1969/70, No.59.
(II 81)

4
Pikeman's corslet and pot
British, probably Greenwich, about 1625–30.

Companies of Pikemen armed with pikes of from fifteen to sixteen feet long continued to be employed to defend musketiers from the attacks of cavalry until the adoption of the bayonet in the second half of the seventeenth century which made the musketier his own pikeman.
A number of similar armours are preserved in the Armouries. Since they are of superior quality to those of the common soldiers it is possible that they are those of the royal bodyguard, the Yeomen of the Guard. This corps was divided into pikemen and musketiers in 1627 (C.R. Beard, 'The clothing and arming of the Yeomen of the Guard from 1485 to 1685', *Archaeological Journal*, LXXXII, 1925, pp. 91–148). The price of these particular armours is not known, but in 1631 a common pike armour cost £1.2s., or £1.4s. if lined with red leather. The brown colour of the steel, known as russetting, was produced by controlled rusting. In 1631 this treatment cost four shillings.

Provenance: at one time in the collection of Sir Guy Laking, Keeper of the King's Armoury; bought by the Armouries in 1974 from the collection of Dr Richard Williams.

Consisting of an open-faced helmet (lacking cheek-pieces), a gorget, a cuirass closed over the shoulders and under the arms by leather straps reinforced with iron plates (restored), and a pair of large one-piece hip-defences (tassets) attached by means of hinged mounts of gilded iron. The decoration consists of iron-headed rivets arranged in rows and rosettes, and an embossed pattern of chevrons. All the edges are followed by two rows of rivets flanking a raised beading. The surface of the metal is russeted.

Weight: pot, 3 lb 5 oz (1.5 kg)   gorget, 1 lb 15 oz (8.79 kg)   breast, 6 lb 2 oz (2.78 kg) back, 5 lb (2.27 kg)   left tasset, 2 lb 11 oz (1.22 kg)   right tasset, 3 lb 1 oz (1.39 kg).
(II 269)

5 (pl. IV)
Field armour of the future King Charles II
Dutch, before 1644.

This armour is depicted in wear by Charles Prince of Wales, when fourteen years of age, in a portrait by William Dobson painted in Oxford in 1644 (property of Her Majesty The Queen). It closely resembles that shown in many Dutch portraits of the period, but is unusual in being cap-à-pie. Improvements in firearms, in gunpowder, and in musketry drill meant that the cavalryman had become increasingly vulnerable to infantry equipped with firearms. Heavier armour could have been made but its weight would have impeded the movement of the cavalry. The solution chosen therefore was to discard parts of the armour to increase mobility. First the greaves were replaced by boots, later the tassets and arm-defences were also discarded (*compare* 6).
At the time of his portrait wearing this armour the Prince of Wales was the nominal commander of a troop of Lifeguards. He had already been under fire at the battle of Edgehill (1642) and was later to lead the Scottish Army in action at the second battle of Worcester (1651). Charles II was the last British monarch, as far as we know, to have complete armour and, because of the decline in its use, it was during his reign (1660–85) that the post of Master of the Armouries was abolished. A harquebus armour of his brother James VII and II is also in the Armouries.

Complete horseman's armour cap-à-pie, consisting of a close-helmet with a two-piece visor, the lower part pierced on each side by S-shaped breaths, and gorget plates; a cuirass made high at the neck rendering a conventional gorget unnecessary, closed by leather shoulder-straps and waist-straps; an articulated skirt defending the rump is hinged at each side to short, articulated tassets at the front which close round the waist by means of a strap and buckle at the centre, the whole resting on the flange at the waist of the cuirass; the tassets can be extended to below the knee by means of articulated extensions to the lower edges of which are attached the greaves and articulated foot-defences (sabatons); a pair of rowel spurs permanently riveted on; symmetrical shoulder-defences (pauldrons) permanently attached to the symmetrical arm-defences by turning joints; and field gauntlets with pointed cuffs and separately articulated fingers. All the plates are decorated with narrow bands of incised and punched foliage, fire-gilt.

Dimensions: Height, 57 in (144.8 cm)   Weight, 43 lb (19.5 kg).

Also exhibited are the plates of the saddle and the defence for the horse's head (the shaffron) as well as the exchange pieces for use when serving on foot, consisting of a pair of short tassets, a round target, and an open-faced helmet.
(VI 117, 118 and 59 respectively)

Weight: saddle, 2 lb 12 oz (1.25 kg)   shaffron, 3 lb 2 oz (1.42 kg)   tassets, 2 lb 10 oz (1.19 kg)
target, 4 lb 13 oz (2.18 kg)   helmet, 2 lb 10 oz (1.19 kg).

Literature: Laking, *Record*, V, pp. 26–8, pls 1442 and 1443; Dufty & Reid, *European armour in the
Tower of London*, pls LIII and CXLIX.
(II 90)

6 (pl. V)
Armour for Light Cavalry (harquebus armour)
British, about 1650.

This is a typical example of the equipment of a cavalry officer after the
abandonment of complete armour. The buff leather of the coat is sufficiently
thick to turn the edge of a sword and stop bullets at extreme range. The
breastplate and skull at least are probably proof against pistol shots at closer
ranges.

The troopers wore similar equipment but of poorer quality. A buff coat at this
period cost between five and ten pounds, the helmet of the ordinary trooper
about seven shillings and his cuirass about thirteen shillings. The type of
cavalry equipped in this way were usually armed with a sword, a pair of
pistols, and a short gun called a harquebus, hence the name given to this sort
of armour.

Provenance: the helmet was presented to the Armouries by Mrs Vivian Ambler in 1958, the
remainder was purchased from the collection of Dr Richard Williams in 1974.

Open helmet consisting of a hemispherical skull to which is riveted an articulated neck-guard of
four lames and, at each side, a cheek-piece (restored); a peak supporting a triple-barred face-
guard is pivoted at each side of the skull. The body-armour consists of a coat of buff leather with
deep skirts to protect the thighs, and long, rather loose sleeves, over which is worn a cuirass with a
broad waist flange and with a rather high neck, making a gorget unnecessary. It closes by means of
a waist-belt, and leather shoulder-straps guarded by iron plate, the decorative ends of which fit
over pins on the breast where they are secured by sneck-hooks. The left elbow-gauntlet, now lacking
its finger lames, was worn to protect the bridle hand; the right hand being protected in action by the
sword hilt.

Weight: helmet, 8 lb 9 oz (3.88 kg)   breast, 10 lb 15 oz (4.96 kg)   back, 13 lb 1 oz (5.93 kg)
gauntlet, 2 lb 5 oz (1.05 kg)   coat, 10 lb (4.54 kg).
(Helmet IV. 332   cuirass III. 1475   gauntlet III. 1476   coat III. 1445)

7 (pl. VI)
Great helm
Possibly English, third quarter of the fourteenth century.

This helm, which has no known provenance, but may come from an English
church, is a recent acquisition chosen to fill a gap in the collections. Another
helm, apparently from the same workshop, now in the Royal Scottish
Museum, Edinburgh (Reg. no. 1905.489) at one time hung over the tomb of Sir
Richard Pembridge, KG (died 1375), in Hereford Cathedral where it formed
part of his funeral achievements. The only other comparable helm is that of
the Black Prince (died 1376) which still forms part of his funeral achievements
in Canterbury Cathedral. Representations of similar helms in stone are found
under the heads of English sepulchral effigies of as early as about 1350, for
instance that at Aldworth, Berkshire, ascribed to Nicholas de la Beche,
Constable of the Tower. It is therefore possible that the Pembridge helm may
have been of some age at the time of its owner's death. He was a veteran of
the battles of Sluys and Poitiers.

Constructed from three plates of plain steel; the low conical crown-plate being overlapped by the
truncated cone of the skull-plate which is itself overlapped by the side-plate. This last, forming the
wall of the helm, is a one-piece tube and is pierced on the right side at the front only by numerous
circular breaths, and at the front near the lower edge on each side by a cross-shaped opening for
the attachment of a toggle-ended chain, by which the helm was secured to the breastplate. The
lower edge of the side-plate is turned in over a wire to strengthen it. The sight is formed by a gap
between the skull and the side-plate, the edges of which are turned out to form a glancing surface
away from the eyes. It is spanned at the centre front by an upward extension of the side-plate. The
front of the helm has a marked vertical keel running up the centre and over the crown. It is much
less pronounced down the centre of the back.
The helm is pierced at twenty-one places with pairs of holes for the attachment of the lining,
mantling, and crest. Three holes arranged in a triangle at the nape of the neck presumably
originally secured the strap by which the helm was attached to the back-plate. The small dome-
headed rivets are of steel, with pointed shanks clinched over inside. Several of the rivets along the
top of the side-plate have diamond-shaped iron washers inside to secure the lining. Three of the six
rivets over the brow have similar washers. The centre of the crown-plate has been roughly
pierced, presumably for the spike on which a funerary crest could be fixed when the helm became
part of a funeral achievement.

Dimensions: Height, 14 in (35.6 cm)   Weight, 5 lb 8 oz (2.49 kg).

Literature: D. Spalding, 'An unrecorded English helm of c. 1370', *Journal of the Arms and Armour Society*, IX, 1977, pp. 6–9.
(IV 600)

8

Visored basinet
German, or North Italian, about 1370–80.

This is a typical fighting helmet of the sort illustrated in numerous paintings and sculpture, in the second half of the fourteenth century, both in the German lands and in North Italy, when the great helm was going out of fashion for use in the field.

Provenance: from the collection of Karl Gimbel (sold R. Lepke, Berlin, 30 May–3 June 1904, lot 38, pl VII), and that of Sir Edward Barry, Bart., presented to the Armouries in 1945 by the National Art-Collections Fund.

Egg-shaped skull, the lower edge and the sides of the face are bordered by a row of small holes for the lining, and by a row of thirteen steel tubular vervelles for the cord attaching the mail tippet (aventail) which originally guarded the neck and shoulders. Above these have originally been riveted five small triangular plates set vertically to deflect blows away from the leather band attaching the aventail. Three of these are now missing. There are five holes arranged vertically on the brow for the attachment of the visor, that in the centre filled with a waisted stud. Vizor of conically pointed form; the horizontal slots forming the sights are strongly boxed and have serrated edges; the snout which is pierced with numerous circular ventilation holes on each side has a similar boxed sight on its underside. The vizor is hinged to a long, narrow plate fitted over the stud on the brow, but the pivoted bar to lock the two pieces together is now missing.

Dimensions: Height, 10 in (25.4 cm)   Weight, skull, 3 lb 2 oz (1.42 kg)   visor, 1 lb (0.453 kg).

Literature: G.F. Laking, 'Mr Edward Barry's collection of arms and armour . . .', *Connoisseur*, XI, 1905, pp. 67–75, illus. on p. 68; Laking, *Record*, I, fig. 278; 'A rare helmet for the nation', *Connoisseur*, CXV, 1944, pp. 57–8; Dufty & Reid; *European armour in The Tower of London*, 1968, pl. LXXIII.
(IV 467)

9

Open-faced helmet (sallet)
Italian, Milanese probably by Domenico dei Barini known as Negroli, about 1490–1500.

This helmet is one of a group of weapons and parts of armour from the castle of Rhodes presumably from a store abandoned by the Knights Hospitaller when the island was captured by the Turks in 1522. A mark similar to that on this helmet occurs on a tilt helm in the State Hermitage, Leningrad (Z.O. No. 3361), and on a sallet belonging either to Philip I of Spain, or to his father the Emperor Maximilian I, now the Royal Armoury at Madrid (1898 *Cat.* No. D 12). has been attributed to Domenico dei Barini detto Negroli, a Milanese armourer of the late fifteenth and early sixteenth centuries.

Provenance: purchased from the castle of Rhodes in 1866, for the Museum of Artillery, Woolwich (1873 *Cat.* No. XVI. 2270), and transferred to the Armouries in 1927.

Forged from a single piece of steel, of graceful form with curved face-opening and low comb pierced at the top by a circular hole. A row of eighteen holes encircles the skull, some still filled with rivets with domed heads capped with brass to attach the lining. The lower edge has an applied gilt-brass border chased with egg-and-dart and acanthus-leaf motifs. On the brow, immediately above the face opening, is riveted a plume-holder consisting of a tube faced with a brass shield of *testa di cavallo* form engraved with a vase of flowers on a hatched ground. A maker's mark is stamped on the back of the skull, consisting of two keys in saltire, the bits downward, all under an open coronet, probably originally of five fleurons. The whole helmet now has a dark-brown rust patina.

Dimensions: Weight: 4 lb 12 oz (2.15 kg)   Height, 9.5 in (24.2 cm)

Literature: C. de Cosson, *Archaeological Journal*, XXXVII, 1881, No.19, pl. II, 16; Laking, *Record*, II, fig. 344; C. ffoulkes, 'Armour from the Rotunda, Woolwich, transferred to the Armouries of the Tower, 1927, *Archaeologia*, LXXVIII, 1928, p. 67, pl. XII, 5, and fig. 4; Dufty & Reid; *European armour in The Tower of London*, p. 12 & pl. LXXVII.

Exhibited, Helmets and Mail, London 1881, No.19, fig. 16.
(IV 424)

10 (pl. VII)
Open-faced parade helmet (burgonet)
German, probably Augsburg, about 1600.

A very similarly decorated cap-à-pie armour in the Electoral Armoury at Dresden was bought in Augsburg in 1602 for the Elector Christian II of

Saxony, and is dated 1599. The plaques in this case show equestrian figures (E. Haenel, *Kostbare Waffen aus der dresdner Rüstkammer*, Leipzig 1923, p. 10, pl. 15). Heavily decorated armour of this sort was intended, like modern full-dress uniforms, for use in parades and for display and would not have been worn on campaign.

Provenance: purchased by the Armouries in 1826.

Constructed of four plates of steel; the high combed skull made in two pieces, and on each side a hinged cheek-piece. The russeted surface of the steel is finely embossed and chased with bunches of fruit and flowers interspersed with birds and insects, all on a matted ground. Around the neck-flange the decoration includes grotesque dolphins. Reserves free from embossing at the back, front, and sides of the skull, and on the comb and cheek-pieces, are overlaid with applied ornament cast in copper, chased, and fire-gilt, consisting of warriors in Roman armour backed by trophies of arms, all framed in elaborately flowing strapwork. The mount at the back also acts as a plume-holder. The edges of the helmet are followed by applied decorative borders also of gilt copper.

Dimensions: Height, 13 in (33 cm)   Weight, 5 lb 3 oz (2.35 kg).

Literature: Laking, *Record*, IV, pp. 180–81, fig. 1262; Dufty & Reid, *European armour in the Tower of London*, pl. XCVII.
(IV 154)

11
Shield or round target with matchlock gun

The shield itself may be Italian about 1540, but the pistol appears to be a later addition although made before 1547 when the post-mortem inventory of Henry VIII records thirty-five 'targetts steilde w^t gonnes' as already being at Westminster. By 1676 there were sixty-six in the Tower, presumably the balance having come from one or more of Henry's other fortresses or palaces. These shields have been connected with one of the inventions offered to the King by Giovanbattista da Ravenna and company in 1544, but so far the evidence that the offer was taken up is lacking (C. Blair, *European armour*, London 1958, pp. 182–3). They were probably intended for the use of Henry's personal guard, but would seem to be more impressive than practical.

Provenance: Tudor Royal Armoury. Tower Armouries since 1676.

Of wood plated with russet steel, of circular and slightly convex form. The front surface is covered by eight segmental plates, the outer edges of which are overlapped by a convex rim of eight plates and the inner edges by a large central disc. The central plate is etched in line and fire-gilt with a scene apparently representing Mucius Scaevola before Lars Porsena. The segmental plates are decorated with scroll-work apparently in gold paint. There are traces of a fringe around the outer edge.

A smooth-bore pistol with a spirally fluted barrel projects through a shield-shaped mount riveted over the upper edge of the central disc. Just above the barrel is a small round sighting hole. Inside is a movable breech, containing a rechargeable steel cartridge, fired by means of a simple matchlock operated by a cord. Below the breech is a carrying-handle.

Dimensions: Diameter, 19.0 in (48.3 cm)   barrel, 6.5 in (16.5 cm)   calibre, 0.495 in (38 bore)
Weight, 10 lb 14 oz (4.93 kg).

Literature: Dufty & Reid, *European armour in the Tower of London*, pl. CXL.
(V 39)

12 (pl. IX)
Shield or round target fitted with a lantern
Italian, about 1550, the lantern probably about 1600.

The usefulness of a lantern fitted to a shield in the narrow, unlit streets of an Italian city at night is obvious, but it could also have been used to dazzle an opponent. Most sixteenth-century fencing books give instructions for the use of sword and round target. Angelo, in *The School of Fencing*, London 1787, gives instructions on the defence against sword and dark lantern (pp. 96–100 and pl. XLV).

Provenance: bought by the Armouries at the Ralph Bernal sale, Christie's, 27 March 1855, lot 2405.

Of circular convex form, made of wood covered on both sides with canvas coated with gesso. The outer surface is painted black with a large circular gold panel in the centre within a border of small circles containing formalised flower heads; a band of similar gold decoration on a larger scale follows the outer edge. Any design which originally existed on the central panel is now obliterated. The inner side of the shield is painted *en grisaille* with a scene showing Camillus attacking the Gauls at the moment when the authorities of the city of Rome were weighing out the tribute which they had demanded. The painting is surrounded by a border of gilt arabesques, a similar border framing the rectangular arm-pad of green velvet which is lined with fine tow. The arm-straps (brases) are missing. At some period a rectangular opening has been cut in the upper edge of the

shield in which has been inserted a cylindrical iron lantern fitted with a rotating shutter with horn window. Each louvre of its conical top is ornamented with a human head in cast brass (two now missing).

Dimensions: Diameter, 22.25 in (56.5 cm)   Weight, 7 lb (3.18 kg).

Literature: Dufty & Reid, *European armour in the Tower of London*, pl. CXLII; L.G. Boccia & E.T. Coelho, *Armi bianche italiane*, Milan 1975, pls 434–5.
(V 16)

13
Sword
Probably Italian, before 1432, possibly late fourteenth century.

An inscription on the blade records that this sword was part of the booty captured by the Egyptian Sultan Barsbêy during his successful attack on John III King of Cyprus in 1424, and was then laid up by him in the Arsenal at Alexandria.
Since the type of guard present on this sword is known to have been in use by the middle of the fourteenth century and an identical blade in the Royal Ontario Museum, Toronto (No. 976) has an inscription recording that it was laid up in the Arsenal at Alexandria in 1368/9, it may be that the Armouries' sword was quite old at the time of its capture. This hilt represents the very beginning of the development of the complex guards which were popular in the sixteenth and early seventeenth centuries.

Provenance: the Arsenal at Alexandria; the collection of the Baron de Cosson; the collection of William Randolph Hearst; bought by the Armouries in 1952 with the help of grants from the National Art-Collections Fund and the Pilgrim Trust.

Blackened iron hilt consisting of hollow, discoid pommel and straight spatulate cross-guard (quillons), of rectangular section, flattened in the plane of the blade. The forward quillon is divided, the smaller, hook-like branch curving to meet the edge of the blade and forming a guard for the forefinger. Wooden grip bound with cord.
Straight, two-edged blade with central fuller; stamped with a mark consisting of the gothic letter M and a cross conjoined, and engraved at the ricasso with an Arabic inscription, which reads in translation: 'Unalienably bequeathed by al-Malik al-Ashraf Barsbêy, – may his victory be glorious! – in the magazines of the victorious arms in the frontier city of Sikandarîya (Alexandria), the well guarded, from what came into his ownership, in the month of al-Muharran, of the year 836'.

Dimensions: Length overall, 41 in (104.1 cm)   Length of blade, 34 in (86.4 cm)
Weight, 1 lb 11 oz (0.765 kg).

Literature: C.A. de Cosson, note in *Proceedings of the Society of Antiquaries of London*, 2 Ser. XIV, 1892, pp. 238–42; Laking, *Record*, II, fig. 667; E. Combe & A.F.C. de Cosson, 'European swords with Arabic inscriptions from the Armoury at Alexandria'. *Bulletin de la Société Royale d'Archéologie d'Alexandrie*, No.31, Alexandria 1937, pp. 13–16, No.VI, fig. 7, who give a translation of the inscription; A.R. Dufty & A.N. Kennard, 'Arms and armour from the Hearst Collection acquired for the Tower of London Armouries, I, *Connoisseur*, CXXXI, 1953, pp. 23–30, fig. XVIII; C. Blair, *European & American arms*, London 1962; fig. 5; Sir James Mann, 'A European sword of the late XIVth Century with Arabic inscription', *Eretz-Israel*, Vol. 7, Jerusalem 1963, pp. 76–7; R.E. Oakeshott, *The sword in the age of chivalry*, London 1964, pl. 39b; H. Seitz, *Blankwaffen*, I, Brunswick 1965, fig. 91; Dufty & Borg, *European swords and daggers in the Tower of London*, HMSO 1974, p. 5, pls 4e & 106; A.V.B. Norman, *The rapier and small-sword*, London 1980, pp. 32–3, pl. 4.
(IX 950)

14
Hand-and-a-half sword
Possibly English, early fifteenth-century.

This is a characteristic knightly sword with a narrow, stiff blade designed almost entirely for thrusting. Such a sword was essential once plate armour became common, making the wearer almost invulnerable to sword cuts. The first six inches just in front of the hilt are not sharpened so that the blade can be grasped by the left hand, indicating that the sword was intended for use with both hands on foot. The relatively long grip and heavy pommel, by acting as a counterbalance, prevent the point from drooping when a thrust is delivered.

Provenance: acquired by the Armouries before 1859.

Tall pommel of octagonal section, long tang, straight cross-guard (quillons) of square section. The grip is missing. Long, straight, two-edged blade of flattened hexagonal section at the forte and thereafter of diamond section. In heavily corroded condition.

Dimensions: Length overall, 47 in (119.4 cm)   Length of blade, 36.5 in (92.7 cm)
Weight, 3 lb 6 oz (1.53 kg).

Literature: J. Hewitt, Official catalogue, 1859, No, IX. 6, without provenance; Laking, *Record*, II, p. 254 & fig. 631, who says that it was found in the Thames; C. Blair, *European and American arms*, London 1962, fig. 34; Dufty & Borg, *European swords and daggers in the Tower of London*, p. 15, pl. 5a, 'found in the Thames near London Bridge'.
(IX 16)

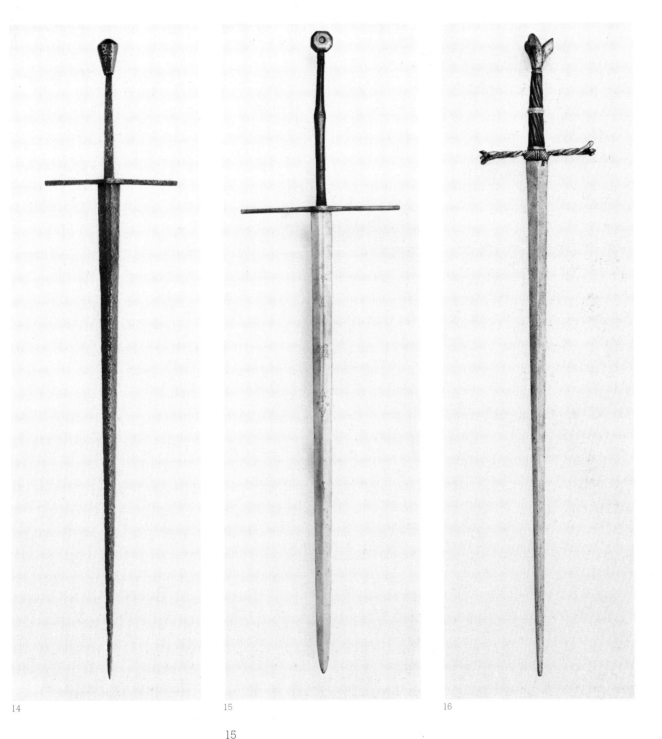

14   15   16

15
Ceremonial bearing sword
Hilt English, the blade German, Passau, early fifteenth century.

The Armouries has a second, very similar sword (Inv. No. IX. 1025). One or other of these has certainly been in the Armouries since the eighteenth century if not before, since it is illustrated by the antiquary Francis Grose in *A treatise on ancient armour and weapons*, London 1786, pl. 22. The Amouries also has the blade of a third re-used about 1600 (Inv. No. IX. 164). A similar sword in Westminster Abbey is traditionally said to be that of King Edward III (Laking, *Record*, II, fig. 707).

This was presumably one of the processional swords of the early Lancastrian Kings, either Henry IV (1399–1413) or his son, Henry V (1413–22).

Of great size for processional use. Steel hilt consisting of an octagonal discoid pommel with a shallow circular recess in each face, and long, straight cross-guard (quillons) of square section expanded slightly at the centre to take the thick tang. Massive, tapering blade of flattened diamond section with a shallow fuller extending for almost half its length; there is a series of symbols on each face at one time inlaid in brass. From hilt to point they are three pairs of parallel lines intersecting, a stylized wolf, the letter M in black letter, and a fleur-de-lis. On one face there is in addition a star of five points. Original grip of wood covered with leather with a slight swelling near its centre from which it tapers sharply towards the pommel.

Dimensions: Length overall, 91 in (231.1 cm)   Length of blade, 65.5 in (166.4 cm)
Weight, 14 lb 6 oz (6.52 kg).

Literature: H. Seitz, *Blankwaffen*, I, Brunswick 1965, fig, 102, who dates it in the last quarter of the fifteenth century; Dufty & Borg, *European swords and daggers in the tower of London*, p. 16, pl. 10a. (IX 1024)

16 (pl. XX)
Sword
North European, probably German, about 1480.

A sword with similarly decorated quillons is held by St Michael on the mid-fifteenth-century painted choir-screen in the parish church of Ranworth, Norfolk.

Provenance: formerly in the Collection of Frédéric Spitzer, the Paris dealer (1815–90). Sold Paris, Chevalier and Mannheim, 10–14 June 1895, lot 230, *repr. in cat.* Purchased by the Armouries from the Collection of William Randolph Hearst in 1952, with the assistance of grants from the National Art-Collections Fund and the Pilgrim Trust.

The hilt of gilt bronze consisting of a pommel and straight quillons chiselled to look as if they were made of three rods twisted together and splayed out at the ends. Wooden grip carved to resemble a gnarled and writhen stave, with a collar of gilt bronze at its centre.
Straight, tapering, two-edged blade of flattened diamond section, with an illegible mark stamped on each face close to the hilt.

Dimensions: Length overall, 43.2 in (109.7 cm)   Length of blade 34.9 in (88.7 cm)
Weight, 2 lb 12 oz (1.25 kg).

Literature: A.R. Dufty and A.N. Kennard, 'Arms and Armour from the Hearst Collection acquired for the Tower of London Armouries, I', *Connoisseur*, 1953, pp. 23–30, fig. XVIII; C. Blair, *European & American arms*, London 1962, fig. 49; R.E. Oakeshott, *The sword in the age of chivalry*, London 1964, pl. 46c; Dufty & Borg, *European swords and daggers in the Tower of London*, p. 15, pl. 5c. (IX 949)

17

17
Sword
Swiss or Swabian, about 1500.

Provenance: formerly in the collection of Sir Samuel Rush Meyrick, the first great English collector of arms and armour in modern times, and later in the Metropolitan Museum of Art, New York; bought by the Armouries at Christie's, 22–23rd November 1960, lot 285, *not repr. in cat.*

17 (detail)

Steel cross hilt consisting of a deep pommel-cap etched with candelabra ornament, modern wooden grip, and long, spatulate quillons of oval section, recurved at right angles to the plane of the blade, and deeply etched with inscriptions: on the outer face: AIN NVWER HAILAG HAIST GROBIAN (A new saint is called Ruffian); on the inner face: DEN WIL IETZ FIREN IEDERMAN (It is he who everyone now wants to celebrate).

Straight blade, two-edged except for the three and a half inches nearer the hilt, of flattened hexagonal section, etched near the hilt on the outside with the Virgin and St Barbara. Along a shallow fuller on the same face is the deeply-etched inscription: .LVOG. VND. SICH. DICH. EBEN. FIR. VOR. AIM. DER. DIR. SCHADEN. DON. WIL. VN. DREW. IST. YETʒ. FAST. EIL (Look around and take care only of he who will harm you. Infidelity is now [prevalent]).

The inner face of the blade is etched with foliate patterns near the hilt and along the fuller with the inscription: HEIETH. DICH: HAB. ACHT. AVF. MICH: TRVF. ICH. DICH. ICH. VERSCHNEID. DICH. (Beware, take care of me, if I catch you I'll mince you).

The dialect throughout is Swiss or Swabian.

Dimensions: Length overall, 35.4 in (89.9 cm)   Length of blade, 30.6 in (77.7 cm) Weight, 1 lb 15 oz (0.879 kg).

Literature: J. Skelton, *Engraved illustrations of antient arms and armour from the collection at Goodrich Court*, Oxford 1830, Vol. I, pl. XXII, and Vol. II, pl. CIII, No.4; Dufty & Borg, *European swords and daggers in the Tower of London*, pp. 17–18, pl. 18 b & c. (IX 1079)

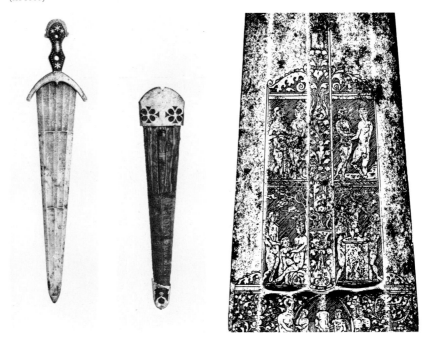

18
Short sword ('cinquedea') and scabbard
North Italian, early sixteenth century.

In Italy it was fashionable about the turn of the fifteenth century for both civilians and the more lightly armoured of the infantry to carry short swords or long daggers. Broad-bladed weapons like this, known today as 'cinquedeas', seem to have been fashionable in the years 1480 to 1520. particularly in Central Italy.

Marks like those found on this blade shaped like the capital letter T, usually with a crenellated upper edge to the crossbar, are common on cinquedeas and spears of various sorts (*see* 50). Pieces marked in this way are normally attributed to Venice, Bologna, Ferrara, or Emilia, but there is no real indication of the exact place of their manufacture (L.G. Boccia and.E.T. Coelho, *Armi bianche italiane*, Milan 1975, Nos. 206, 229, 242, 259, 261, 297, and 306).

Provenance: from the collection at Norton Hall formed by Beriah Botfield the well-known antiquary (1807–1863); presented to the Armouries by the National Art-Collections Fund in 1942.

The crescentic cross-guard of iron is edged with gilt brass engraved with a laurel wreath bound with fillets. The pattern is repeated on the arched, gilt-brass pommel-cap, the top of which is recessed to take a rectangular panel of some material now missing. The grip is formed of two scales of wood one on each face of the tang, covered in threadbare red velvet secured by silver nails. Each face is decorated with ivory stars, of which one is missing, and a copper Roman coin bearing the head of, on one side, the Emperor Trajan and on the other, the Emperor Nero. Two holes in the grip probably held the tubes with rose-window-like decoration normally found on cinquedeas. The

gap between the scales at the sides is filled by two engraved pieces of ivory or bone which continue along the top of the quillons, one of the pieces on the quillon is missing.
Broad, two-edged blade, fluted longitudinally with four flutes near the hilt, three in the middle, and two near the tip. It is etched on both sides with small naked human figures illustrating scenes the meaning of which is obscure, presumably from some as yet unidentified story. Slight traces of fire-gilding survive near the hilt. Traces of a mark resembling a capital letter T remains on one side. Scabbard of parchment covered with tooled black leather, with small sheath for a byeknife. The chape and the locket are both of steel and pierced decoratively

Dimensions: sword, length overall, 26.8 in (68.1 cm)   Length of blade, 21 in (53.3 cm)
Weight, 2 lb 9 oz (1.16 kg)   Scabbard. Length. 21 in (53.3 cm)   Weight, 10 oz (0.283 kg).

Literature: Sir James Mann, 'The Norton Hall arms and armour for the Tower', *Connoisseur.* CXI, 1943, pp. 3–11, fig, XVI; C. Blair, *European and American arms*, London 1962, fig, 63; Dufty and Borg, *European swords and daggers in the Tower of London*, p. 18, pl. 19b, 20a, and 107.
(IX 767)

19
Hunting sword
British, early seventeenth century.

Claude Blair has shown that this type of hilt is almost certainly English since a number have been found in England, and others occur in English portraits, including that of Henry, Prince of Wales, and John, Lord Harrington, dated 1603, in the Metropolitan Museum of Art, New York. (*The James A. de Rothschild collection at Waddesdon Manor, arms and armour and base-metalwork*, Fribourg 1974, Cat. 19).

Provenance: purchased for the Armouries at Christie's, 19th February 1975, lot 31, *repr. in cat.*

Hilt entirely of iron, the tubular grip made in one with a pommel shaped like the stylised head of a parrot or falcon. Small tang-button. Behind the bird's beak on each side is a projecting globular stud. Quillons of flattened rectangular section recurved in the plane of the blade, the front one forming a partial knuckle-guard. On the outside of the quillon-block is a shell curved slightly towards the blade. The hilt is engraved, and counterfeit-damascened all over in silver and gold, with foliate scrolls ending in animal heads.
Straight, single-edged blade, with a fuller near the spine and a ricasso which is engraved and gilt with foliage. An orb and cross mark is stamped in each fuller.

Dimensions: Length overall, 34.9 in (88.7 cm)   Length of blade, 30 in (76.2 cm)
Weight, 1 lb 11 oz (0.765 kg).
(IX 1424)

20
Military sabre
Hilt British, probably about 1625–30, the blade possibly Persian.

The presence of an oriental blade on a sword bearing on its hilt the arms used by several branches of the Shirley or Sherley family, is interesting because of the connection between Persia and the branch of the family established at Wiston in Sussex. Sir Anthony Shirley and his brother Robert Shirley travelled to Persia in 1598, Sir Anthony returning in 1600, Robert in 1608 having in the previous year married a Circassian. Both men acted subsequently as ambassadors from the Shah of Persia and both frequently adopted a Persian style of dress. Robert returned to Persia between 1613 and 1615 and again in 1627, dying in Persia on 13 July 1628. Sir Anthony died in Granada in 1633, having lived mainly in Spain since 1606.
However, because of the date of the hilt, this sword is perhaps more likely to have belonged to one of the sons of the third brother, Thomas, who was imprisoned in Constantinople between 1603 and 1606 for his attack upon a Turkish island, and in the Tower between 1607 and 1608 for attempting to undermine English trade with Turkey. Of his eighteen children, the most likely to have owned this sword was probably Thomas, a professional soldier, who served in the army of the United Provinces, took part in the English expedition to the Ile-de-Ré in 1627, and fought for the King in the Civil War, being knighted by him at Oxford in 1645. On the other hand if the sword belonged to a different branch of the family, another possible owner might be Sir Robert Shirley, a Royalist who died a prisoner in the Tower during the Interregnum.

Provenance: presented to the Armouries in 1978 by the Danish collector Master Goldsmith Holger Jacobsen and his family.

Hilt of iron, consisting of a pommel in the form of a blackamoor's head, a knuckle-guard, and a rear quillon curled towards the blade, supporting on the outside a side-shell curved towards the pommel and linked to the knuckle-guard by a scroll-guard. The shell is pierced and chiselled with

vigorous foliage scrolls surrounding a coat of arms, which also occurs on the knuckle-guard; paly of six, a canton ermine, with as a crest, placed on a barred helmet, a blackamoor's head, and the motto LIBERTATE ET PATRIAE. The inner shell has been replaced, apparently in the working life of the sword, by a smaller shell pierced with trellised decoration. Quillon-block chiselled with acanthus scrolls, and the end of the quillon with a monster's head.
Curved, single-edged blade with plain flat faces, in the Persian style.

Dimensions: Length overall, 35.5 in (90.2 cm)　　Length of blade, 30.125 in (76.2 cm)
Weight, 2 lb 3 oz (0.992 kg).
(IX 1800)

21　　　　　　　　　　　　　　　　　22　　　　　　　　　　　　　　　　　23

21
Rapier
The hilt British, the blade possibly North Italian, by Vicenzio Ginam, about 1634–50.

A number of blades signed by different members of the Ginam family are recorded but nothing is known about where they worked.
This hilt and that of No. 23 are characteristic of those worn by civilians and soldiers off duty in the period leading up to the British Civil Wars and the years of the Wars themselves, 1642–6 and 1650–4 (A.V.B. Norman, *The rapier and small-sword*, London 1980. pp. 162–3).

Provenance: presented to the Armouries by Miss E. Mallett, 1947.

Steel hilt, now bright, consisting of a pommel, a pair of quillons recurved in the plane of the blade supporting a knuckle-guard which is linked by a loop-guard on each side to a side-ring on the quillons both inside and outside the hand. The blade passes through the centre of a hexafoil saucer the edges of which are linked to each quillon by a short strut and to each of the side-rings by a pair of small winged terminal figures. The decoration includes foliage, grotesques, strapwork, and human heads some of which appear to represent Charles I and his Queen, Henrietta Maria, all chiselled in relief and pierced. Traces of silver-plating and fire-gilding remain. Wooden grip bound with a basket-weave of copper wire and steel foil.
Narrow, straight, two-edged blade of flattened hexagonal section changing to diamond section toward the point, with a fuller at the forte in which is stamped: VICENCIO GIИAM.

Dimensions: Length overall, 46.5 in (118.1 cm)　　Length of blade, 38.7 in (98.3 cm)
Weight, 2 lb 4 oz (1.02 kg).

Literature: Dufty & Borg, *European swords and daggers in the Tower of London*, p. 20, pl. 28d.
(IX 883)

22 (pl. XXI)
Military backsword
British, about 1640.

This sword is traditionally that of Oliver Cromwell. Two marks on one side of the blade appear to have been made by musket balls.
Oliver Cromwell (1599–1658), a country gentleman of Puritan persuasion, became Member of Parliament for Huntingdon in 1628, and sat in the Long Parliament as member for Cambridge. At the outbreak of the first Civil War in 1642 he served as a Captain of Horse in the Parliamentary Army, rising by 1644 to be Lieutenant-General. He commanded the left wing of the Parliamentary cavalry at Marston Moor (1644), and the right wing at Naseby (1645). In 1649 he was appointed Lord-Lieutenant and Commander-in-Chief in Ireland, where he subdued the Royalist forces with great severity. He defeated the Scots at Dunbar in 1650. Appointed Lord Protector in 1653, he held the balance between the Army, the true centre of power in the country, and Parliament, more narrowly Puritan in outlook.

Provenance: Museum of the Royal United Service Institute (1908 *Catalogue*, No.209); acquired by the Armouries in 1963.

Basket-hilt of so-called 'Mortuary' type, japanned black, with foliage and trophies on the pommel and guard painted in gold, consisting of a bud-shaped pommel; pierced boat-shaped guard, with short, pointed langets, one broken off; three knuckle-guards attached by screws to the pommel, the outer and inner one each linked to the main knuckle-guard by a scroll-guard. Wooden grip covered with fish-skin; copper wire turk's-head ferrules. Straight single-edged blade, with single fuller near the spine.

Dimensions: Length overall, 38.2 in (97 cm)   Length of blade, 31.9 in (81 cm)
Weight, 2 lb 6 oz (1.08 kg).

Literature: Dufty & Borg, *European swords and daggers in the Tower of London*, pp.46–7, pl.46a & b.
(IX 1096)

23

Rapier and scabbard
The hilt and scabbard British, the blade probably German, about 1640–55.

The bilobate shell-guard suggests a late date within the group to which this hilt belongs (*compare* No.21).
Sahagun, the correct spelling of the name on this blade, is the surname of at least four Toledo swordsmiths, Alonso I and his sons Alonso II, Juan, and Luis. However, the name was widely forged by the swordsmiths of Solingen and this blade is probably an example of their work.

Provenance: from Norton Hall, the collection of Beriah Botfield; presented to the Armouries by the National Art-Collections Fund in 1942.

Steel hilt consisting of a pommel, a pair of quillons recurved at right angles to the plane of the blade, supporting a knuckle-guard which is linked by a scroll-guard to a side-ring mounted on the quillons outside the hand. The blade passes through the centre of a bilobate shell-guard which is linked to each of the quillons by a short strut and to the knuckle-guard inside the hand by a scroll-guard. The hilt is chiselled with stylised acanthus foliage in relief, blued and fire-gilt. Wooden grip covered in white ray-skin and spirally bound with gilt wire; turk's-head ferrules.
Straight, slender two-edged blade of flattened hexagonal section, stamped in a fuller on each face of the forte: X SAHAGOM X.
Scabbard of wood (not illustrated), covered with tooled leather and with steel top-locket and chape.

Dimensions: Sword: Length overall, 47.2 in (119.9 cm)   Length of blade, 39.5 in (100.3 cm)
Weight, 2 lb (0.907 kg)   Scabbard: Length, 40 in (101.6 cm)   Weight, 3 oz (0.085 kg).

Literature: Sir James Mann, 'The Norton Hall arms and armour for the Tower', *Connoisseur*, CXI, 1943, pp. 3–11, fig. XVIIIc; Norman, *The rapier and small-sword*, London 1980, pl. 85.
(IX 794)

24

Small-sword and scabbard
Hilt North European, the blade German, probably Solingen, dated 1651.

According to family tradition, this sword belonged to Charles Worsley, Major-General under Cromwell, who commanded the detachment which expelled the Long Parliament in April 1653. Worsley died at St James's on 12 June 1656 and was buried in Henry VII Chapel in Westminster Abbey.
The date of the hilt is confirmed by the appearance of a very similar one in the portrait of Cornelis van Aerssen by Adriaen Hanneman, dated 1658 (Amsterdam, Rijksmuseum, No.1104).

Provenance: Wing Commander Carill-Worsley by family descent; bought by the Armouries in 1975.

Hilt of iron now russet, decorated overall with arabesques in gold counterfeit-damascening. Bud-like pommel of facetted section, with prominent tang-button. Guards of flattened rectangular section, consisting of knuckle-guard and single rear quillon, mounted on a quillon-block supporting small arms of the hilt. Separate double shell-guard. Grip of wood covered in basket-work of silver-gilt wire and foil; copper ferrules.
Straight two-edged hollow-ground blade of flattened diamond section, etched in line and fire-gilt with figures and inscriptions; on the outside *Vincere aut mori* and *Si Deus Pro/Nobis/quis Contra nos/1651* above the figure of a mounted trooper; below this is a classicising figure identified by the words *Achilles Grae/cus*. On the inside the inscriptions are *Fide sed Cui vid* and *Regere seipsum/Summa Est sa/Pientia* above a trooper on horseback, and a classicising figure identified as *Anibal Car/tagus* (Hannibal).
The scabbard is of wood covered in leather, with its original locket, decorated *en suite* with the hilt, and a modern chape. The separate belt-hook is missing.

Dimensions: Sword: Length overall, 39.2 in (99.5 cm)   Length of blade, 32.5 in (82.5 cm)
Weight, 1 lb 5 oz (0.595 kg)   Scabbard: Length, 33.3 in (84.6 cm)   Weight, 4.5 oz (0.127 kg).

Literature: A.C.N. Borg, 'The Sword of Major-General Charles Worsley', *The Antiquaries Journal*, LV, 1975, pp. 413–4, pl. LXXXVIII.
(IX 1428)

25
Cup-hilted rapier
Italian, probably Brescian, about 1660–70.

This type of hilt is usually called Spanish because it is frequently depicted in Spanish portraits. However, no hilt of this precise form signed by a Spanish maker is recorded, those that are signed invariably bearing the names of Italian makers, Brescian or Milanese. The style of decoration of this particular hilt and of a few others like it, being very similar to the steel inlay on Brescian firearms of the period, has led to the suggestion that they may also be of Brescian manufacture. (A.V.B. Norman, *The rapier and small-sword*, London 1980, p. 178).

Provenance: the collection of William Meyrick; presented to the Armouries by Miss E. Mallet in 1947.

Steel hilt consisting of a pommel, long straight quillons supporting a knuckle-guard and two arms of the hilt their ends linked by an oval plate to which the cup is screwed. The cup has its edge turned outwards to form a trap for the point of an opponent's sword (*rompepuntas*). This part is chiselled in low relief, while the remainder of the cup is delicately pierced and engraved with foliage patterns involving hunting scenes and grotesque animal masks. The pommel, quillon ends, and the centre of the knuckle-guard are writhen. The wooden grip is bound with copper wire and has steel ferrules and four longitudinal strips. Narrow, straight, two-edged blade, of flattened hexagonal section with a short fuller at the forte.

Dimensions: Length overall, 50 in (127 cm)   Length of blade, 42.5 in (107.9 cm)
Weight, 2 lb 2 oz (0.963 kg).

Literature: *Illustrated catalogue of weapons and detached specimens of armour from the collection of William Meyrick, Esq*, London 1861, No. 49; Dufty & Borg, *European swords and daggers in the Tower of London*, p. 21, pl. 33b.
(IX 887)

26
Military sword of King George II
The hilt probably British, about 1700, the blade German, Solingen, by Johannis Brach.

King George II (1683–1760) was the last British Sovereign to lead his troops in action, which he did with great personal courage at Dettingen in 1743. This sword belongs to an earlier part of his life, but it could have been used in his first campaign in 1708 when he led a cavalry charge at Oudenarde. He did not live to see the victorious outcome of the Seven Years War (1756–63) which with the battles of Plassey and the Heights of Abraham eventually secured India and Canada respectively for the British Empire.
A number of swordsmiths named Johannis Brach are recorded in Solingen at different times. Two other Brach signatures, that of Jan and Arnoldt, are recorded with the mark of a unicorn walking along.

Provenance: the Royal Collection, transferred to the Armouries in 1938 by H.M. King George VI.

Steel hilt, consisting of pommel, knuckle-guard and short rear quillon supporting on each side a side-ring filled with a pierced plate. The knuckle-guard which is screwed to the pommel, is linked to each side ring by a small scroll-guard. The wooden grip is covered in grey ray-skin and spirally bound with twisted copper wires.

Straight, two-edged blade, with two short fullers in the forte. In each fuller is struck IOHANNIS BRACH, with the mark of a very stylised running wolf between the words. Beyond the fuller a mark consisting of the letter S combined with a cross is struck three times. On each face near the hilt is a partially defaced mark struck twice, apparently a unicorn walking along. The remainder of the blade, which has been shortened, is etched with a calendar.

Dimensions: Length overall, 41.2 in (104.6 cm)   Length of blade, 35.2 in (89.4 cm)
Weight, 2 lb 2 oz (0.963 kg).

Literature: Dufty & Borg, *European swords and daggers in the Tower of London*, p. 33, pl. 92a.
(IX 1243)

27
Horseman's sword
The hilt British, probably London, between 1702 and 1714, the blade probably German.

The Royal Arms on the hilt are those used by James II and VII until the loss of his throne in 1688, and by his daughter Queen Anne from 1702 to 1714. Comparable hilts are known, one bearing the monogram of Queen Anne, and others the regimental devices of the Royal Horse Guards as used from 1661 to 1703 and of Schomberg's Horse as used from 1693 to 1711.
The inscription on the blade purports to be the signature of Andrea dei Ferari, a sixteenth-century bladesmith working at Belluno on the river Piave, at the edge of the mountains to the north of Venice. His name, which is found on a very large number of blades, many of much later date, seems to have been widely forged.

Provenance: purchased by the Armouries in 1957.

Hilt of cast brass, with traces of silvering; consisting of a pommel, a knuckle-guard and a short rear quillon supporting on each side an oval side-shell. The knuckle-guard is linked to each shell by a small scroll-guard. A second pair of scrolls links the centre of the knuckle-guard to the curl of the other scroll on the same side. The pommel and shells bear, in low relief, the arms of the Royal House of Stuart as used in England and the arms of the City of London.
Straight two-edged blade with two deep fullers and prominent central full-length rib; stamped in one fuller on each side is the name ANDREA, and in the other the illegible remains probably of the name FERARA.

Dimensions: Length overall, 43 in (109.2 cm)   Length of blade, 36.2 in (91.9 cm)
Weight, 1 lb 15 oz (0.878 kg).

Literature: Dufty & Borg, *European swords and daggers in the Tower of London*, p. 24, pl. 49b.
(IX 1010)

26 (detail)

27   28   29

28
Hanger
The hilt British, post 1717, the blade probably German.

This is No.8 of a set of similar hangers most of which are still in the armoury at Boughton House, the home of John, Duke of Montagu (1688–1749) whose device they bear. He was Master General of the Ordnance from 1740 to 1741 and from 1743 to 1749. These swords are presumably intended for the use of the Duke's huntsmen or footmen. The Duke was created a Knight of the Garter in 1717. A similar but plainer set also survives at Boughton.

Provenance: purchased by the Armouries in 1980, partly because of the association with a very distinguished Master General of the Ordnance.

The hilt of gilt brass, decorated in relief, consisting of a pommel-cap, knuckle-guard and rear quillon supporting a side-shell outside the hand and a smaller shell inside. The knuckle-guard is linked to the outer shell by a short loop-guard. Stag-horn grip with a brass ferrule at the end nearer the blade. The sides of the pommel-cap and the ferrule are both decorated with a band of ducal coronets, the top of the cap with four human heads amid scrolls; the knuckle-guard has a central knob decorated with acanthus calyxes; the quillon ends in a grotesque ram's head. The outer shell is cast and pierced with spiralling scrolls surrounding on the side towards the pommel the crest of the Dukes of Montagu, the head and wings of a griffin, within a Garter and beneath a ducal coronet. On the side towards the blade is engraved the figure 8 in a cartouche fringed with palm-leaves. Gradually curved, single-edged blade slightly shortened at the tip, with a broad, central full-length fuller and a narrow fuller close to the spine running out six and a half inches from the tip.

Dimensions: Length overall, 31 in (78.7 cm)   Length of blade, 26 in (66 cm)
Weight, 1 lb 6 oz (0.623 kg).
(IX 2016)

29
Basket-hilted back-sword (claymore)
Hilt British, Stirling, by John Allen II, about 1750, the blade probably German, Solingen.

The basket-hilted broadsword, known since the seventeenth century as the claymore ('great sword' in Gaelic), is the characteristic weapon of the Highlanders of Scotland, and is still carried by the officers of the Scottish Line Regiments on ceremonial occasions.
The letters J.A. over S stamped on this hilt stand for John Allen, Stirling, the maker. John Allen II, armourer, admitted burgess of Stirling on 1 August 1741, was probably the second son of John Allen I, and brother of Walter admitted in 1732 (C.E. Whitelaw & S. Barter, *Scottish arms makers*, London 1977, pp. 283–4, & 304–5).

Provenance: acquired in 1953, from the collection of Lord Ashburnham.

Steel basket-hilt of characteristic Scottish type with bars of rectangular section inlaid with various patterns in brass. The edges of the larger pierced plates are cusped and indented. The conical pommel is also inlaid with brass. Grip of wood covered in grey fish-skin and bound with a spiral of twisted brass wire; brass ferrules. There is a stout buff-leather pad at the end of the grip nearer the blade. On the face of the quillon towards the blade are stamped the letters J.A. over the letter S. Straight, heavy, single-edged blade with a broad, central, full-length fuller, and a narrower fuller close to the spine running out some 11 inches from the tip. A mark is stamped near the hilt, resembling the letter O with a dart through it.

Dimensions: Length overall, 41 in (104.2 cm)   Length of blade, 35.8 in (91 cm)
Weight, 3 lb 2 oz (1.42 kg).

Literature: C. Blair, *European & American arms*, London 1962, fig. 180; Dufty & Borg, *European swords and daggers in the Tower of London*, p. 25, pls. 54c and 108.
(IX 958)

30
Small-sword and scabbard
The hilt British, London, by Joseph Clare II, dated 1766–7, the blade probably German, Solingen.

It is believed to have belonged to a member of the Shortland family, ancestors of the donor, possibly Commander John Shortland, Royal Navy (1739–1803). Although this is a civilian weapon, portraits of naval officers indicate that swords of this sort were often worn in full dress. An example occurs in the portrait of Admiral Lord Hawke by Francis Cotes painted about 1768–70 (National Maritime Museum, Greenwich, No. G.H. 30).

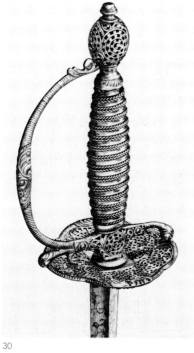

30

Joseph Clare II, whose mark occurs on the hilt, was a goldsmith who specialised in making sword furniture. He was apprenticed to Jeremiah Marlow II on 6 June 1732. His first recorded mark was entered in 1763, when he gave his address as Deans Court, St Martin's le Grand. He had apparently ceased to trade by 1773, since his name does not occur in the list of goldsmiths prepared for Parliament in that year. (A. Grimwade, *London Goldsmiths, 1697–1837*, London 1976, p. 465, marks Nos.358 and 1208–9).

Provenance: presented to the Amouries in 1979 by Miss Phoebe Lowe.

Silver-gilt hilt consisting of an oval pommel, with pronounced tang-button, a pair of quillons supporting vestigial arms of the hilt and a knuckle-guard, and a separate shell, its outline formed by four arcs of a circle to make a lobated oval. The pommel and shell are pierced with spirals of formalized foliage. Wooden grip spirally bound with silver wire and silver-gilt foil. The knuckle-guard bears the London hallmark and the date-letter for 1766–7, and the mark of the maker, Joseph Clare II.
Straight, hollow-ground, blade of triangular section now much pitted; etched in line with symmetrical neo-classical scroll-work, sun bursts, and trophies of arms.
Scabbard of wood (not illustrated) covered in black leather (probably a replacement) with a nineteenth-century gilt-brass top-locket and loose brass ring, but original gilt brass chape and mid-locket also with a loose brass ring.

Dimensions: Sword: Length overall, 39 in (99.1 cm)   Length of blade, 32.5 in (82.5 cm)   Weight, 12 oz (0.340 kg)   Scabbard: Length, 32.625 in (83.1 cm)   Weight, 4 oz (0.115 kg).
(IX 1861)

31
Hanger and scabbard of an officer of the Hudson's Bay Company
The hilt and scabbard British, London, 1783/4, the blade probably German, Solingen.

Hilts of this form are characteristic of those fitted on the light, curved swords used by officers on both sides in the American War of Independence (1775–83).
The firm of William and Edward Loxham, probably father and son, who supplied this sword, were established at 88 Cornhill, close to the Royal Exchange, in London, by 1755. William, who had been Master of the Cutlers' Company in 1742, died in 1780, and the firm was continued by Edward alone until about 1790, when he was joined by Robert Loxham, presumably his son. Edward was Master of the Cutlers' Company in 1758, and Robert in 1797 and 1811. At a committee meeting of the Hudson's Bay Company held on 30 June 1784 a payment of £9.19s to Edward Loxham Sword Cutler was recorded (H.B.C. Archives A. 1/46, fol. 25d: information kindly supplied by Mrs S.A. Smith, Keeper of Archives, H.B.C.). This payment may refer to this sword. It was presumably presented by the Board of the Company to one of their officers as rewards for some outstanding service.

Provenance: presented to the Armouries by Messrs J.R. Gaunt and Son, Limited, Birmingham, in 1956.

Silver hilt consisting of a lion's head pommel, knuckle-guard expanding to form a wide guard at the base of the grip, pierced and fretted in irregular patterns including a flaming sword in the knuckle-guard. The writhen grip is of ivory stained green. Curved, single-edged blade with broad, central, full-length fuller, and a narrow fuller close to the spine running out some eight inches from the tip. It is etched in line with the sun, the moon, a hand emerging from a cloud holding a sword, and trophies of arms. Black leather unlined scabbard with top-locket and mid-locket of silver, the top-locket has an oval stud for the belt-frog, the chape missing. The outside of the top-locket is engraved with the crest, arms and motto PRO PELLE ET CUTEM, of the Hudson's Bay Company. The inside of the top-locket is engraved LOXHAM/*Royal Exchange*. On the guards towards the blade is stamped the London hall-mark and the date-letter for 1783/4, but no maker's mark.

Dimensions: Sword: Length overall, 32.8 in (83.3 cm)   Length of blade, 27.1 in (68.8 cm)   Weight, 1 lb 4 oz (0.567 kg)   Scabbard (incomplete): Length 24.8 in (63 cm)   Weight, 4 oz (0.113 kg).

Literature: Dufty & Borg, *European swords and daggers in the Tower of London*, p. 26, pl. 57b.
(IX 1034)

32
Cavalry sabre and scabbard
United States of America, about 1785.

For a curved sword this has a blade of exceptional length; the standard British Light Cavalry sword of 1796 had a comparable blade but it was only 32 inches long. The design of the arms of the blade is similar to that approved by Congress as the Seal of the United States in June 1782.

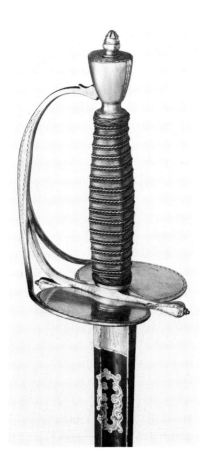

It is not known when or under what circumstances this sword entered the Armouries.
Russet steel half-basket hilt, originally blued, consisting of a vertically facetted pommel of truncated conical form, two stirrup-like knuckle-guards one in the usual position and one outside the hand, linked to each other by three parallel bars at right angles to the main axis of the hilt. The guard is completed by a short quillon and, on each side, a curved bar forming a side-ring. Written wooden grip covered in black leather.
Exceptionally long, single-edged curved blade with a broad fuller for most of its length, etched in line, on the outside with a scroll bearing the word *WARRANTED*, the arms of the United States of America supported by an eagle bearing in its beak a scroll inscribed *E PLURIBUS UNUM*, all surrounded by sixteen stars; above are trophies of arms and floral ornament. On the inside is the monogram J H. The decoration at the forte is blued and gilt, the remainder is in 'bright work'. Unlined scabbard of tooled black leather with three steel mounts, the top and mid-lockets having loose-rings for the slings.

Dimensions: Sword: Length overall, 48.5 in (122.5 cm)   Length of blade, 42 in (106.7 cm)
Weight 3 lb (1.36 kg)   Scabbard: Length, 42.3 in (107.4 cm)   Weight, 1 lb 11 oz (0.765 kg).

Literature: Dufty & Borg, *European swords and daggers in the Tower of London*, p. 29, pl. 71c.
(IX 955)

33
Military dress sword of King George III
The hilt British, London, about 1790, the blade probably German.

George III (1738–1820) succeeded to the throne in 1760 on the death of his grandfather George II. The greater part of his political life was spent in a struggle for the royal prerogative and for what he believed to be best for his subjects, against the undoubted encroachments of the great Whig families and their adherents on whom his predecessors had relied too much. A stubborn and misguided insistence on his rights over the American colonists, in which at first he was supported by the majority of his subjects, led to the outbreak of war in 1775, the Declaration of Independence on 4 July 1776, and the eventual freedom of these colonies by the Treaty of Versailles in 1783.
The King was personally brave as is shown by his conduct during the Gordon Riots of 1780, and on other occasions when he was endangered by rioters and assassins. He formed a collection of antique arms and armour which, having been incorporated with that of his son George IV, is now at Windsor Castle. Several swords comparable to this are still in the Royal Collection at Windsor Castle, in particular No.618 in the 1904 *Catalogue*, for which a receipted bill survives, dated 1789.

Provenance: the Royal Collection; transferred to the Armouries by H.M. King George VI in 1938.

Gilt brass hilt consisting of a vase-shaped pommel, two straight cross-guards (quillons) supporting a knuckle-guard and, on each side, a side-shell. The knuckle-guard is linked to each shell by a short loop-guard. The edges are decorated with bright-cut engraving. Grip of wood bound in silver wire and foil. Turk's head ferrules.
Straight single-edged spadroon blade, etched in line, blued, and fire-gilt at the forte with the royal arms of England as used until 1801, scrolls, and trophies of arms.

Dimensions: Length overall, 38.2 in (97 cm)   Length of blade, 32.0 in (81.3 cm)
Weight, 1 lb 4 oz (0.567 kg).

Literature: Dufty & Borg, *European swords and daggers in the Tower of London*, p. 33, pl. 92b.
(IX 1244)

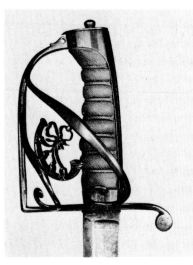

34
Sword of an officer of Light Infantry
Probably British, made for the United States market, late eighteenth century.

The bugle-horn stringed of the type decorating the guard of this sword was the characteristic badge of Light Infantry in most European armies.

Provenance: purchased by the Armouries in 1965.

Half-basket stirrup hilt of steel probably originally blued. The head of the back-plate is oval in plan. The back-plate is longitudinally facetted. The guards consist of a stirrup-like knuckle-guard and a rear quillon with a discoid terminal knob, supporting a side-guard linked to the knuckle-guard by two scroll-guards which support between them a bugle-horn stringed. Wooden grip covered in grey fish-skin and bound with two strands of twisted copper wire. Facetted steel ferrule at the end nearer the blade. The ring for the sword-knot is now missing from the end of the knuckle-guard. Straight, single-edged spadroon blade, etched in line at the forte with foliage scrolls and on the outside with a shield bearing the arms of the United States of America supported by an eagle displayed and the motto E PLURIBUS UNUM, and on the inside with a trophy of arms. There are traces of fire-gilding and blueing.

Dimensions: Length overall, 37.6 in (95.4 cm)   Length of blade, 32.1 in (81.4 cm)
Weight, 24 oz (0.680 kg).
(IX 1108)

35
Military dress sword and scabbard of the 1st Duke of Wellington
British, General Officer's dress pattern 1796, the blade German, Solingen.

Arthur Wellesley (1769–1852), later 1st Duke of Wellington, known as 'the Iron Duke', was one of the great British heroes of the nineteenth century. The fourth son of Garret Wellesley, first Earl of Mornington, he joined the army in 1787. The formative years of his military career were passed in India culminating with a brilliant campaign against the Mahrattas whom he defeated crushingly at Assaye and Argaum in 1803. From 1809 he commanded the British and allied forces in the Iberian peninsula and by 1813 had driven the French armies occupying Portugal and Spain back across the Pyrenees into France. He was created Viscount Wellington in 1809 after his victory at Talavera, and Earl after the storming of Ciudad Rodrigo in 1812. Later in the same year he was created Marquis. In the following year, after the victory at Vitoria, he was appointed Field-Marshal, and a Knight of the Garter. He was created Duke of Wellington in 1814. After Napoleon's return from exile in 1815 he commanded the British and allied forces in Belgium and on 18 June, with the aid of his Prussian allies under Marshal Blücher, crushingly defeated the French at Waterloo, after a long and furiously contested action. He was showered with honours, titles, land, art treasures, and wealth, both by a grateful nation and by the allied sovereigns. He was Master General of the Ordnance with a seat in the Cabinet from 1818 to 1827 when he resigned. He was Prime Minister from 1828 to 1830 and again in 1834, and Commander-in-Chief from 1827 to 1828 and again from 1842 until his death. Appointed Constable of the Tower in 1826, he did much to improve its organisation and efficiency.
John Justus Runkel, who signed the blade of this sword, was a merchant who imported Solingen blades to England where he is first recorded in 1786. From 1795 to 1808 his business was situated at 8 Tookes Court, Castle Street, Holborn, London.

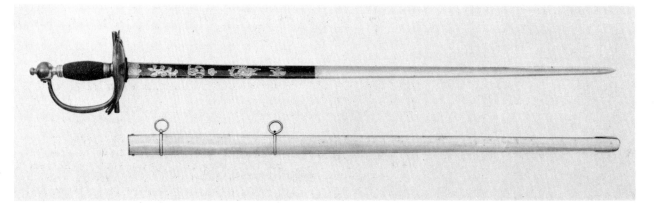

No order exists for the introduction of this sword for the use of General Officers but examples appear in wear in their portraits shortly after the introduction of an identical sword for cavalry officers in 1796. In 1816 the Royal Accounts refer to a similar sword which is described as a 'Fine Large Boatshell Field Marshals Sword'. It cost fifteen guineas. (*see* Norman, *The Rapier and small-sword*, London 1980, pp. 213–4).

Provenance: presented to the Armouries in 1968 by the 6th Duke of Wellington.

Brass hilt with traces of gilding, consisting of an oval pommel, straight quillons supporting a knuckle-guard screwed to the pommel, and a boat-shaped shell. Wooden grip bound with twisted silver wire. Gilt brass ferrules.
Straight, single-edged spadroon blade, etched in line, blued and fire-gilt at the forte with trophies of arms, foliage, and inside with the royal arms as borne from 1801 to 1816, and outside with the monogram GR crowned. On the spine is engraved the name *J.J. Runkel Solingen*.

Dimensions: Sword: Length overall, 39.3 in (99.8 cm)   Length of blade. 32.5 in (82.5 cm)   Weight, 1 lb 13 oz (0.822 kg)   Scabbard: Length, 33 in (83.8 cm)   Weight 14 oz (0.396 kg).

Literature: Dufty & Borg, *European swords and daggers in the Tower of London*, p. 30, pl. 76a.
(IX 901)

36
Presentation small-sword and scabbard of Lieut. J. Allen
British, London, about 1800.

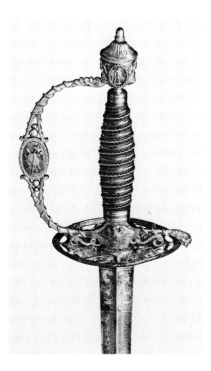

John Allen is recorded in *Wilson's Dublin Directory* of 1807 as a wholesaler and linen factor of 15 Gardiner's Place and as a member of the Society of the Ouzel Gallery.
Richard Clarke, the retailer of this sword, was a jeweller and toyman who supplied swords of the very highest quality mounted either in heavily gilded copper or in gilded silver. He was recorded, at first in partnership with a man called Green, at 102 Cheapside, London, in 1784, and thereafter until 1829 at 62 Cheapside. Green left the partnership in 1792. From 1796 Clarke was joined in the company by his sons.
This sword dates from between 1796, when the first volunteers were raised in Ireland, and 1801, when the royal arms were changed at the time of the Union with Ireland.

Provenance: purchased by the Armouries in 1980.

Thickly fire-gilt brass hilt, consisting of vase-shaped pommel, knuckle-guard with large flattened oval knob at its centre, rear quillon curving towards the blade and ending in a lion's head with a bomb in its jaws, and an oval, slightly dished shell. The place of the arms of the hilt is taken by two small scrolls.
The decoration, which is in neo-classical taste, is partly cast and chased, and partly applied. On either side of the pommel are applied ovals containing the figure of Hercules, elsewhere the decoration consists largely of military trophies, applied, chiselled and pierced, with some acanthus foliage. Wooden grip bound with silver wire and silver foil. Gilt-brass ferrules.
Straight, double-edged, hollow-ground blade of diamond section, etched in relief at the forte, bright on a false-watered ground, with symmetrical foliage involving on the outside the royal arms of England as used until 1801 and the inscription: PRESENTED BY THE OFFICERS AND PRIVATES OF THE LINEN HALL/CORPS TO *John Allen Esqʳ* THEIR LIEUTENANT AND ADJUTANT AS A/TOKEN OF ESTEEM AND GRATITUDE FOR HIS UNREMITTED ATTENTION/TO THEIR INTEREST AND DISCIPLINE.
On the inside is the royal monogram GR crowned and a female figure symbolic of Justice.
Unlined scabbard of black leather tooled with saltires and stamped with the feathers of the Prince of Wales. It has three gilt-brass mounts consisting of two lockets with loose-rings and a chape. The lockets are engraved with trophies of arms and the inside of the top-locket with the inscription R. Clarke/and *Son*/CHEAPSIDE.

Dimensions: Sword: Length overall, 38.25 in (97.1 cm)   Length of blade. 31.25 in (79.3 cm)   Weight, 1 lb 1 oz (0.481 kg)   Scabbard: Length, 31.65 in (80.4 cm)   Weight, 5 oz (0.141 kg).
(IX 2025)

37 (pl. XXIII)
City of London gold presentation small-sword and scabbard of Vice Admiral Lord Collingwood
British, London, dated 1806/7.

Cuthbert Collingwood (1750–1810), a Northumbrian by birth, entered the Royal Navy in 1761. He was a contemporary and a close friend of Horatio Nelson. For his actions at Bunkers Hill in 1775 he was promoted to Lieutenant. He also distinguished himself at the battles of the Glorious 1st of June (1794) and Cape St Vincent (1797). As Vice Admiral he served Nelson as Second in Command at Trafalgar (1805), and succeeded to the command on the latter's

PRESENTED BY THE Corporation of the City of London pursuant to a Vote of Common Council Passed the 26th Novr 1805. The Right Honble James Shaw Mayor; to VICE ADMIRAL LORD COLLINGWOOD for the brilliant & decisive Victory obtained by his Majesty's Fleet under his Command (upon whom it devolved upon the ever to be lamented Death of Vice Admiral Lord Viscount Nelson) over the Combined Fleets of France & Spain, off Cape Trafalgar, on the 21st October 1805. Thereby affording to the World at large an additional & lasting proof of British Valour.

death in the course of that action. Created Baron Collingwood of Coldburne and Hethpoole for his part in this battle. Among the many gifts showered upon him at this time was this sword presented by the Corporation of the City of London. As Nelson's successor he served as Commander in Chief in the Mediterranean until shortly before his death at sea in 1810.

The maker's mark, which is unfortunately partly defaced, appears to be that of John Ray and James Montague of 22 Denmark St, London, who were the leading craftsmen in this sort of work at the time. Thomas Harper, who retailed this sword, was born about 1735/40 in Bristol, England. By 1773, if not earlier, he was established as a goldsmith in Broad Street, near the Exchange, Charlestown, South Carolina, where he remained until 1778, when, as a loyalist, he left for St Eustatius in the Dutch West Indies. He was in Charlestown once again in 1781, but two years later was in permanent exile in London, where he set up as a goldsmith, at first at 207 Fleet Street, and later at 29 Arundel Street. The City of London paid him £211.1s.0d. for this particular sword. He died in 1832. (A. Grimwade, *London Goldsmiths*, London 1976, pp. 536–7).

Provenance: bequeathed to the Armouries in 1948, by Sir Bernard Eckstein, Bart.

Gold hilt, consisting of an oval pommel, a knuckle-guard and a rear quillon, and an oval shell. In place of the arms of the hilt are two small anchors. The whole is chased with laurel wreaths and trophies of arms and set with oval plaques of dark-blue enamel. On the outside of the grip the plaque is painted with the arms of Lord Collingwood, that on the inside with the arms of the City of London, each surrounded by small diamonds; those on the pommel are painted with trophies of arms. The knuckle-guard is inscribed in letters set with diamonds against a dark-blue enamel ground, on the outside: ENGLAND EXPECTS EVERY MAN TO DO HIS DUTY; and on the inside: TRAFALGAR.
The shell is engraved on the face towards the blade with details of the presentation (*see* plate).

Plain straight, hollow-ground blade of triangular section. Wooden scabbard covered in black fish-skin with three gold mounts signed: Thos. Harper/207/Fleet St/LONDON.
The gold mounts bear in various places a group of marks including: 1) the maker's mark IM below some illegible letters; 2) a closed crown; 3) the number 18 in a square; 4) the king's head; 5) the crowned leopard's head; 6) the London date-letter L for 1806–7.

Dimensions: Sword: Length overall, 40 in (101.6 cm)   Length of blade, 33.2 in (84.3 cm)
Weight 13 oz (0.368 kg)   Scabbard: Length, 33.5 in (85.1 cm)   Weight 3 oz (0.085 kg).

Literature: C. Blair, *Three presentation swords in the Victoria and Albert Museum and a group of English enamels*, Victoria and Albert Museum Brochure No.1, London 1972, p. 51, No.33; Dufty & Borg, *European swords and daggers in the Tower of London*, pp. 27–8, pl. 65.
(IX 909)

38

Presentation small-sword and scabbard of Sir Samuel Whittingham
British, London, 1825, the hilt by Thomas Prosser.

Lieutenant-General Sir Samuel Ford Whittingham K.C.B. (1772–1841), to whom
this sword was presented, was a distinguished soldier. He served with
honour in Spain and Portugal throughout the Napoleonic Wars. He was
appointed Governor General of Dominica in 1819 and served there until
1821. He ended his life as Commander-in-Chief of the Madras Army.
Thomas Prosser, sword-cutler and goldsmith, not only retailed this sword but
also made the mounts, since it is his mark which they bear. He is first
recorded in April 1796, at 9 Charing Cross, where he remained until about
1853, when he moved to 37 Charing Cross. He is last recorded in 1860. He
was sword-cutler to both George III and George IV, and a number of swords
by him are still at Windsor Castle (A. Grimwade, *London Goldsmiths*, London
1976, p. 634, Mark No. 1590).

Provenance: purchased by the Armouries in 1978.

Gold hilt consisting of an oval pommel flattened in the plane of the blade; straight quillons ending in
knobs and supporting a broad knuckle-guard; and a pair of separate asymmetrical shell-guards, the
larger outside the hand inclined towards the blade. Cast and chased all over with relief
decoration in late neo-classical style, including a British crown flanked by serpents on the pommel,
a laurel wreath forming the knuckle-guard, and a pine-apple between sprays of oak-leaves on the
outer shell. The gold grip is decorated *en suite*, at its centre is a palm-tree.
Slender, straight, two-edged blade of flattened diamond section etched in relief against a bright
ground; outside at the hilt on a shield 'RESTORED/by/WILKINSON/Pall Mall/London', above
which are scrolls of stylised foliage enclosing panels in one of which is the inscription:
'PRESENTED BY THE PLANTERS RESIDENT IN GREAT BRITAIN/TO SIR S.
WHITTINGHAM G.C.H. IN TESTIMONY OF HIS SERVICES/DURING HIS RESIDENCE
AND GOVERNMENT AS HIS MAJESTY'S/REPRESENTATIVE IN DOMINICA JANUARY
31st 1822'.
Wooden scabbard covered with black leather with gold locket and chape decorated *en suite* with
the hilt. On the reverse of the locket is engraved PROSSER/LONDON.
The gold mounts bear at various points some or all of these marks: 1) An eight-pointed star; 2) the
king's head; 3) the leopard passant; 4) the maker's mark IP in an oval; and on the shell and locket in
addition; 5) the London date-letter f for 1821–2.

Dimensions: Sword: Length overall, 37.5 in (95.2 cm)
Length of blade, 31.3 in (79.4 cm)   Weight, 15 oz (0.425 kg)
Scabbard: Length, 32.15 in (81.6 cm)   Weight, 3 oz (0.085 kg).
(IX 1796)

39 (pl. XXII)

Presentation sabre, scabbard and case of Sir William Fenwick Williams
British, London, 1856, mounts by Antoine Vechte.

Sir William Fenwick Williams (1800–83), born at Annapolis, Nova Scotia,
joined the Royal Military Academy in 1815. He was commissioned in 1825,
and rose to the rank of General in 1868. His greatest military achievement
was the defence of the Turkish town of Kars, which under his leadership held
out from 7 June until 22 November 1855, against overwhelming Russian
forces. Although eventually he was obliged to capitulate, since no relief was

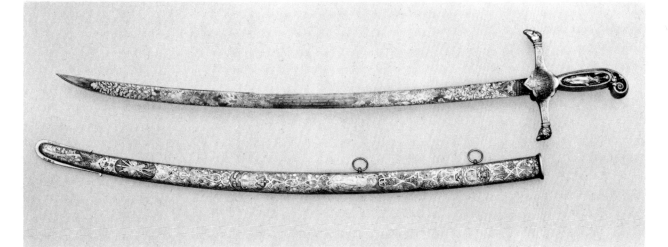

possible, his achievement was recognised in 1856, upon his return from captivity in Russia, when he was created baronet 'of Kars', made a Knight Commander of the Order of the Bath, and voted a pension of £1,000 a year by Parliament. He also received the freedom of the City of London, together with a sword of honour, and his fellow countrymen of Nova Scotia presented him with this sword. His later appointments included the governorship of Nova Scotia between 1865 and 1870, and the post of Constable of the Tower of London in 1881.

John Samuel Hunt, who was not a practising goldsmith, succeeded Paul Storr in the firm of Storr and Mortimer in 1839, and went into partnership with Robert Roskell, a Liverpool goldsmith in 1844, to form one of the most important firms of London goldsmiths of the nineteenth century. They held warrants from almost all the members of the Royal Family, and won prizes at the Great Exhibition of 1851 and many subsequent exhibitions. In the 1880s they were taken over by the firm of J. W. Benson which is still active today.

Antoine Vechte (1800–68) was a French goldsmith-designer who, having been recruited by Mortimer in 1844, set up his studio in London after the 1848 Revolution. He was undoubtedly one of the most important artist-craftsmen of the period, frequently described by his contemporaries as 'The Cellini of the nineteenth century'. The vase and shield he exhibited in the Great Exhibition of 1851 are now in Goldsmiths Hall, London.

Provenance: purchased by the Armouries in 1978 as an example of high Victorian design and because of its association with both Canada and the Tower of London.

Hilt of silver parcel-gilt. Straight quillons of square section decorated with engraved leaf-scrolls, and ending in the cast heads of a camel and a bear. The trilobate langets are decorated with applied addorsed monograms of the letters FW surrounded by engraved leaf and scrolls. The grip terminates in a ram's-horn pommel, with a spray of applied foliage on each side, and also bears a silver female figure in an oval niche on each side, one representing Minerva, goddess of Wisdom, and the other Truth.

Curved, single-edged blade, etched in bright work with scrolls and strapwork, including on the outside the royal monogram, and the arms and motto of Sir William Fenwick Williams. On the inside the decoration includes the inscription: THE LEGISLATURE OF NOVA SCOTIA PRESENTS THIS BLADE/FORMED OF NATIVE METAL TO HER DISTINGUISHED SON MAJOR GENERAL/SIR WILLIAM FENWICK WILLIAMS K.C.B.; and the words HUNT & ROSKELL/156/New Bond Street/LONDON.

Silver scabbard parcel-gilt, with two loose rings, decorated in low relief with floral scrolls and strapwork surrounding silver cartouches, including on the outside a representation of the seal of Nova Scotia and Cape Breton Island, and various allegorical devices. On the inside of the scabbard the cartouches contain the arms and motto of Sir William, and the Royal Arms of England. The chape is stamped on the inside HUNT & ROSKELL and with the maker's mark of J.S. Hunt, the London hall-mark, and the date-letter for 1856/7. The top of the locket and the quillons bear similar marks. The oak case (not illustrated), which is lined with blue velvet, bears a brass plaque stamped: HUNT & ROSKELL/SILVERSMITHS & JEWELLERS/TO THE QUEEN/156 NEW BOND STREET, LONDON, and a label printed HUNT & ROSKELL/LATE STORR AND MORTIMER/JEWELLERS AND GOLDSMITHS TO THE QUEEN 156 NEW BOND STREET.

Dimensions: Sabre: Length overall, 35.125 in (189.2 cm)   Length of blade, 29.65 in (75.3 cm)
Weight, 1 lb 10 oz (0.737 kg)   Scabbard: Length, 31.4 in (79.7 cm)
Case: Length, 39.125 in (99.3 cm)   Width, 8.65 in (22 cm)

Literature: illustrated and described in the *Illustrated London News*, 20 September 1856.
(IX 1841)

40
Dagger and sheath mounts
Probably North European, fifteenth century.

This dagger is believed to have come from the River Scheldt in Antwerp but at least five others of this general form have been excavated in England. The group has generally been dated to the late fourteenth or early fifteenth century. This particular dagger, however, has always been considered to be of late fifteenth-century date. In 1933, Charles Beard compared the monstrous head which forms the finial of the silver scabbard chape of this dagger to a very similar monstrous head on the tip-mount of a drinking horn, in the collection of Viscount and Viscountess Lee of Fareham, which he believed to date from the second half of the fifteenth century. A ballock dagger, formerly in the collection of Sir Guy Laking, which he dated for no apparent reason to about 1460, also had a scabbard with a similar chape cast with an identical monstrous head (see Laking, *Record*, London 1920–2, III. p. 37).

Monstrous heads of this particular type, however, can be found on objects of very varying dates. For instance, two very similar appear on the quillon ends of the ceremonial sword made in about 1433 for the Emperor Sigismund I (Vienna, Waffensammlung, No. A 49); and another is on the quillon-block of a bronze-hilted dagger from the Thames at Wallingford (now in the Armouries, No. X.689), which is almost certainly of early sixteenth-century date.

Provenance: believed to be from the Scheldt at Antwerp; collection of Frans Claes (sold Antwerp, 29 November 1933, lot 969); purchased by the Armouries in 1955 from Major H.D. Barnes.

Residual guard consisting of two rhombus-shaped sheets of copper, originally silvered, which are rivetted to either side of the blade. The sheets are engraved one with a Gothic S, the other with a spray of foliage on a hatched ground. Grip formed of two scales of wood, secured to the tang by five silver-headed rivets, and pierced through the spherical pommel by a large, hollow rivet of silver. Long, straight, single-edged blade, the tang shaped to form a ring at the pommel. The scabbard is reconstructed but the silver mounts are original. The chape terminal is cast in the form of a long-eared monstrous head.

Dimensions: Length, 22.4 in (56.9 cm)   Length of blade, 15.5 in (39.4 cm)   Weight, 10 oz (0.283 kg).

Literature: C.R. Beard 'Early silver in the collection of Viscount and Viscountess Lee of Fareham', *The Connoisseur*, CI, 1937, pp. 63–4.
(X 284)

41
Rondel dagger
European, possibly English, late fifteenth century.

Both soldiers and civilians usually carried daggers in the Middle Ages, and to meet the demand many different types were developed. This one is of a type, now called a rondel dagger because of its round pommel and guard, which apparently first appeared about 1300 and remained one of the most popular forms of dagger until the early sixteenth century. This example, with its long blade and small but equal-sized rondels, is of a kind which appears most frequently in illustrations of the second half of the fifteenth century. It was found in the River Thames in London and it is possibly an English-made dagger for, although daggers of this general type appear to have been used throughout Europe, two others with very similar low-domed pommels and guards have also been found in the Thames (Museum of London, Nos. 37.99 and XVII.87). This dagger is in exceptional condition for an excavated piece, and its grip, which is perfectly preserved, is unusual in being reinforced and decorated with spiralling bands of iron edged with twisted brass wire. A rather similar decorative feature appears on the wooden grip of another rondel dagger of about the same date in the Musée de l'Armée, Paris (No. P.O.1193), which is carved with raised longitudinal chevron bands bordered by twisted brass wire.

Provenance: excavated from the Thames foreshore at Queenhithe, London, in 1976; acquired by the Armouries in 1979.

In excavated condition, the metal covered with a blue-black patination. The rondels are apparently formed of solid pieces of iron. The guard has a conical taper to the hilt and a domed taper to the blade. The pommel is of similar form with the appearance of a button. Wooden grip reinforced with two longitudinally spiralling bands of iron, pinned to the grip at either end and in the middle, and bordered on either side by twisted brass wire. Long, straight, double-edged blade of flattened diamond section, tapering to a point, with the remains of a circular mark on one side.

Dimensions: Length overall, 24.12 in (61.3 cm)   Length of blade, 19.5 in (49.5 cm)
Weight, 1 lb (0.453 kg).
(X 599)

42
Dagger
Spanish or Italian, about 1650.

In the Middle Ages the sword was generally used by itself but sometimes in conjunction with a small shield which was held in the left hand and used to

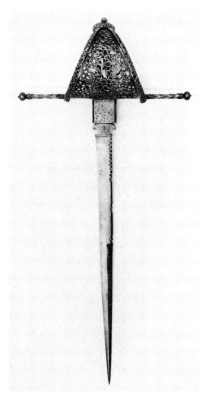

parry the opponent's blade. From the beginning of the sixteenth century, with the development of more scientific forms of fencing, the sword was often used together with a parrying dagger, and many fencing manuals appeared advocating the best ways of fighting with sword and dagger. Generally these daggers, which are usually known today as 'left-hand daggers', followed the hilt styles of the swords they were made to accompany, although, certainly at first, matching pairs of swords and daggers seem to have been uncommon. Daggers of this particular type, which were designed to accompany the distinctive 'Spanish' cup-hilt rapier (see 25), first appeared in the second quarter of the seventeenth century. They were used in the particular form of fencing, developed in Spain, in which the opponents circled each other with almost dance-like steps and used their weapons both for cutting and thrusting. Although styles of fighting changed rapidly elsewhere in Europe this type of fencing remained popular in Spain itself well into the eighteenth century, and consequently cup-hilt rapiers and parrying daggers of this general form continued to be made and used until late in that century. This dagger, as many of its type, has two features specially designed to catch the blade of an opponent's sword – the outward turn of the rim of the guard (*rompepuntas*) and the scroll-shaped inlets on each side of the blade just in front of the ricasso. This dagger probably came from a Spanish or Portuguese collection, as it appears as No. 352 in a catalogue album of photographs entitled *Oeuvres d'art en photographie; Espagne et Portugal*, which was at one time obtainable from J. Laurent & Cie of Paris and Madrid.

Provenance: acquired by the Armouries in the 1950s.

The hilt is of steel. The triangular shell-guard is finely pierced and chiselled with scrolling foliage, the edges with a strong outward turn (*rompepuntas*). The hollow pommel is of flattened spherical shape and, together with the hollow steel grip, is chiselled and pierced to match the guard. The long, straight quillons are chiselled with a design of overlapping leaves and end in knobs chiselled with scrolls. The straight blade is single-edged at the forte where the back is bevelled and notched, but half-way along its length it becomes double-edged with a prominent medial ridge. It has a broad ricasso, the inner side with an oval depression for the thumb, the outer side punched with small engrailed circles. Just beyond the ricasso the blade has a scroll-shaped inlet on either side, and is stamped on both faces with a mark in the form of a Maltese cross above a dot.

Dimensions: Length overall, 22 in (55.9 cm)   Length of blade, 17.25 in (43.8 cm)   Weight, 1 lb 8 oz (0.68 kg).

Literature: Dufty & Borg, *European swords and daggers in the Tower of London*, p. 34, pl. 99. (X 367)

43
Pollaxe
European, about 1500.

The pollaxe was a popular weapon in the fifteenth and sixteenth centuries for use on foot both in battle and in the tournament, where it was frequently used in combats in which two opponents fought within a fenced enclosure known as the barriers. Despite the fact that a very similar pollaxe to this is illustrated, carried by a man-at-arms, in the 'Pageant of the Birth, Life and Death of Richard Beauchamp Earl of Warwick K.G.', a manuscript of about 1485 in the British Library, it seems probable that decorated pollaxes of this form were intended for use in the tournament rather than on the battle-field. The distinctive feature of this pollaxe is the fluke emerging from the flat hammer-head which balances the blade. This feature also appears on a number of similar pollaxes, and it has often been suggested that these weapons might be of English origin. There is even a tradition (*see Gothic Art in Europe*, London 1936, p. 27) that this particular pollaxe came from the Musée d'Artillerie, Paris, where it was known as the axe of Edward IV, a tradition later borne by another axe in the same museum, No. K.84, which is almost certainly of the time of Henry VIII. This type of pollaxe, however, was certainly not confined to England, and is illustrated, for example, on the inside panel of the right wing of Hans Memling's tryptych 'The Mystic Marriage of St Catherine', in St John's Hospital, Bruges. Wherever they were made, however, such weapons do seem to have been popular in England for many years and one, with the distinctive fluke emerging from the hammer-head, is illustrated in a series of drawings of the Guard of King Henry VIII in the British Library.

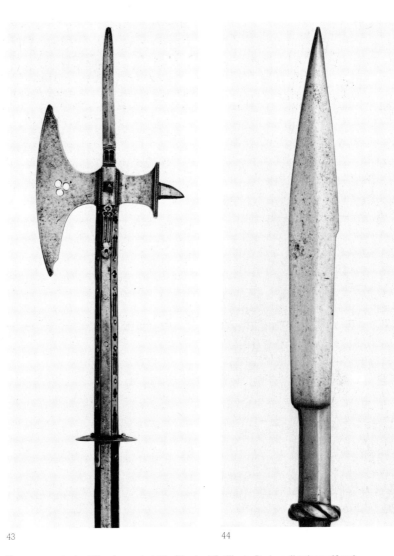

43   44

Provenance: by tradition formerly in the Musée d'Artillerie, Paris; collections of Lord
Londesborough, Sir Noel Paton (who apparently acquired it from a house in Lancaster), Mr George
Coates, Dumfries, Major H.D. Barnes (who purchased it from the dealer, H. Furmage in 1928);
bequeathed to the Armouries in 1955 by Major Barnes.

Narrow, crescentic axe blade, pierced in the centre with a trefoil, the upper and lower edges
cusped just behind the leading edge and tapering in a concave curve to the socket which is
decorated with roping. Attached through the socket are side-spikes in the form of elongated
pyramids. The blade is balanced by a large flat-ended hammer-head from which emerges a
slightly down-curved fluke or beak. Surmounting the head is a quadrangular spike struck twice
with a mark, probably a script *f*, and decorated at the base with gothic piercings. Four long cheeks
of steel extend down alternate faces of the octagonal wooden haft. The intervening spaces are
reinforced with brass strips decorated with gothic piercings, which extend as far as the round,
slightly dished hand-guard approximately 2 feet from the tip of the top spike.

Dimensions: Length overall, 70 in (177.8 cm)   Length of head including cheeks, 33.5 in (85.1 cm)
Weight, 6 lb 7 oz (2.92 kg).

Exhibited: 'Gothic Art in Europe', Burlington Fine Arts Club, London 1936. Cat. No.9.

Literature: F.W. Fairholt, *Miscellania Graphica*, 1857, p. 52; G.F. Laking 'The Noël Paton Collection
of Arms and Armour', *The Burlington Magazine*. Vol. XVII, 1910, p. 157.
(VII 1542)

44
Glaive
European, about 1500.

It is not certain by what name this type of staff weapon was known in the
fifteenth century, but most modern writers use the term 'glaive' to describe
it, and it is possible that this is a contemporary term. Weapons of this type are
quite frequently illustrated in fifteenth-century manuscripts, especially those

of French origin, but there is no real evidence to suggest that this was a peculiarly French weapon, and indeed this example is thought to have come from Rhodes (*see* 9). However, the large roped moulding at the base of the blade is a feature found on a number of staff weapons believed to have been made for the Guard of King Henry VIII (*see* 54), and it is therefore possible that the Rhodes provenance has been misapplied to this weapon and that it came instead from the Tudor Royal Collection. This is by no means certain, however, since this feature is not found exclusively on weapons made for Henry VIII.

Provenance: possibly from Rhodes; transferred to the Armouries in 1978 from the Rotunda Museum, Woolwich (1873 *Cat.*, No.1597).
Iron head consisting of a single-edged blade with a medial rib, the back-edge sharpened and tapering to a spear point for 10 inches (25.4 cm) from the tip. Hexagonal socket, with a large, roped collar at the base. The head is secured to the modern haft by two long cheeks.

Dimensions: Length overall, 97 in (246.4 cm)   Length of head, 23.5 (59.7 cm)
Weight, 9 lb 1 oz (4.11 kg).
(VII 1727)

45
Lance head
German, early sixteenth century.

The term 'lance' is now used exclusively to describe a horseman's spear, but originally it appears to have been a synonym of the term 'spear', which was used generally to describe both cavalry and infantry weapons of this type. The lance was the major arm of the cavalry throughout the Middle Ages and, because tournaments began as training for war rather than as sport, lances also became the most common tournament weapon. Generally, jousting lances followed the same development as those designed for war, but from at least the thirteenth century they were often equipped, for reasons of safety, with rebated heads, often shaped like a crown and, because of this, usually known as coronels. By the late fifteenth century jousting was no longer regarded as a training for war and had become much less dangerous than before. Lances were often made hollow so that, although they looked heavy, they broke easily on impact. Especially in German lands, and due in part to the interest of Emperor Maximilian I (reigned 1493 to 1519), many very specialised forms of jousting were developed, and for many of these special lances and lance-heads were made. This particular form of lance-head, with a slightly down-curved tip was used in a number of these special courses including the *Rennen* (*see* 1). Similar heads are illustrated, for example, in the *Tournament Book* produced in 1529 by Hans Burgkmair the Younger, where they are shown being carried for use in various different *Rennen* courses.

Provenance: transferred to the Armouries in 1927 from the Rotunda Museum, Woolwich (1873 *Cat.*, No.1709).

The head is of steel and consists of a small, down-curved tip of hexagonal section, decorated with incised cabling, and a large socket decorated at either end with double incised lines. The lower edge of the socket is also pierced for the nails by which it was attached to the haft.

Dimensions: Length overall, 8.5 in (21.6 cm)   Weight, 10 oz (0.28 kg).
(VII 1365)

46
Pollaxe
European, first half of the sixteenth century.

Although often known today as a pole-hammer, the term pollaxe seems to have been applied to this form of weapon in the fifteenth and sixteenth centuries. Long-handled hammers of this general type, with the hammer-head in the form of a claw, were used both in battle and in the tournament. They were especially popular with the Swiss cantonal levies from the fifteenth to the seventeenth centuries and, because many are preserved in the old Zeughaus in Lucerne, Swiss weapons of this form are usually known as 'Lucerne Hammers'. Nevertheless, this general type of pollaxe was popular throughout Europe including England. This particular example was almost certainly intended for use not in battle but in the form of tournament known as foot combat, and it is here exhibited with the foot-combat armour of

King Henry VIII (2). There is no evidence that this particular pollaxe formed part of King Henry's arsenal but it is certainly of the type which he would have used, and it dates from about the period of his reign (1509–47). A comparable weapon is illustrated in the portrait of either John or William Palmer, attributed to Andrew White, which dates from between 1538 and 1544. Both Palmers seem to have been members of the Royal bodyguard known as the Band of Gentlemen Pensioners, and J.L. Nevinson ('Portraits of Gentlemen Pensioners before 1625', *Walpole Society*, XXXIV, p. 6) has tentatively suggested that this form of pollaxe may be a Gentleman Pensioner's weapon.

Provenance: presented to the Armouries in 1950 by Major H.D. Barnes.

Head of steel consisting of a broad, leaf-shaped spike with a pronounced medial ridge. From the base of the spike two long cheeks extend down the modern haft. Wedged between the spike and the iron cap to the haft is the hammer-head consisting of three claws set on a long neck, and, in one with it, a back-spike in the form of a triangular-sectioned fluke. The upper part of the haft is reinforced by longitudinal strips of iron between the cheeks and by a spiral binding of iron strips. At the butt is an iron spike.

Dimensions: Length overall, 93.5 in (237.5 cm)   Length of head, 11.25 in (28.6 cm)
Weight, 7 lb 11 oz (3.49 kg).
(VII 1510)

47 (pl. XII)
Partizan
Italian, early sixteenth century.

The partizan seems to have developed in Italy in the early fifteenth century, and was presumably based on the type of spear with a simple triangular head which appears in Italian paintings from the beginning of the fourteenth century. Its use soon spread throughout Europe and it rapidly became one of the most popular of parade weapons. This is one of three similar partizans in the Armouries bearing the Tudor Royal Arms, which were probably intended for one of the Guards of King Henry VIII. The pointillé decoration on this weapon is Italian in style and it is probable that it and its fellows were purchased through Italian merchants, such as Leonardo Frescobaldi of Florence, who supplied all manner of military equipment to the Crown in the early years of Henry's reign. Over 1,500 decorated partizans are recorded in the great Inventory of Henry VIII's possessions drawn up after his death in 1547, including two in the Tower which were 'party gilte with the kings armes graven uppon them, garnyssed with grene pasements and fringed with grene and whit silke' (the Tudor colours). When the German traveller Hentzner visited the Tower in 1598, he was shown 'a great many rich spears, commonly called partizans, with which the guard defends the royal person in battle'. This partizan and its companions have been on public display in the Tower ever since, from the late seventeenth century to the mid-nineteenth century in the Spanish Armoury (later Queen Elizabeth's Armoury), which purported to show weapons and instruments of torture captured from the Spanish Armada of 1588, but which, in fact, was largely composed of weapons from Henry VIII's arsenal. They are described in late eighteenth-century Tower Guides as 'Spanish Officers' Lances'.

Provenance: Tudor Royal Armouries; probably the 'Spanish Javelins' of the 1676 Tower Inventory.

Very long tapering head of steel with a pronounced medial rib flanked on either side by a broad fuller. The lower edges of the head extend outwards in a gentle curve to form small wings. The base of the blade is decorated with a panel of pointillé scroll-work, involving on one side the Tudor Royal Arms, and on the other a helmeted profile head. Tapering octagonal socket decorated with pointillé rope-work, secured to the modern haft by two short cheeks.

Dimensions: Length overall, 83.12 in (211.2 cm)   Length of head, 37 in (94 cm)
Weight, 4 lb 12 oz (2.15 kg).

Literature: A. Borg, 'The Spanish Armoury in the Tower', *Archaeologia*, CV, 1976, pp. 339.
(VII 147)

48
Partizan
Probably Italian, early sixteenth century.

A much smaller partizan than No. 47, but this too was probably made in Italy and supplied by Italian merchants for one of Henry VIII's companies of

Guards. The dragon, the national symbol of Wales, was a favourite emblem of the Tudors, and one of the supporters of the royal arms. Its presence on this partizan seems to confirm that it was made for King Henry. There are another 25 similar small partizans in the Armouries, all presumably part of the same purchase, and all with similar pointillé decoration, the subjects including dolphins, dragons, helmeted human heads, winged cherubs, scroll-work, strapwork, and foliage. The large bulbous moulding at the top of the socket and the longitudinal line decoration along its length are reminiscent of the similar features which occur on a large group of pikes which are also believed to date from the time of King Henry VIII (*see* 56). It is not possible to relate this group of partizans to any particular entry in the 1547 Inventory of King Henry's possessions, but as they were certainly decorated with gilding over the panel of punched decoration they are probably included amongst the many 'partie'- or 'parcell'-gilt partizans mentioned.

Provenance: probably Tudor Royal Armouries; in the Armouries since before 1859.

Head of small size with a straight tapering steel blade of flattened diamond section. On either side of the blade just above the wings is a semi-circular inlet. The wings are small and up-curved with a cusped inlet on their lower edges. The base of the blade and the wings are decorated in pointillé work on either side with a panel containing a dragon. A bulbous moulding joins the blade to the octagonal socket. Both moulding and socket are decorated with four pairs of longitudinal lines, between each of which on the socket is pointillé serpentine line. Two cheeks secure the head to the modern haft.

Dimensions: Length overall. 100.75 in (255.9 cm)   Length of head. 16.5 in (41.9 cm)
Weight. 4 lb (1.81 kg).
(VII 204)

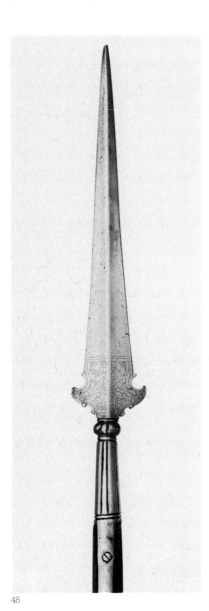

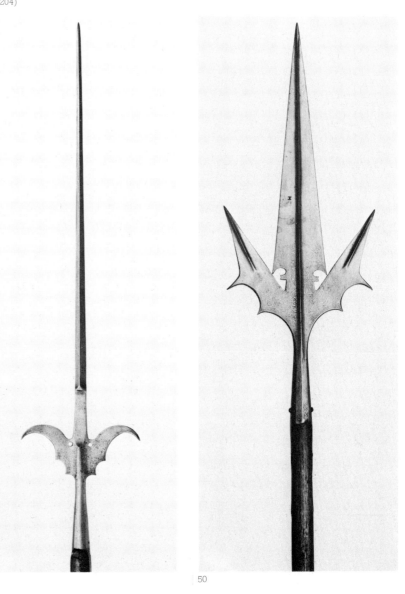

48   49   50

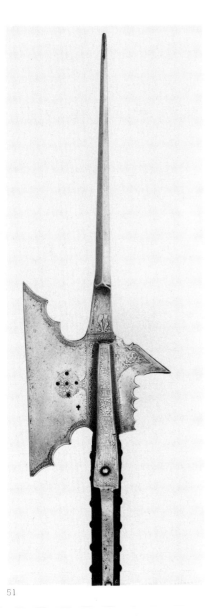

49
Corsèque
Italian, early sixteenth century.

The term corsèque, although not a contemporary English term, is now generally applied to this form of three-bladed spear, popular during the sixteenth and early seventeenth centuries, which derived from the medieval lugged spear. This is one of six similar 'corsèques' in the Armouries, which may have been supplied by Italian merchants for the use of one of King Henry VIII's companies of Guards. It has generally been accepted that the English term 'rawcon' was applied to this type of weapon and if this is so, these weapons may possibly be related to the 84 rawcons listed as being in the Palace of Westminster in the 1547 Inventory of Henry VIII's possessions. However, Alan Borg (see Literature) has recently suggested that this attribution is incorrect, that the term rawcon probably derived from the Italian *roncone*, meaning bill, and that these three-bladed spears were simply listed as partizans in the 1546 Inventory. Even the attribution to Henry VIII's arsenal is by no means certain, for the decoration of one of the other similar corsèques in the Armouries includes the Imperial Eagle and another almost identical in the Rijksmuseum, Amsterdam, is decorated with the Pillars of Hercules and PLUS ULTRA, the badge and motto of Charles V, Holy Roman Emperor. It appears, therefore, that this type of weapon and this style of decoration was not confined to one market only, and because of this the origins and history of these weapons remain uncertain. What is certain, however, is that these weapons or others like them were on display in the Tower's Spanish Armoury (see p. 3) in the eighteenth century when they were described as 'Spanish Spears'.

Provenance: uncertain, possibly Tudor Royal Armouries; probably on display in the Tower since at least 1676.

Long top-spike of square section flattened at the base from which spring two down-curved flukes, sharpened on their upper and cusped on their lower edges. Tapering socket with two short cheeks extending down the modern haft. The base of the top-spike, the flukes, and the socket bear patterns of strapwork and foliage in pointillé work.

Dimensions: Length overall, 97.75 in (248.3 cm)   Length of head, 34 in (86.4 cm)
Weight, 4 lb 11 oz (2.13 kg).

Literature: A. Borg; 'The Spanish Armoury in the Tower', *Archaeologia*, CV, 1976, pp. 339, 344–5, pls LXXXIV, XCa.
(VII 837)

50
Three-grained staff
Italian, early sixteenth century.

This is almost certainly one of the 'three-grayned staves' mentioned in the 1547 Inventory of the possessions of King Henry VIII. The word 'grayne' was sometimes used in Medieval English to describe the blade of a weapon, and it is therefore likely that some form of three-bladed spear is being referred to in the Inventory. 279 are listed in all, 188 apparently with plain heads, 25 with 'partlie gilt' heads, and a further 66 similarly gilt heads without staves. Considerable traces of gilding remain on the head of this example and it therefore presumably related to one of the latter two entries. The maker's mark stamped on the blade is of a design frequently found on Italian edged weapons of the early sixteenth century (see 18) and it also occurs on various other staff weapons which are believed to have been supplied for the use of one of Henry VIII's Guards.

Provenance: transferred to the Armouries in 1927 from the Rotunda Museum, Woolwich (1906 *Cat.*, No. XII. 1); said to have been presented by King George IV.

Steel head consisting of a long triangular blade with a pronounced medial ridge, stamped on either side with a maker's mark roughly in the form of a capital T with a crenellated top. On either side of the neck of the blade is a small, flat-ended lug. From the base of the neck spring two wings, projecting upwards at an angle of approximately 45°. The inner edges of the wings are straight, the outer edges are cusped to form two acute points. Each wing has a pronounced medial ridge for about half its length from the point. The decagonal socket has two cheeks extending down the modern haft. The base of the blade and the wings, and the socket are etched with figures of saints, putti, and centaurs, a grotesque male figure, foliage, strapwork, and scroll-work, the main figures against a finely hatched ground. Considerable traces of fire-gilding remain.

Dimensions: Length overall, 76 in (193.1 cm)   Length of head, 22 in (55.9 cm)
Weight, 3 lb 3 oz (1.45 kg).
(VII 1340)

51
Halberd
Italian, early sixteenth century.

The halberd, derived from the long-handled axe, grew in popularity during the later Middle Ages, and by the beginning of the sixteenth century it was widely used throughout Europe. This example was made in Italy, and was probably purchased for the use of one of King Henry VIII's companies of Guards. Only 306 halberds are recorded as being in the Tower in 1547, but such weapons were certainly used by Henry's Guards, for instance the painting at Hampton Court of Henry's embarkation from Dover in 1520 shows his Guard carrying halberds of this sort, some with similar decorative roundels on the blade. It is known that the Florentine merchant Leonardo Frescobaldi supplied some halberds, with the King's Arms engraved upon them, in 1513, but none of these has survived. This halberd is probably the one described in Tower Guides from the mid-eighteenth century as 'The Spanish General's Halbert', which formed part of the Tower's Spanish Armoury. (*see* p. 3).

Provenance: Tudor Royal Armouries; probably one of the 'Spanish Halberts' listed in the 1676 Tower Inventory.

Head of steel, consisting of an axe-blade with a straight cutting edge, triply cusped on its upper and lower edges, opposed by a short fluke set on a wide, cusped base at the rear, and surmounted by a top-spike of flattened rectangular section at the base and stiff diamond section above. Attached to the haft by an open-sided socket and cheeks. The head is etched with panels of scroll-work, the figures of St Sebastian and St Barbara, and, at the centre of the blade, with a medallion, pierced with five holes, bearing on one side a classical head, and on the other a floral design. The haft, which is not original, is covered in red velvet and studded with brass nails.

Dimensions: Length overall, 91.5 in (232.4 cm)   Length of head, 20.5 in (52.1 cm)
Weight, 5 lb 14 oz (2.66 kg).

Literature: A. Borg, 'The Spanish Armoury in the Tower', *Archaeologia*, CV, 1976, pp. 347, Pl. XCIc. (VII 962)

52
Bill
English, sixteenth century.

The military bill developed out of the agricultural implement of the same name and it is often difficult to tell them apart. It was especially favoured as a weapon in England where there is literary and pictorial evidence of its continued and growing popularity from the beginning of the fourteenth century. By the sixteenth century a distinctive English form of bill had developed, quite different from the tall, elegant, and often richly decorated bills made chiefly in Italy (*see* 53). Barbaro, the Venetian Ambassador, was struck by this difference in 1551 and he wrote that English bills 'have a short thick shaft with an iron like a peasant's hedging bill, but much thicker and heavier than what is used in the Venetian territories; with this they strike so heavily as to unhorse the cavalry, and it is made short because they like close quarters'. This bill is a good example of this English type, a plain, rather crude, but very functional weapon. Large quantities of these English bills were stored in the Tower in the sixteenth century, the greatest number being the 8,000 recorded in the 1540 Inventory.

Provenance: found at Horsham, Surrey; presented to the Armouries in 1950 by Major H.D. Barnes.

The iron head has a recurved cutting edge, a top-spike which angles away from the blade, and a short triangular fluke towards the base of the back-edge. Tapering socket of oval section, completely opened down one side except for a ring at the bottom. Modern wooden haft.

Dimensions: Length overall, 80.5 in (204.5 cm)   Length of head, 19.2 in (48.8 cm)
Weight, 5 lb 1 oz (2.3 kg).
(VII 1493)

53 (pl. XII)
Bill
Italian, early sixteenth century.

The bill (*see* 52) was a popular military weapon through the Middle Ages but this particular type, chiefly made in Italy, was widely used, especially for

parade and ceremonial purposes, in the early sixteenth century. This example is one of a group of about twenty in the Armouries which were almost certainly supplied by Italian merchants to King Henry VIII for use by one of his Guards (*see* 47). The 1547 Inventory of Henry VIII's possessions lists no fewer than 6,700 bills stored in the Tower as well as many in other places, including a small number of decorated bills to which those now in the Armouries may relate, such as the 'three billes ptely guilte with longe brassell (brazil wood) staves garnished with white and grene vellet and Silke' (the Tudor colours).

Provenance: transferred to the Armouries in 1927 from the Rotunda Museum, Woolwich (1864 *Cat.*, No. XII 14); said to have been presented by King George IV.

Long, elegant head of iron. The blade has a long cutting edge sloping out to a low point in the centre opposite the fluke which is of diamond section and expands at the shoulder into two flat-ended lugs. Above the fluke the rear edge is also sharpened. At the top of the cutting edge is a large, curved, double-edge hook. Long top-spike with a pronounced medial rib flanked on either side by a fuller or flute. At the base of the blade are two flat, slightly up-turned lugs. Rectangular-sectioned socket with bevelled corners, and two short cheeks. The blade is decorated below the back-spike with a panel of pointillé work consisting from top to bottom of the figure of a saint (on one side St Catherine, and on the other St Barbara); a profile head within an oval cartouche; and an oblong cartouche with scrolled corners bearing a cypher, composed slightly differently on either side, of the letters HENRI. The socket is decorated to match with a panel of symmetrical floral scroll-work. The haft is modern.

Dimensions: Length overall, 85.5 in (217.2 cm)   Length of head, 32 in (81.3 cm)
Weight, 9 lb 15 oz (4.51 kg).
(VII 1341)

54 (pl. XII)
Holy-water sprinkler
Possibly English, early sixteenth century.

The term 'holy-water sprinkler' appears frequently in sixteenth- and seventeenth-century English inventories and seems to refer to a long, spiked club, of this general form. It was apparently a peculiarly English weapon, for the Venetian Ambassador, Nicolo di Savri, writing in 1513, notes that 12,000 of the English army were armed with 'a weapon never seen until now, six feet in length, surmounted by a ball with six steel spikes'. 493 plain 'hollywater sprinckles' are listed in the 1547 Inventory of the possessions of King Henry VIII, and this example, together with another similar one in the Tower, may be a survivor of these. From the late seventeenth to the mid-nineteenth centuries they were displayed in the Tower's Spanish Armoury, as Danish or Saxon clubs, with the story that they had been used by the Danes in the conquest of England. The Tower Guides from 1750 to 1796 relate that the Yeoman Warders 'call 'em Women's Weapons, because, they say, the British Women made Prize of them, when in one Night, they all conspired together and cut the Throats of 35,000 Danes', adding sarcastically that this was 'the greatest Piece of Secrecy the English Women ever kept'.

Provenance: possibly Tudor Royal Armouries; probably one of the four 'Danish Clubbs' mentioned in the 1676 Tower Inventory.

Large, heavy iron head, consisting of six flanges, each cusped twice to form three spikes, the spikes of alternate flanges having pyramidal tips. Above is a thick top-spike of diamond section and, below, a hexagonal neck ending in a large roped roundel. Wooden haft of square section with chamfered corners reinforced for its entire length by four steel straps.

Dimensions: Length overall, 74.5 in (189.2 cm)   Length of head, 15.5 in (47 cm)
Weight, 11 lb 9 oz (5.24 kg).

Literature: A. Borg, 'The Spanish Armoury in the Tower', *Archaeologia*, CV, 1976, pp. 341–2, pl. LXXXIIIc, LXXXIV, no.32, LXXXVIIb.
(VII 1642)

55
Spear
Possibly English, first half sixteenth century.

One of a group of twenty-four similar small spears in the Armouries all of which bear the same mark. In form they closely resemble the group of pikes in the Armouries which are believed to date from the time of King Henry VIII (*see* 56). It is probable that these spears too were made during Henry's reign and they were probably intended for use by light cavalry. The 1547

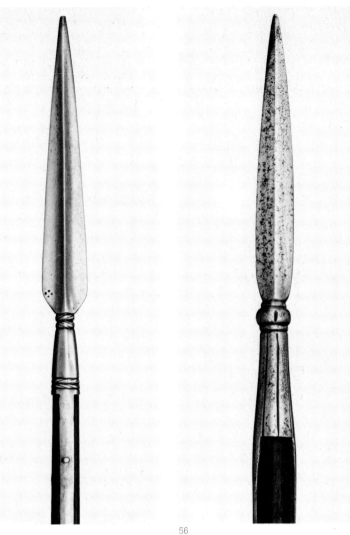

55   56

Inventory of Henry VIII's property lists four different types of light cavalry
spear – 'javelyns', 'demy launces', 'northeron staves', and 'Colin cleves', but
it is not now possible to attribute these terms to any particular type of
surviving spear. Nor is it possible to be certain where spears such as this one
were made. There is evidence that Henry VIII acquired light spears both
from English merchants and armourers such as John Crochet, and from
foreign, notably Italian and German suppliers; and in 1551 the 'Colin cleves'
mentioned above were described as weapons 'commonly bought at the city
of Cologne'.

Provenance: probably Tudor Royal Armouries; in the Armouries since before 1859.

Head of steel consisting of a small, leaf-shaped blade of hollow diamond section, stamped on either
side with a mark in the form of a four-leaf clover. Short, tapering socket of round section with a plain
ring at the top and bottom. Short cheeks, one now missing, secure the head to the modern wooden
haft.

Dimensions: Length overall, 91 in (231 cm)   Length of head, 11.7 in (29.6 cm)
Weight, 3 lb 1 oz (1.39 kg).
(VII 104)

56
Pike
Early sixteenth century.

The term pike is generally used to describe the very long, small-headed
spear, used chiefly in massed formations as defence against cavalry, which
was especially popular in Europe for the 200 years between the mid-fifteenth

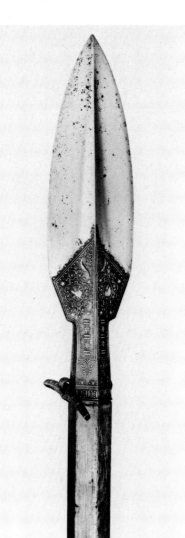

57

and mid-seventeenth centuries. This example, mounted on part of its original haft, is one of a group of over 80 similar pikes in the Armouries which range in length between 16 and 20 feet. In form and decoration they are related to some of the groups of staff weapons from the armouries of King Henry VIII (*see* 48 & 55), and it seems likely that they too date from Henry's reign. They may have been among the 20,100 'Morris Picks' listed among the stores in the Tower in the 1547 Inventory of the possessions of King Henry VIII. Morris pikes first appear in the Tower Inventories of the late fifteenth century, and are last mentioned in the Inventory of 1559, after which the term 'pike' is used without any prefix. The name Morris (or Moorish) pike suggests a Spanish origin for the weapon, but it appears that most of the Morris pikes acquired for King Henry VIII were purchased from Italian merchants, such as the Florentines Franciscus Taunell and Francis De Barde, who supplied large quantities in 1512 and 1513 (see *Letters and papers Henry VIII*, 1, pt. 2, 3613). At a later date, Morris pikes were probably made in England, since the 1559 Inventory of the Tower contains an entry proposing the purchase of another 1,000 of these weapons to which is added the recommendation that 'the said morrispikes are best made wth in the Realme'.

Provenance: Tudor Royal Armouries.

Steel head consisting of a narrow leaf-shaped blade of flattened diamond section and a tapering socket of round section, to which are attached two long cheeks. Between the head and the socket is a bulbous moulding. Both the moulding and the socket are filed with 8 longitudinal lines. The head is fitted to approximately 3 feet of the original haft.

Dimensions: Length overall, 46.62 in (118.4 cm)   Length of head, 8 in (20.3 cm)
Weight, 1 lb 2 oz (5.103 kg).
(VII 1715)

57
Hunting spear
French, or possibly Italian, about 1600.

Hunting spears of this general type were in use in Europe from at least the fifteenth century until the middle of the eighteenth century. Although commonly known as 'boar spears' they were, in fact, used for hunting most large game, although spears the size of this one were almost certainly intended for use against either boar or bear. The toggle at the base of the socket acts in the same way as a fixed cross-bar to prevent the wounded prey from closing with the hunter by rushing up the shaft of the spear. The gold and silver encrusting of this spear links it with a group of similarly decorated objects, including a number of wheel-lock pistols which exhibit various constructional features commonly found on wheel-locks made in France. Mainly because of this, the entire group has been thought to be of French origin. Claude Blair, however, has recently tentatively suggested that these pistols may have been made in the French style by Gasparo Mola, a goldsmith and medallist, who was born in 1567, died in 1640, and spent much of his life working for the Medici family in Florence. If this is true the similarity of the decoration suggests that the entire group of related weapons including this spear, may also have been made in Mola's workshop.

Provenance: acquired by the Armouries before 1859 (in the 1859 *Catalogue* of the Armouries it is probably VII.388, 'Boar spear, the head damaskined in gold and silver. 16th century').

Large leaf-shaped blade with a pronounced medial ridge and a short hexagonal socket pierced to receive the fixed ring by which a steel toggle is attached. The toggle, socket, and lower part of the blade are encrusted in gold and silver on a blackened ground with trophies of arms, crossed palms, strapwork, and stars. The haft is modern.

Dimensions: Length overall, 73.37 in (186.4 cm)   Length of head, 15.9 in (40.4 cm)
Weight, 5 lb (2.27 kg).

Literature: E. von Koerner, 'Französische Stangenwaffen in der dresdener Rüstkammer' *Zeitschrift für historische Waffenkunde*, XII, 1929–31, pp. 12–13; J.F. Hayward, *The art of the gunmaker*, London 1962, I, pp. 102–4; Sir James Mann, *Wallace Collection Catalogues: European arms and armour*, London 1962, II, p. 557; C. Blair, review of N. di Carpegna, *Arma de fuoco della collezione Odescalchi*, Rome 1968, in *The Connoisseur*, August 1969, pp. 256–7; A.V.B. Norman, *The rapier and small-sword*, London 1980, pp. 328, 362.
(VII 81)

58 (pl. XI)
Partizan
Possibly Italian, about 1600; decorated about 1650, probably in Lyons.

Staff weapons of many different sorts were made for the special troops and guards raised by towns and cities. Some were plain, functional, and often rather crude weapons intended for use by those, such as night watchmen, whose job it was to preserve order. Others, such as this example, were highly decorated weapons intended for use only on ceremonial occasions. This partizan appears to be one of a group of 24 acquired by the City of Lyons in 1650 for its *Corps des Arquebuziers*, a body-guard which escorted the City Fathers on both formal and festive occasions. The decoration of the head includes not only the arms of France and Lyons but those of the Lyonnaise family of Rouannes, and this suggests that this particular partizan belonged to Charles Rouannes who is recorded as an official of the *Corps des Arquebuziers* in the 1650s. There is, however, some doubt about where and when this partizan was made, for it bears a maker's mark that also appears on a group of halberds and 'corsèques', apparently dating from about 1600, which have generally been considered to be of Italian origin. It is possible, therefore, that this is a plain Italian partizan which was later decorated, perhaps in Lyons itself, for the use of the civic guard.

Provenance: collection of Ralph Bernal; purchased by the Armouries at Christie's sale of his collection, 27 March 1855, lot 2369.

Long, tapering blade, with a pronounced medial rib, expanding at the base in two small, pointed wings. Struck on one side with a maker's mark, the letter V within an inverted heart. Round, tapering socket with two cheeks extending down the modern haft. On either side of the blade are four etched and formerly gilt panels which, from top to bottom, are decorated as follows: formal scroll-work involving a human mask and surmounted by ogival arches and a fleur-de-lis; the arms of France and Navarre surrounded by the collars of the Orders of Saint Michel and the Saint Esprit; a classical figure scene depicting on one side Mars and Pallas Athena, and, on the other side, Apollo; and another classical scene depicting on one side Orpheus riding a dolphin, and, on the other, a landscape with Muses. The socket is similarly etched with formal scroll-work involving the arms of Lyons and the family of Rouannes.

Dimensions: Length overall, 80.37 in (204.1 cm)   Length of head, 32.25 in (81.9 cm)
Weight, 4 lb 7 oz (2.01 kg).

Literature: E. Vial, *Gens et choses de Lyon*, Lyons 1945, p. 56; Sir James Mann, *Wallace Collection Catalogues; European arms and armour*, London 1962, II, p. 475.
(VII 216)

59 (pl. XI)
Partizan
French, about 1670.

During the sixteenth, seventeenth and eighteenth centuries elaborately decorated staff weapons were carried by the guards and retainers of many noblemen and monarchs. This partizan, richly decorated in gold counterfeit-damascening on a blued ground, was made for the Gardes de la Manche, part of the Gardes du Corps (body-guard) of King Louis XIV of France. The Gardes de la Manche was the senior of the French Royal Guards dating back to the early fifteenth century and, originally, it was composed entirely of Scots. The decoration of this partizan includes the arms and emblems of France and Navarre and the motto NEC PLURIBUS IMPAR (nor unequal to many) which the King apparently adopted about 1668. Other details of the decoration confirm that this partizan cannot have been made before 1667 but that it is unlikely to have been made much later than 1670 (*see* C. Aries, *Armes blanches militaires françaises*, XXII, Paris 1974). Two similar partizans made for the Gardes de la Manche are in the Armouries and at least twelve others are known to survive in other collections.

Provenance: brought from Paris in 1816; transferred to the Armouries in 1927 from the Rotunda Museum, Woolwich (1864 *Cat.*, No. XII.90).

Flamboyant blade of blued steel with a pronounced medial rib and up-curved wings at the base. It is decorated from top to bottom on either side in gold counterfeit-damascening as follows: the motto, NEC PLURIBUS IMPAR; the sun in splendour; a trophy of arms surrounded by four fleurs-de-lis; the arms of France and Navarre surmounted by a crown and surrounded by the collars of the Orders of the Saint Esprit and Saint Michael; and a panel of foliate scroll-work involving two opposed figures of Fame. The top of the octagonal socket is chiselled with acanthus foliage, the remainder is blued and counterfeit-damascened in gold with fleurs-de-lis. The cheeks have broken off and the transverse peg, for which the base of the socket is drilled, is missing. The haft is modern.

Dimensions: Length overall, 75.62 in (192.1 cm)   Length of head, 22.8 in (58 cm)
Weight, 4 lb 8 oz (2.04 kg).

Literature: Sir James Mann, *Wallace Collection Catalogues; European arms and armour*, London 1962, II, pp. 469–71.
(VII 1358)

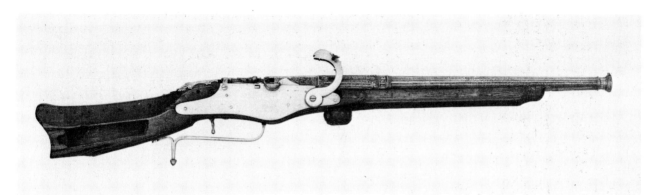

60
Breech-loading gun
Probably English, dated 1537.

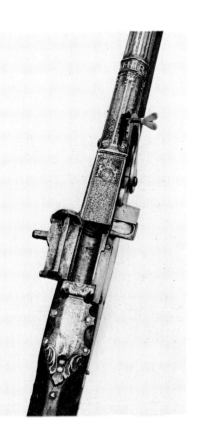

This is the smaller of two breech-loading guns in the Armouries which were made for King Henry VIII. Both were originally equipped with wheel-locks, which have now disappeared, the lock of this gun being replaced by a plain matchlock with an automatic sliding pan-cover, which was probably made in the nineteenth century. Both guns employ reloadable steel chambers which are pushed into the breech in the same way as a modern cartridge. The side-hinged breech-block of both these guns bears a striking resemblance to the breech action, developed by the American Jacob Snider, which was adopted by the British Army in 1864. Breech-loading hand-guns using reloadable chambers were produced intermittently from the fifteenth to the nineteenth century, the earliest ones apparently being modelled on contemporary breech-loading cannon, the chambers simply lying in a trough at the breech end of the barrel and secured by lugs and pins or simple wedges. The guns of Henry VIII are the earliest-known examples of this type to have hinged-breech-blocks. Henry, who, like many of his contemporary princes, seems to have been fascinated by new mechanical contrivances, had no fewer than 139 breech-loading guns in his collection at the time of his death, including 116 Italian guns, and it is now impossible to be certain which if any of the entries in the 1547 Catalogue Inventory of his possessions, relates to this gun. However, as this gun obviously had a velvet-covered cheek pad it may be the 'chamber pece in a Stocke of woode, lyned in the Cheke with vellet' which is listed as being in the Palace of Westminster along with another chambered gun, perhaps the larger of the two now in the Armouries. Henry's interest in breech-loading guns is further attested by the series of curious gun-shields from his arsenal which are also preserved in the Armouries and which are equipped with breech-loading matchlock pistols of an otherwise unknown type (*see* 11). The fine barrel of this gun, which is chiselled in the form of a column and bears the devices and initials of Henry VIII, illustrates the quality of craftsmen Henry could call upon. Hayward (*see* Literature) has tentatively suggested that it may have been imported from Antwerp where barrels of comparably complex designs were being made at this time, but it seems more likely that it was made in England by one of Henry's own gunmakers. It is stamped with a mark which may be that of William Hunt who in 1538 was appointed Keeper of the King's Handguns and Demi-Hawks and was 'emplo'd about the makeing and furnishing of the King's Highnesses' devices of certain pieces of artillery'. It was perhaps this gun which Joseph Platter, a Swiss traveller, saw in the Armouries in 1599 and described as a pistol 'very like a musket', which 'could be loaded at the breech, that by this means it might be the less readily exploded'.

Provenance: Tudor Royal Collection; in the Armouries, probably since 1599, certainly since 1691 when it was described in a valuation as 'King Henry Eights Carbine'.

Plain replacement matchlock with an automatic sliding pan-cover. The stock has a slightly upcurved shoulder-butt with a butt-box on the right side and another smaller box beneath; the covers of both now missing. The left side has been fitted with a cheek-pad of which only the brass securing-nails remain. The side-flat is slightly carved with foliage. Immediately behind the breech is an applied shield-shaped plaque of brass, formerly gilt, engraved with figures of St George and the Dragon. Ahead of the lock there is a projecting boss on the underside of the stock, carved with acanthus foliage, which is intended to act as the grip for the left hand. The fore-end, which would originally have continued to the muzzle, has had the final 3½ inches trimmed away. The letters GT are incised twice on the right side behind the lock-plate. The steel trigger-guard is probably a replacement. The barrel is of square section at the breech and then round to the moulded muzzle. The breech-block, which is hinged at the left side, has a short operating lever on the right and is secured when closed by a transverse pin at the front. It is chiselled with acanthus foliage, stamped with a maker's mark, WH above a fleur-de-lis, and incised at its forward end with the date 1537. The breech, which is chambered for a reloadable steel cartridge, is chiselled on the top face with a crowned Tudor Rose with lion supporters, and is engraved with foliage, which is now almost obliterated. It retains traces of gilding. The beginning of the round section of the barrel is chiselled with three slender columns framing at the base two medallion heads, the capitals supporting a frieze bearing the initials HR. The remaining length of the barrel is fluted as far as the mouldings at the muzzle which carry a brass fore-sight.

Dimensions: Length overall, 38.37 in (97.5 cm)   Length of barrel, 25.6 in (65 cm)
Calibre, .54 in (30 bore)   Weight 9 lb 5 oz (4.22 kg).

Literature: J.F. Hayward, *The art of the gunmaker*, London 1962, I, pp. 106–10; H.L. Blackmore, *Guns and rifles of the world*, London 1965, p. 65, pl. 350–1; W. Reid, *The lore of arms*, London 1976, pp. 114–5.
(XII 1)

61 (pl. XVII)
Wheel-lock pistol or short carbine
Probably French, about 1590.

This richly decorated weapon was almost certainly intended for show rather than for use. Although it has a lock of German form it was probably made in France. The form and decoration of the stock is very similar to that of a carbine with a lock of French construction in the Musée de l'Armée (No. M.98), and Hayward (*see* Literature) has suggested that the two stocks may have been made in the same workshop. The form of the chiselling on the lock, mounts, and barrel closely resembles that on a wheel-lock pistol from the *Cabinet d'Armes* of Louis XIII, now in the Hermitage Museum, Leningrad. The most unusual features of the decoration of this gun are the two *verre églomisé* plaques, set one on either side of the butt, which are painted in gold on a red ground with a shield bearing a sprig of forget-me-not, in the centre of which is the Sacred Monogram within a heart, and above which is the German inscription *VER GIS MEIN NIT* (forget me not) and the date 1581. Such plaques are usually found set in rings and cannot be regarded as providing evidence either for the date or origin of the gun itself – they might for instance have been imported by the maker or acquired abroad by the owner. However the forget-me-not motif and inscription perhaps suggest that the gun may have been a presentation piece.

Provenance: by tradition the property of an English family since the sixteenth century; purchased by the Armouries with the aid of the National Art-Collections Fund at Sotheby's, 22 December 1960, lot 177.

Wheel-lock chiselled and gilt with a satyr, a human-headed and bird-bodied monster, and a grotesque mask. The arm of the dog is formed as a merman. The dog-spring and pan-cover release-button are missing and the bearing plate of the wheel is a restoration. Walnut stock with down-curved butt of what is commonly known as petronel form, inlaid with decoration in white and green-stained stag-horn, and mother of pearl consisting of running foliage inhabited by human figures, birds, centaurs, and satyrs. In addition the stock is inset with a number of silver medallions embossed with human and grotesque masks, two miniatures of bearded men, one wearing an open coronet, painted on ivory and set beneath glass or rock-crystal, and on either side of the butt a *verre églomisé* plaque (*see* above). The stag-horn butt-plate is engraved with the figures of Venus and Cupid. Gilt-steel mounts, the wooden ramrod a restoration. Barrel chiselled and gilt for its entire length with human masks and demi-figures, strapwork, canopies, and stylised floral ornament, with a monster's head at the muzzle.

Dimensions: Length overall, 29.5 in (74.9 cm)   Length of barrel, 21.6 in (54.9 cm)
Calibre, .37 in (90 bore)   Weight, 4 lb 6 oz (1.98 kg).

Literature: J.F. Hayward, *The art of the gunmaker*, London 1962, I, pp. 100–1, pl. 25b; C. Blair, *Pistols of the world*, London 1968, p. 90, pl. 55.
(XII 1764)

·62
Snaphance pistol
English, about 1600.

The snaphance lock differs from the later flintlock principally in having a pancover which is separate from, rather than combined with, the steel, and a horizontally acting external sear. The earliest recorded evidence for the existence of this type of lock occurs in Swedish and Italian documents dated 1547, but it appears likely that it was a German invention. By about 1580 the snaphance lock was in use in most parts of Europe and national styles were becoming apparent. It has generally been accepted that the snaphance was introduced into England from Holland and that English snaphances are thus of Dutch style. In fact, however, some of the earliest surviving English snaphance guns pre-date any recorded Dutch ones, and it is possible that the English snaphance influenced Dutch designs rather than vice versa. The earliest reference to snaphance guns in England dates from 1580, and relates to the arming of troops to be sent to Ireland, and the earliest surviving example, now in the National Museum, Copenhagen (Inv. No. 10428) is dated 1584. This pistol is the type of firearm which in the sixteenth and seventeenth centuries was known as a 'pocket dag'. Because of their small size, which made concealment easy, such pistols were commonly regarded as the weapons of footpads, thieves and assassins, and so from the time of Henry VIII onward, they came under royal prohibition. However often they were repeated, however, such legal bans on the use of these pistols seem to have been generally ineffective. Nor was the use of these small guns confined to the dishonest, for as Holinshed wrote in 1587 'for self protection the honest traveller is now inforced to ride with a case of dags at his saddle bow, or with some pretie short snapper'. This pistol is very similar to a small pair in the Kremlin, Moscow (Nos. 8243–4), which probably formed part of a gift of firearms sent by James I to Tsar Boris Godunov in about 1604. The form of decoration on this pistol, however, seems to relate more closely to that on late sixteenth-century English firearms and accessories than to those of early seventeenth-century date.

Provenance: collection of J.T. Hooper, purchased by the Armouries at Christie's 27 October 1971, lot 119.

Snaphance lock of Anglo-Dutch form, with a separate pan-cover and steel, and a horizontally operating sear which engages the heel of the cock. The flat lock-plate, now much russetted, is shaped at the rear as a monstrous head, and is counterfeit-damascened in gold with foliate scroll-work, now much rubbed. Attached to the outside of the pan is a round, convex flash-guard. Walnut full-stock with a writhen, lemon-shaped pommel. The stock is inlaid with engraved bone and mother of pearl. The major surfaces are bordered by strips decorated with guilloche ornament and similar strips divide the top of the butt into diagonal bands. The intervening spaces are filled with bone scrolls and mother-of-pearl bands, with, on either side of the barrel-tang, a bearded profile head. The fore-end and rammer pipes are of bone engraved to match. The iron button trigger is not protected by a trigger-guard. A long belt-hook, running almost to the muzzle, is fitted on the left side, the tip now broken off. The surface is now russetted but bears traces of counterfeit-damascening in gold. Its finial is in the form of a monstrous head, and bears a spring and guide for the missing safety catch. The round barrel has a transverse moulding at the breech and another almost half-way to the muzzle. The expanding muzzle is decorated with coarse spiralling lines. The barrel is now russetted but bears traces of foliate scroll engraving and of gold counterfeit damascening to match that on the lock.

Dimensions: Length overall, 11.25 in (28.6 cm)   Length of barrel, 6.25 in (15.9 cm)
Calibre, .45 in (51 bore)   Weight 1 lb 3 oz (0.538 kg).

Literature: I.D.D. Eaves, 'Further notes on the pistol in early 17th century England', *Journal of the
Arms and Armour Society*, 1976, VIII, No.5, pp. 283–5.
(XII 1823)

63
All-brass sporting gun
British, Dundee, dated 161?, the lock about 1700.

All-metal pistols, both of steel and brass, were made in considerable
numbers in Scotland throughout the seventeenth and eighteenth centuries,
but only two Scottish all-metal long-guns are known, of which this is one. The
other, which is almost a pair to this, was purchased by the National Museum
of Antiquities of Scotland, Edinburgh, in 1973. The Edinburgh gun bears the
mark attributed to James Low of Dundee, at this time the principal centre of
firearms manufacture in Scotland, and there can be little doubt that the
Tower's gun was also made by Low. James Low is first recorded working as a
lockmaker in 1587, and a large number of guns bearing his mark survive,
ranging in date from 1602 to 1627. The most unusual feature of both these
guns is the adjustable extension to the butt, presumably intended to facilitate
their use by people of varying stature, for whom the guns could be adjusted
as necessary. Such adjustable butts seem to have been one of Low's
specialities, and they also occur on a pair of brass, lemon-butted, snaphance
pistols dated 1614 which bear his mark (collection of R.T. Gwynn). Similar
devices are, however, recorded on a number of other early firearms,
including a late sixteenth-century English-type snaphance gun bearing the
arms of the Scottish family of Spens (Livrustkammaren, Stockholm, No.1349),
which perhaps suggests that the idea was introduced to Scotland from
England. The Edinburgh gun retains its original snaphance lock, but the
original lock of the Tower's gun has been replaced, probably during its
working lifetime, by a later plain flintlock. Unfortunately this conversion
necessitated cutting away part of the raised breech of the barrel, on which
would have been the maker's mark. The last numeral of the date has also
been partially lost, but what remains is an upper loop suggesting that the date
must have been either 1612, 1613, 1618 or 1619. The Edinburgh gun is dated
1624. The butt extension of both guns is crudely fretted with an English royal
crown, and the decoration of both guns involves pairs of addorsed C's which
are especially prominent on the Tower's example. Similarly conceived
addorsed C's are also found on a richly engraved and gilt armour in the
Armouries which is believed to have been made for King Charles I (No. II.91),
and the weight of evidence suggests that both guns were made for Charles
when he was still Prince of Wales. However, Maxwell (*see* Literature) has cast
some doubt on this attribution by calling attention to the blank shields on both
guns, obvious places to acclaim royal ownership which he argues 'was
surely not something to be hidden'.

Provenance: believed to have come from Bolton Hall, Yorkshire; collection of Mrs M.H. Pinkerton, The Manor House, New Place, Pulborough, Sussex; sold by John D. Wood & Co., London, 14 September 1965, lot 574; collection of Mr F.A. Turner; purchased by the Armouries together with an ancestral scrap-book, perhaps relating to the family which owned the gun before 1852, in 1965.

The replacement flintlock has a flat brass lock-plate, originally gilt, and is made unusually long in order to occupy the space of the original snaphance lock. The stock is entirely of brass, originally gilt all-over, traces of gilding now surviving only in sunken parts of the decoration. The butt is engraved with scrolling foliage, and a frieze of palmette ornament. The fore-end bears on either side a band of ribbon ornament and another resembling a form of compressed key-pattern. The short butt is fitted with an extension consisting of a solid brass plate crudely pierced in the form of a royal crown, which is mounted on a flat brass bar which slides into the butt and is cut with six squared notches to engage with the spring-catch on the underside of the butt. The trigger-guard has an extension for the fingers, the solid scroll-shaped end being engraved with a rose. The present brass ramrod is probably not original. The slender barrel is of round section with a flat on either side running nearly to the flared and moulded muzzle. There is a raised flange at the base of the breech into which is cut the back-sight notch. The barrel is engraved with panels of scrolling foliage, involving addorsed C scrolls, together with chequered and herring-bone ornament framed in looped ribbon-like bands, the loops enclosing roses and other conventional flowers. Towards the breech, between two low mouldings, is a blank shield beneath a crowned helmet. The ground to the engraving is hatched and the entire surface has originally been gilt. At the breech is engraved the date 161?, the last digit partly obliterated.

Dimensions: Length overall, 46.31 in (117.6 cm)   Length overall (butt extended), 52.31 in (132.9 cm)
Length of barrel, 35.8 in (90.9 cm)   Calibre .476 in (43 bore)   Weight, 8 lb 2 oz (3.69 kg).

Literature: W. Reid, 'A Prince's Gun from Dundee', *The Connoisseur*, 1966, CLXIII, pp. 148–50; C. Blair, 'Scottish Firearms', *American Society of Arms Collectors Bulletin*, 1975, No. 13, pp. 70–1 S. Maxwell, 'A brass sporting gun dated 1624', *Proceedings of the Society of Antiquaries of Scotland*, 1975, CVI, pp. 215–8.
(XII 1786)

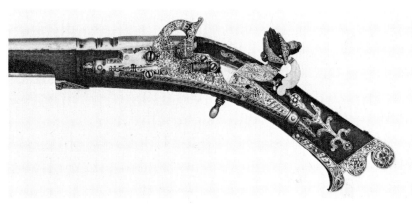

64 (pl. XVI)
Snaphance pistol
British, made in Lowland Scotland, dated 1619.

By the end of the sixteenth century a recognisably Scottish style of firearm had appeared. For many years it was generally accepted that this style derived, like that of contemporary English guns, from Continental, and probably Dutch prototypes. However, it now seems far more likely that the Scottish and English styles, which display very close similarities, evolved as a result of an interchange of ideas between the two nations, probably with the English influencing the Scottish style rather more than the reverse. The decoration of Scottish firearms is one of their more distinctive characteristics, the metalwork often being engraved, with a mixture of Romanesque scroll-work and Celtic patterns. This pistol appears unusual because it is mounted with a lock on the left side of the stock, for use in the left, rather than the right hand. This was, however, a very common feature of early Scottish pistols, which were often made in pairs for use in both hands. It is almost certain, therefore, that this pistol was originally one of a pair. This pistol has a snaphance lock (*see* 62) and is of the earliest-known Scottish type, which is distinguished by the 'fish-tail' form of the butt. The earliest dateable Scottish pistols of this form are a pair, perhaps the work of John Kennedy of Edinburgh, which have left- and right-hand locks and are dated 1598 (Historisches Museum, Dresden). Whether this style derived from that of contemporary English pistols or whether the Scottish form influenced the design of English guns it is impossible to tell, but certainly pistols of this particular form, although lacking the typically Scottish decoration, were also made and used in England (*see* for instance: two plain pistols of early seventeenth-century date in the Palazzo Ducale Venice, Nos. 930, 932, and a pistol, lavishly decorated in the Anglo-Dutch style which is illustrated in the 1594 portrait of Captain Thomas Lee on loan to the Tate Gallery, London). This pistol has two features in common with the English snaphance pistol No.62, the ball-trigger without a trigger-guard, and the long-belt hook. It bears the initials of a maker who has not yet been identified. ffoulkes (1916 *Cat.*), however, compared this pistol with a Scottish long-gun in the Armouries (No. XII.63) which was made in 1614 by the Dundee gunmaker Robert Allison, and suggested that the maker of this pistol came from the same family. As this long-gun was then believed to have belonged to Charles I when Prince of Wales, ffoulkes suggested that this pistol might also have belonged to Charles. There is, however, no real evidence to support either of these conclusions.

Provenance: collection of Lord Londesborough; sold Christie's, 4 July 1888, lot 55; Gurney collection, sold Christie's, 9 March 1898, lot 264; purchased by the Armouries later in 1898 from Mr Harding.

Left-hand snaphance lock with a separate steel and pan-cover and a horizontally acting sear which engages the heel of the cock. The lock-plate is of brass, and together with the outer faces of the cock and steel, is engraved with foliate scroll-work and bands of guilloche ornament. Ahead of the stock the lock-plate is stamped with the maker's initials C A. The fence or flash-guard attached to the outside of the pan bears the date 1619. The finial or comb attached to the back of the cock is a restoration. The walnut stock is mounted in brass decorated to match the lock, and is inlaid on the butt with cut-out and engraved brass sheet in the form of symmetrical palmette ornament. A silver strip engraved with strap ornament is inlaid along the back of the grip. A short section of wood is missing from the tip of the fore-end. The button-trigger, the ramrod with moulded ends, and the belt-hook are of steel. The steel barrel is of octagonal section at the breech and then round to the slightly tulip-shaped muzzle, with a wide double moulding at the change of section.

Dimensions: Length overall, 16.2 in (42.2 cm)   Length of barrel, 11 in (27.9 cm)
Calibre, .35 in (95 bore)   Weight, 1 lb 5 oz (0.595 kg).

Literature: *Proceedings of the Society of Antiquaries*, 1897, 2 Series, XVII, No.107, pp. 2–3; C.E. Whitelaw, *A treatise on Scottish firearms*, London 1923, p. 90; C. Blair, 'Scottish firearms', *American Society of Arms Collectors Bulletin*, 1975, No.31, Fig. 14.
(XII 737)

65 (pl. XVIII)
Flintlock sporting gun
German, Alsace, dated 1646.

The richly decorated stock of this gun was made by Jean Conrad Tornier of Masevaux, one of a number of sixteenth- and seventeenth-century gun-stockers who are also known to have made small articles of furniture which could be decorated in the same manner as gun stocks. The stock is unsigned, but the decoration is undoubtedly by the same hand as that on a wooden casket in the Wallace Collection, London (Cat. No. A. 1345), which is signed FAIT EN MASSEVAUX PAR JEAN CONRAD TORNIER MONSTEUR D'HARQUEBISSES L'EN 1630 (made in Masevaux by Jean Conrad Tornier, gun-stocker, in the year 1630). Three other firearms stocked by Tornier have also been identified, all decorated, like this example, with intricate inlaid designs based on the engraved ornament of Michel le Blon who was working in Amsterdam from about 1610, and whose designs seem to have been used mainly by gunmakers working in the Low Countries and Northern France. Masevaux (German: Massmünster), the town in which Tornier worked, is approximately 11 miles from Belfort, in that part of Alsace which was transferred from Germany to France by the treaty of Westphalia in 1648. The lock of this gun bears the mark of Franz Kruter of Solothurn, Switzerland, who is known to have been working in the 1640s.

Provenance: the property of a Viennese collector, sold at Sotheby's, 2 July 1936, lot 89; purchased by the Armouries in 1952 from the collection of W.R. Hearst, St Donat's Castle, with the assistance of grants from the National Art-Collections Fund and the Pilgrim Trust.

Flat lock with a ring-necked cock, ahead of which is stamped a mark – within a shield the initials FK above two stars above a flower. Stock with deep-bellied butt inlaid in plain and yellow- and green-stained stag-horn with intricate designs of bunches of fruit and flowers interspersed with birds, animals, and hunting scenes. Scrolling lines of stag-horn fill the areas between the decoration and act as terminals to blossom and leaves. Pierced steel trigger-guard and plain brass butt-plate. Around the tang of the barrel is a brass plate pierced with foliate scrolls. The forward rammer pipe is a restoration. Long, slender, octagonal barrel engraved I.S., probably the initials of the maker, and with the date 1646. The sights are of brass.

Dimensions: Length overall, 59.37 in (150.8 cm)   Length of barrel, 44 in (111.8 cm)
Calibre, .39 in (78 bore)   Weight, 6 lb 5 oz (2.86 kg).

Literature: A.N. Kennard, 'Jean Conrad Tornier', *The Burlington Magazine*, 1940, LXXVII, pp. 127–8; J.F. Hayward, *The art of the gunmaker*, I, London 1962, p. 152; Sir J. Mann, *Wallace Collection Catalogue: European arms and armour*, London 1962, II, pp. 513, 627; H.L. Blackmore, *Guns and rifles of the world*, London 1965, No.177.
(XII 1549)

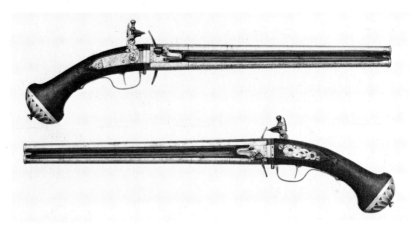

66
Double-barrelled flintlock pistols
British, London, about 1660.

The over-and-under barrels of these pistols are both equipped with pan and frizzle, and can be rotated by hand to bring each in turn to the firing position. The term 'turn-over' is usually applied to this type of weapon, although the German word *Wender* is also used to describe it. 'Turn-over' pistols seem first to have appeared in Holland and France in the 1640s and were produced in considerable numbers during the second half of the seventeenth century. Harman Barne, the maker of this pair of pistols, was an immigrant gunmaker, perhaps of Dutch origin, who came to England in about 1642 as gunmaker to Prince Rupert, nephew of Charles I. During the Civil Wars and Commonwealth he suffered periods of imprisonment for his support of the royalist cause, but in 1655 he was allowed to begin making guns once more. In 1657 he was elected a freeman of the London Gunmakers' Company and in 1661, shortly before his death, he was made Gunmaker-in-Ordinary to King Charles II. It is not possible to date these pistols precisely. Harman Barne is known to have been making guns during the Civil Wars, but it is more likely that these pistols date from after his rehabilitation in 1655. A pair of 'turn-over' pistols by Claude Cunet of Lyons, who is known to have been working in the 1650s, now in Skokloster Castle, Sweden (see T. Lenk, *Flintlåset*, Stockholm 1939, pl. 26.2) is very similar to this pair by Barne and has the same fluted butt caps and telescopic rammer.

Provenance: purchased by the Armouries from an English private collection in 1979 after an export licence had been refused by the Department of Trade.

Each pistol has a single back-action lock, engraved on the tail of the flat lock-plate and on the flat cock with floral decoration and sea-monsters. The lock-plate is signed in elaborate script HARMAN BARNE. Walnut butts with flattened mushroom pommels covered with fluted brass caps. The prominent screws which apparently secure these caps are the ends of telescopic ramrods. Steel side-plates pierced and engraved as sea-serpents. Two strips of walnut, one either side, act as the fore-end of each pistol. Double over-and-under barrels, which can be revolved when the front of the trigger-guard is pressed upwards, each with its own pan and frizzle. A double muzzle-ring helps to hold the ends of the barrels together.

Dimensions: Length, 25.5 in (64.8 cm)   Length of barrel, 16.5 in (41.9 cm)
Calibre, .526 in (32 bore)   Weight, 2 lb 15 oz (1.33 kg)
(XII 4743–4)

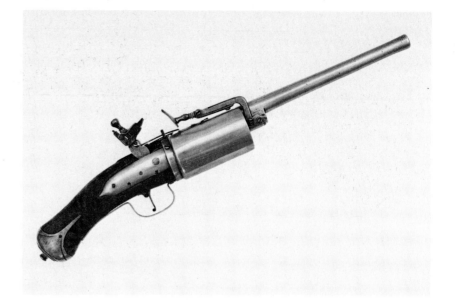

67
Snaphance revolver
British, London, about 1680.

This pistol is the earliest known single-action revolver. The action of cocking the hammer also revolves the cylinder bringing a ready-loaded chamber in line with the barrel. The mechanism is in principle the same as that patented by Samuel Colt in 1835, and still used to this day. According to his own accounts, however, Colt did not know of this pistol until after 1835, and it therefore seems that it did not provide Colt with his inspiration. Indeed, in a lecture given in London in 1851, Colt was rather disparaging about this revolver, which was then in the United Services Museum, describing it as '. . . evidently only a model of a proposed construction, which has never been practically tested, as if it had been used it would have been blown to pieces by the first discharge'. His main objection to the construction of this revolver, was the lack of a proper seal between cylinder and barrel, a problem which was to hinder the development of the revolver until Colt's own day, and he wrote: 'In as much as it possesses no means of regulating the contact of the breech and the barrel, so as to prevent the spread of lateral fire, it offers no security against the simultaneous discharge of all the chambers'. The revolver is unsigned but, because of its resemblance to a revolving carbine in the Milwaukee Museum, which is signed by the London gunmaker John Dafte, it has been suggested that it may have been made by the same maker. Dafte is recorded as working between 1668 and 1697 and it is probable that this revolver dates from about 1680. The remains of another pistol of this type are in the Brighton Museum.

Provenance: Museum of the Royal United Service Institute (1908 *Catalogue* No. 2363); transferred to the Armouries in 1963.

The ring-necked cock is mounted on the inside of the brass lock-plate. Linked to the front of the cock is a pawl which acts upon a ratchet cut in the base of the cylinder to revolve it one-sixth of a turn whenever the action is cocked. The brass cylinder has six chambers, and is held in proper alignment with the barrel by an external spring bolt. Each chamber has a sliding pan-cover, opened automatically by a link attached to the neck of the cock. Surrounding the revolving cylinder is a fixed brass casing which prevents the pan-covers from being opened accidentally. The steel is hinged to the end of a long-angled arm, and was originally provided with a link which pulled it down over the pan each time the hammer was cocked. Walnut pistol-grip with brass mounts and a steel belt-hook on the left side. Smooth-bored brass barrel.

Dimensions: Length 21.7 in (55.1 cm)   Length of barrel, 9.5 in (24.1 cm)
Calibre, .497 in (38 bore)   Weight, 6 Lb 4 oz (2.84 kg).

Literature: S. Colt, 'On the application of machinery to the manufacture of rotating chambered-breech fire-arms and the peculiarities of those arms', *Inst. of Civil Engineers*, London 1851, No.862, p. 36; J.N. George, *Engllsh pistols & revolvers*, Onslow County 1938, pp. 144–7; J.F. Hayward, *The art of the gunmaker*, London 1962, I, p. 219; H.L. BLackmore, *Firearms*, London 1964, p. 118; Blackmore, *Guns & rifles of the world*, London 1965, p. 81; A.W.F. Taylerson, *Revolving arms*, London 1976, pp. 1–2; C. Blair, *Pistols of the world*, London 1968, pp. 44, 128.
(XII 1780)

68
All-steel flintlock sporting gun
Italian, Brescia, about 1680.

All-metal firearms, especially pistols, were quite common in the sixteenth century, but less so in the seventeenth century. A number of early seventeenth-century brass-stocked Scottish guns are known (*see* 63), and there is also a small group of German all-steel guns, mainly pistols, dating from the second half of the century, most of which were produced by members of the Cloeter family in Mannheim and Grevenbroich. Most common, however, are all-steel guns made in and around the town of Brescia in northern Italy, of which this is a fine example. The great majority of these Brescia all-steel guns, including this example, were made by Stefano Scioli (Cioli or Sioli), a gunmaker of Brescia, who is recorded as working between 1633 and 1685. Scioli apparently made both the locks and the stocks of the majority of these guns but not the barrels. The barrel of this gun is signed by Gironimo Mutto, a barrel-maker of Gardone whose name is more than once associated with that of Scioli (*see* for instance, the pair of all-steel pistols in the Wallace Collection, London, Cat. Nos. A. 1227 and A. 1228, and the pair of pistols in the Musée de l'Armée, No. M.1723). Scioli was by no means the only maker of these Brescian all-steel guns, however, and examples either exist or are recorded by a number of other Brescian gunmakers including Hieronimo Zucolo and Francesco Garatto.

Provenance: from the collection of Major H.B.C. Pollard; purchased by the Armouries in 1959.

Rounded lock with swan-necked cock, chiselled in places with acanthus foliage and engraved, behind the cock with foliate scroll-work, and ahead of the cock with the words IN BRESCIA. All-steel stock with long fore-end and shoulder-butt, engraved all-over with scrolling foliage and flowers except by the ramrod tail-pipe where the decoration is in relief. The heads of the screws securing the butt-plate are chiselled with classical busts, a similar bust being placed on the bow of the trigger-guard. The rear finial of the trigger-guard is engraved STEFANO SCIOLO F. IN BRESCIA. The side-plate and escutcheon are pierced and chiselled with scrolling foliage, involving on the latter a coronet and a classical bust. The barrel is octagonal at the breech, where it is engraved with foliage and the name of the maker GIRONIMO MVTTO, and then round to the muzzle. The barrel-tang, to which the trigger is pivoted, is concealed inside the stock.

Dimensions: Length overall, 59 in (149.9 cm)   Length of barrel, 43.75 in (111.1 cm)
Calibre, .645 in (17 bore)   Weight, 8 lb 4 oz (3.74 kg).

Literature: J.F. Hayward, *The art of the gunmaker*, London 1962, II, pp. 136–7; Sir J. Mann, *Wallace Collection Catalogues: European arms and armour*, London 1963, II, pp. 583–4; H.L. Blackmore, *Guns and rifles of the world*, London 1965, p. 32, pl. 188.
(XII 1752)

69
Flintlock sporting gun
French, Paris, about 1685.

This magnificent sporting gun is believed to have been a gift from King Louis XIV of France to Charles Lennox, 1st Duke of Richmond and Lennox (1672–1723), natural son of Charles II by Louise de Keroualle, Duchess of Portsmouth. It was made by the French gunmaker, Bertrand Piraube, who appears to have been working in St Germain-en-Laye from 1663, and who in 1670 was granted a patent of *logement* in the *Galeries du Louvre*, where the best of the craftsmen attached to the Royal Court worked: Piraube retained

his royal appointment until his death in 1724/5. Most of the surviving examples of his work are dated, and this enables a reasonably precise date to be given to this undated gun. It most closely resembles the sporting gun in the Royal Collection at Windsor Castle (Laking, *Catalogue* No. 425) which was almost certainly made for Louis XIV himself, and which is dated 1682. The decoration on the locks, side-plates and breeches of the two guns differ only in small details, and some of the inlays on the stocks are also of the same pattern. It seems possible, therefore, that this gun was made for presentation to the Duke of Richmond during his visits to Paris in 1681/2 or, perhaps, in 1685. Such a fine weapon was in reality the result of the co-operation of a number of craftsmen, members of different guilds, forbidden to intrude on each others *métiers*. For a gun of this exceptional quality a professional designer would probably be called upon to prepare drawings for the patron's approval. In this case it is possible that he was Jean Bérain who came from a gunmaking family and became *Dessinateur de la Chambre et du Cabinet du Roi* to Louis XIV, designing such things as coaches, the *décor* of state rooms, royal theatricals, and state funerals.

The silver mounts were almost certainly made by a silversmith, and engraved by a specialist engraver while the lock and other steel parts were probably chiselled by a medalist such as Jerôme Roussel, who is thought also to have worked on sword-hilts. The chiselled decoration on the lock is based closely on the designs of the French gunmakers Thuraine and Le Hollandois, which were published in 1660. The barrel is not of steel but of silver, a very unusual but not unique feature, which confirms that this gun was made for presentation rather than for sustained use. Such silver barrels, however, were certainly strong enough to be fired occasionally, and examples bearing London proof-marks are found on a number of English pistols of the second half of the eighteenth century.

Provenance: collection of the Duke of Richmond and Gordon; purchased by the Armouries with the aid of the National Art-Collections Fund at Christie's, 31 March 1958, lot 167, for 2,100 guineas, then a world record price for a gun at auction.

The lock-plate is chiselled with the figures of Mars, in a chariot drawn by lions, and Jupiter astride an eagle, and engraved PIRAVBE AVX GALLERIES. The swan-necked cock is chiselled with a figure of Fame and a classical head. The upper jaw and screw are restorations. The frizzle is chiselled with monsters' heads. Silver mounts, showing traces of gilding, chased with classical figures including, on the butt-plate, a victorious Roman general in armour, and, on the side-plate a figure, perhaps Apollo, in a chariot drawn by four horses. Walnut stock decorated with inlays of engraved silver and with scroll-work in fine silver wire. On either side of the butt is an oval medallion engraved with a camp scene, surmounted by the Sun God in his chariot, holding a sceptre topped by a fleur-de-lis. Other inlays take the form of classical figures, masks, and grotesques. Silver barrel, octagonal at the breech, where it is chased and engraved with trophies of arms, foliate scrolls, and a figure of Mars. Silver-gilt back-sight in the form of a band which slips over the barrel. From the back-sight a flattened sighting rib extends to the fore-sight.

Dimensions: Length, 57 in (144.8 cm)   Length of barrel, 42 in (106.7 cm)   Calibre, .58 in (23 bore)   Weight, 7 lb 13 oz (3.54 kg).

Literature: C. Blair, *European and American arms*, London 1962, p. 88, pl. 317; J.F. Hayward, *The art of the gunmaker*, London 1963, II, pp. 44, 326, pl. 7; H.L. Blackmore, *Royal Sporting Guns at Windsor*, London 1968, p. 55.
(XII 1690)

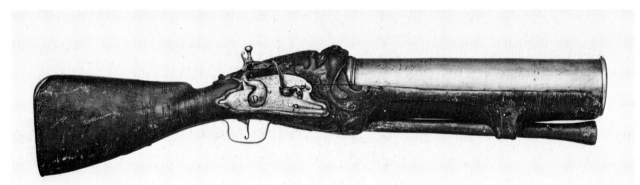

70
Flintlock firework gun
British, London, about 1690.

This is one of two almost identical guns in the Armouries which were made by the London gunmaker James Ermendinger for Prince George of Denmark, consort of Princess, later Queen Anne. They can probably be identified as two of the eight 'Granade' guns which are listed in a manuscript catalogue of Prince George's collection of arms, which appears to have been drawn up at the time of his death. James Ermendinger, a German by birth, was granted English nationality in 1689, but he had been working in London for a number of years previously, certainly from 1679 and probably from 1677. He worked as a gunmaker to Prince Rupert until the latter's death in 1682, and is also recorded as a gunmaker to the Hudson's Bay Company. In 1689 he was appointed to the prestigious post of Chief Gunmaker to the Tower of London, but his appointment was rescinded by the House of Commons following a petition from the London Gunmakers' Company. He died in 1693. The stock of a third gun of this type is also in the Armouries (No. XII. 1033), and another of the same form, dated 1686, is in the Tøjhusmuseum, Copenhagen (Cat. No. B. 1071:1). This latter bears on the barrel the monogram of Christian V of Denmark (1670–99) and is crudely signed on the muzzle by Christian Nerger. Nerger, a native of Saxony who spent most of his working life in Copenhagen as a sculptor, both in wood and stone, to the Danish Court, was apparently the inventor and maker of a new sort of 'grenade' gun which was adopted by the Danish cavalry in 1677. A number of similar plain guns also exist, and it seems likely that it was this plainer type of gun which Nerger supplied for military use. All these guns, whether plain or decorated, are characterised by the very weak construction of their barrels, and it seems likely, despite the apparent documentary evidence to the contrary, that they were intended to shoot not grenades but fireworks, the ornamented guns probably launching decorative fireworks for festive occasions, and the plain guns military fireworks such as flares.

Provenance: collection of Prince George of Denmark; sold Christie's, 11 December 1975, lot 195; purchased by the Armouries in 1976.

The rounded lock-plate is engraved with foliate scroll-work and the name of the maker I ERMENDINGER. An iron ignition tube within the stock connects the pan with the centre of the breech of the barrel. The two-piece stock of pine is covered with layers of paint and varnish giving the surface a natural brown colour. Originally, however, it was almost certainly painted black. Around the breech the stock is carved in the form of a lion's head, from the mouth of which issues the barrel. The iron furniture is decorated in places with engraving. The side-plate is of foliate outline and is engraved with leaf scrolls. The trefoil-shaped reinforcing strap on the rammer pipe is now missing. To the left-hand side of the fore-end was originally attached a sling-bar, now missing. The barrel is of very large calibre, but is constructed of thin sheet metal beaten into a cylinder round a former and then brazed and riveted together. The breech is in the form of a domed cap brazed to the end of the barrel. It is pierced in the centre to accept the ignition tube. On the top of the barrel at the breech is the name of the maker IAMES ERMENDINGER and, above, the monogram of Prince George of Denmark, addorsed G's within palm-leaves.

Dimensions: Length overall, 37 in (94 cm)   Length of barrel, 16.5 in (41.9 cm)
Calibre, 3.25 in (8.25 cm)   Weight, 11 lb 12 oz (5.33 kg).

Exhibited: Ironmonger's Hall, 1861.

Literature: *A Catalogue of the antiquities and works of art exhibited at Ironmonger's Hall, London in the month of May 1861*, London 1868–9, II, pp. 173; G. Boothroyd, 'Gunmaker to Prince Rupert', *Shooting Times and Country Magazine*, October 4, 1969, p. 1613.
(XII 3913)

71 (pl. XV)
Pair of flintlock holster pistols
British, London, about 1695.

These magnificent pistols, the result of the combined skills of a number of artist-craftsmen (*see* 69, 77, 80 & 84) are perhaps the most highly decorated firearms ever made in England. They are, however, entirely French in style and bear the name of the French Huguenot gunmaker Pierre Monlong. Monlong began his career as a gunmaker in Anger, probably in about 1660.

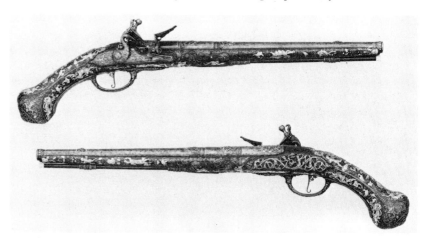

In 1664 he was appointed one of the gunmakers to the French Royal Household, and moved to Paris. Despite his appointment as a Royal Gunmaker Monlong did not set up on his own in Paris, but instead went into partnership with the Parisian gunsmith Pierre Frappier. In 1684 Monlong emigrated to London with his wife and three children, and in 1688 they were granted denization. He established a business near Charing Cross in an area favoured by immigrant craftsmen because, being both outside the City of London and close to the Court at Whitehall, it offered them some protection from the City Companies which jealously guarded their privileges and fought hard against the competition from foreign craftsmen. Monlong's great talent was soon recognised by the Court and in 1689 he was appointed 'Gentleman Armourer to His Majesty-in-Ordinary'. He died in 1699 and was buried in the parish church of St Martin-in-the-Fields on 23 November. These pistols are decorated on the lock with a portrait bust which appears to be based on a medallion of William III, and it is therefore possible that they may have been made for the King himself. The general style of much of the ornament seems to derive from the pattern books of Claude and Jacques Simonin, published in Paris in 1685 and 1693; the style of the rest, together with the form of the lock, seems to relate to earlier pattern books such as those published by Jean Bérain in 1659 and by C. Jacquinet in 1660. It is probable that for pistols of this quality a special set of designs was made, although it is impossible to tell whether these were produced by Monlong himself. Hayward (*see* Literature) has suggested that they may have been furnished by Simonin before Monlong left Paris.

Provenance: collection of the Duchess of Westminster; purchased by the Armouries in 1975 with the aid of the National Art-Collections Fund, the Pilgrim Trust, the Worshipful Company of Goldsmiths, and a public appeal.

The lock-plates are chiselled with demi-figures, masks, and delicate scrolls terminating in heads, and are engraved MONLONG LONDINI. The cocks, one of which is cracked across the neck, have restored top jaws and screws, and are engraved with demi-figures and foliate scrolls. The cock-screws are chiselled with a bust portrait, possibly of William III. The frizzles and pans are chiselled with scrolls and lion's masks. The frizzle-springs terminate in a foliate head and scroll finial. The full-length figured walnut stocks are carved in low relief with scrolls terminating in heads, and are profusely inlaid in silver wire, and cut and engraved silver-sheet, with scrolls, birds, animals, and figures including, on the butt, Diana flanked by hounds; in front of the trigger-guard, Apollo driving the Sun chariot; and near the fore-end, Fortitude. The steel furniture is chiselled to match the lock-plate, and with acanthus foliage. The butt-caps terminate in a grotesque mask within a cartouche of masks and scrolls. The side-plates are pierced with scroll-work terminating in a demi-figure and grotesque masks. The ramrods are restoration. The barrels are in three stages separated by mouldings and are chiselled with masks, foliate scrolls, and figures, and damascened with gold scrolls. The muzzles are chiselled with a ring of acanthus foliage, and the fore-sights are in the form of a mask surrounded by gold scrolls. Under the breech is stamped the mark of the maker, an M under a heart and within a circle.

Dimensions: Length overall, 21 in (53.3 cm)   Length of barrel, 13.9 in (35.3 cm)
Calibre, .527 in (32 bore)   Weight 2 lb 11 oz (1.22 kg).

Exhibited: 'Iron and Steel Work', Burlington Fine Arts Club, 1900. Victoria and Albert Museum 1960–70.

Literature: J. Starkie Gardner, *Iron and steel work*, London 1900, pl. LXIII, J.F. Hayward, *The art of the gunmaker*, London 1963, II, pp. 66–7, H.L. Blackmore, 'The Monlong pistols', *Huguenot Society Proceedings*, 1975, pp. 463–4; Blackmore, 'The Monlong pistols', *The Connoisseur*, CLXXXIX, No. 762, September 1975, p. 72.
(XII 3829–30)

72
Flintlock sporting gun
British, London, dated 1721.

This single-barrelled sporting gun was made for Thomas, 1st Earl Coningsby (1656?–1729) while he was imprisoned in the Tower in 1721 for libelling the Lord Chancellor Thomas Parker, the Earl of Macclesfield. The libel was contained in the first page of a pamphlet entitled 'The First Part of Earl Coningsby's Case relating to the Vicarage of Lempster in Hertfordshire . . .', in which the Earl complained that his right to present the living of the Church of Lempster had been disallowed in favour of the King at Hereford Assizes in the previous year because the court had been packed and rigged by the Lord Chancellor. Coningsby was imprisoned in the Tower on 27 February 1721 by order of the House of Lords and remained in prison until the House was prorogued on 29 July. This gun was made by William Mills, a 'Barrell Forger and Frobisher within the Tower', who in 1718 was described as one of the twenty best-qualified and most deserving of the gunmakers employed by the Board of Ordnance. In the following year he was dismissed for a 'breach of trust' – losing six muskets which he had been directed to repair – but was restored to his post after only 23 days. According to the rhyming inscription on the barrel this gun was made from the blades of 'Rebel Swords'. This is apparently a unique reference to the use of sword-blades to make gun barrels. Tower Guides of the second half of the eighteenth century record that weapons captured during the Jacobite rebellion of 1715 were on show in the Tower, and it is therefore possible that others which had been captured and stored in the Tower were re-worked in some way. The reference in the inscription to the 'South Sea Bubble', the popular name for the wild financial speculation in the South Sea Company which had led to ruin for many in 1720, is obscure. However, Sir George Caswall, a former director of the Company had been a member of the Assize Court which had disallowed Coningsby's case. The final line of the inscription is probably intended to be read in two ways, both as a plea by Coningsby for royal clemency (Hampton Court was one of the major Royal Palaces), and as a request for Coningsby to look after the gun (Hampton Court was also the name of his country seat in Herefordshire).

Provenance: collection of the Viscount Hereford, Hampton Court, Leominster, Herefordshire; purchased by the Armouries in 1967.

Plain lock, of advanced form. The pan has a raised edge, and a water-drain in the fence, and the frizzle-screw has a bridle. The lock-plate is engraved W MILLS. Silver-mounted stock with short fore-end. The side-plate is in the form of a dragon and the escutcheon is engraved with an earl's

coronet and the arms and supporters and motto of Earl Coningsby. The ramrod is a restoration. The round, browned barrel has two moulded silver bands near the breech, a silver fore-sight in the form of a grotesque mask, two silver ramrod pipes, and a silver ramp below the muzzle to secure the ramrod. The top of the breech is inlaid in gold with an earl's coronet and an inscription (*see illus.*), and is stamped with the proof-marks of the London Gunmaker's Company and the mark of the barrel-maker. The barrel hooks into a false breech and is secured to the fore-end by a screw.

Dimensions: Length, 54.12 in (137.5 cm)   Length of barrel, 38.5 in (97.8 cm)
Calibre, .75 in (11 bore)   Weight, 7 lb 5 oz (3.32 kg).

Literature: H.L. Blackmore, 'Lord Coningsby and his gun', *Strange stories from the Tower of London*, London 1976, pp. 27–31.
(XII 1789)

73–76
Sporting garniture
Russian, Tula, parts dated 1752.

Hunting garnitures usually consisting of a selection of matching firearms and accessories, and sometimes including edged weapons as well, were produced in some numbers in the eighteenth century, especially in Germany and Russia. In Russia such garnitures became the speciality of the state small-arms factory established in 1712 in the central Russian town of Tula, which had been a centre of the gunmaking trade since the end of the sixteenth century. The state factory at Tula was principally intended to manufacture the service arms of the Russian army, but it soon began to produce luxury arms, especially those intended for presentation by the Russian government to foreign monarchs, nobles and dignitaries. A number of Tula garnitures survive, varying in date between 1745 and 1781. This garniture consists of a shotgun and a pair of pistols, all three firearms bearing the monogram of Empress Elizabeth of Russia (reigned 1741–62) and dated 1752, together with a powder flask and a pair of stirrups, neither of which are either dated or marked with the imperial monogram, and which were probably associated with the guns in the late eighteenth century. Other items with the same provenance, including a powder or tobacco box of Tula manufacture, were also associated with the garniture when it was sold in 1950. The steel parts of the entire garniture are decorated with the chiselled ornament on a gold ground which is characteristic of the Tula factory. As with most Russian weapons of this period, all of the decoration is in the French style, and is here based closely upon the designs published by De Lacollombe about 1706 and by Nicholas Guérard in 1719. Indeed the inlaid silver decoration on the butt of the shotgun is an almost exact copy of one of Guérard's designs. The history of this garniture is uncertain, but it appears that it was brought from Moscow in 1812 by the Chevalier Louis Guérin de Bruslart, a colourful character, who at that time appears to have been acting as a Bourbon agent attached to the invading French army. Shortly afterwards, on a visit to London, Bruslart befriended one William Vardon, an ironmonger of Gracechurch Street, with whom he left the garniture, probably as security for a loan, and the garniture remained in his and his descendants possession until its sale in London in 1950. In 1883 William Vardon's nephew claimed that the garniture had been entrusted to Bruslart's care in 1812 'by a Russian nobleman to be given to some member of the French nobility on his or her personal application', and this is perhaps confirmed by a number of letters (now in the Armouries archives) dated 1814, which suggest that the arms deposited with Vardon by Bruslart were the property of the Vicomtesse de Richemont.

Provenance: from Russia in 1812; deposited with William Vardon; collection of D.A. Burnett-Hitchcock; purchased by the Armouries at Sotheby's, 21 April 1950, lots 1, 3, 5 & 6.

Literature: H.L. Blackmore, *Hunting weapons*, London 1971, p. 245; Blackmore, 'Les armes de l'Impératrice de Russie', *Gazette des Armes*, 1978, No.62, pp. 25–7.

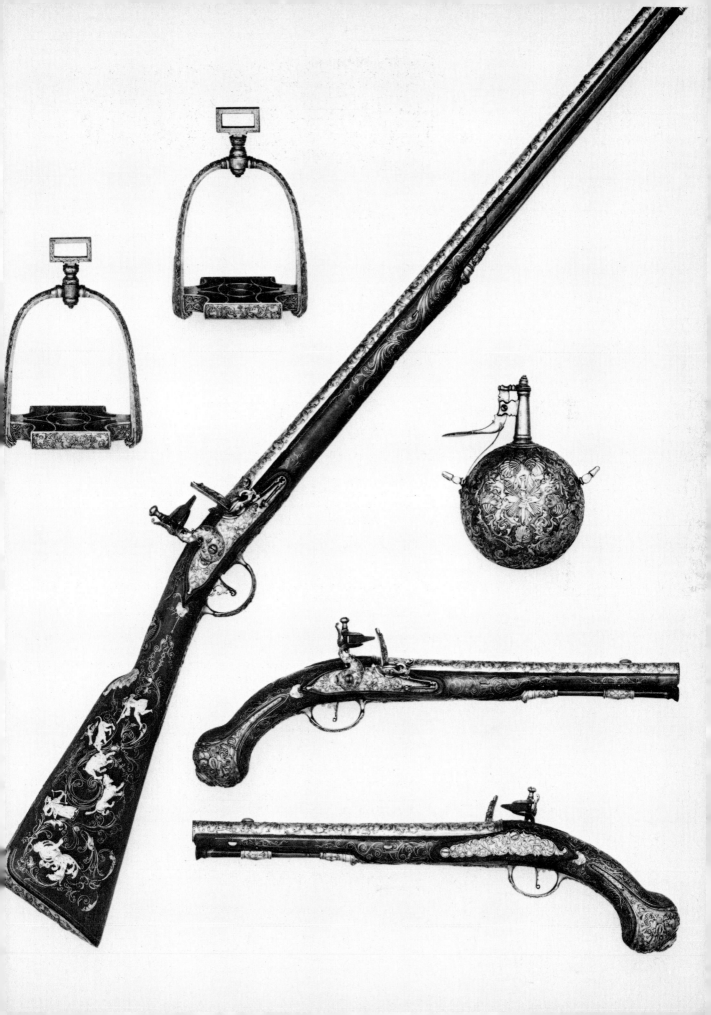

The garniture consists of:

73 (pl. XIII)
Flintlock sporting gun

The lock is chiselled with rococo scroll-work and trophies of arms on a gilt ground. There is a sliding safety-catch to the rear of the cock and the frizzle incorporates an additional pan-cover operated by a lever in the back of the steel, which may be closed separately to act as a further safety device. This ingenious feature was not confined to arms produced in Tula, and may also be found on a number of other guns in the Armouries, notably a sporting gun signed LORENZONI FIRENZE dating from about 1695 (Inv. No. XII.1692) and a pair of pistols by the London gunmaker John Twigg, with mounts bearing the date-letter for 1773–4 (Inv. Nos: XII,1486–7). The stock is inlaid in silver wire with scroll-work, and in addition on the butt with silver plates cut-out and engraved with trophies of arms, classical figures and sporting scenes. The steel furniture is decorated to match the lock and barrel. The silver-gilt escutcheon is formed as the Imperial Russian Eagle with, in the centre, a cartouche decorated with the figure of a horseman. The barrel is decorated for its entire length with symmetrical scroll-work and trophies on a gold ground, matching the ornament of the lock and furniture. Near the breech is the crowned monogram of Empress Elizabeth, and half-way down its length the inscription TULA 1752.

Dimensions: Length overall, 59.5 in (151.1 cm)   Length of barrel, 44.125 in (112 cm)
Calibre, .61 in (20 bore)   Weight, 7 lb 9 oz (3.43 kg).
(XII 1504)

74
Pair of flintlock holster pistols

Locks of identical form to that of the sporting gun, incorporating both the sliding safety and the double pan-cover, and decorated to match. The inscription TULA 1752 is engraved on the edges of the lock-plates. The stocks are inlaid in silver wire with scroll-work to match that on the sporting gun and, on the underside ahead of the trigger, with a silver plaque cut out and engraved as the bust of a classical warrior. The steel furniture is decorated to match the lock, the large butt-plate bearing trophies of arms and a helmeted classical warrior. The pistols bear the same escutcheon as the sporting gun. The barrel is similarly decorated to match, but is not inscribed with the place or date of manufacture as is the barrel of the sporting gun.

Dimensions: Length overall, 18.75 in (47.6 cm)   Length of barrel, 11.6 in (29.5 cm)
Calibre, .6 in (20 bore)   Weight, 2 lb 10 oz (1.19 kg).
(XII 1505–6)

75 (pl. XIII)
Powder-flask

Made of steel. The circular body is convex at the front and flat at the back, and has a suspension swivel on each side. The body is surmounted by a tall, moulded nozzle, topped by a sprung cap with a large curved lever. The front of the body is chiselled on a gilt ground with rococo shells, foliate scroll-work, and trophies of arms.

Dimensions: Length, 7.2 in (18.3 cm)   Weight, 1 lb 2.5 oz (0.524 kg).
(XIII 150)

76
Pair of stirrups

All-steel stirrups of arched form, the sides of convex section widening towards the treads. The swivel-loops for the stirrup leathers are of oblong shape. The broad treads are pierced with a geometric pattern, the outer edges straight in the middle and joined to the sides by short, concave curves. The sides of the stirrups, and the edges of the treads are chiselled in low relief on a gilt ground with foliate scroll-work, rococo shells, and trophies.

Dimensions: Height, 7.75 in (19.7 cm)   Weight, 1 lb 11 oz (0.765 kg).
(VI 356–7)

77
Pair of flintlock holster pistols
British, London, about 1760.

These magnificently decorated pistols are of the highest quality and were obviously intended for presentation or show rather than for every-day use. They are signed by the London gunmaker Henry Hadley, whose name also appears on four other similar pairs of pistols, but it is unlikely that all the parts of these pistols were made in his workshop. High-quality firearms such as these embody the work of many craftsmen – a barrel-forger, a locksmith, a wood-carver, a steel-engraver and a silversmith. The gunmaker who finally signed and retailed the result of these combined skills often did little more than assemble the parts provided to him by all these other craftsmen. Henry Hadley worked at various addresses in London from sometime before 1735

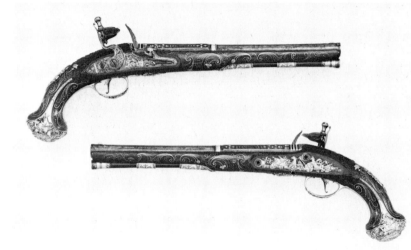

until his death in 1773, but he never became a member of the Gunmakers'
Company. At first the Company, which was at this time attempting to gain
complete control of gunmaking in London, tried unsuccessfully to stop
Hadley trading, but later it tacitly accepted his right to work as a gunmaker,
and even allowed him to train apprentices. It was for this reason that the
barrels of his guns are usually stamped, as are these, with the crowned
capital F mark indicating that the barrel had been proved for a 'Foreigner',
or a maker who was not a freeman of the Company. It is impossible to be
certain which other craftsmen were involved in the manufacture of these
pistols. However, the stocks are stamped with the initials TM, perhaps the
mark either of Thomas Mead the Younger, who became a freeman of the
Gunmakers' Company in 1749, or of Hadley's own workman Theobald
Michell. The engraving of the lock is perhaps the work of the 'London
Ingraver' William Sharpe, who was one of the beneficiaries of Hadley's Will.
The barrels may have been made either by Hadley himself or by Thomas
Hudson, whose name appears on the barrels of a sporting gun by Hadley in
the Royal Collection at Windsor Castle (1904 *Cat.* No.427), and who always
seems to have been closely associated with Hadley. The barrels of these
pistols are made in the Spanish style and bear stylized versions of the marks
of the gunmakers Geronimo Fernandez of Madrid and Pedro Esteva of
Barcelona. At this time Spanish barrels were famed for their accuracy and
strength and it was not unusual for English gunmakers to use imported
Spanish barrels, but these barrels are instead deliberate copies of the
Spanish product. On the escutcheons of these pistols is the crest of the
Spencer family, surmounted by a ducal coronet, and it is probable that they
were made for George Spencer, fourth Duke of Marlborough (1739–1817), or
perhaps for Charles, third Duke of Marlborough (1706–1758).

Provenance: collection of H. W. Arthurton; purchased by the Armouries in 1956.

The locks are engraved with foliate scroll-work and classical figures including two representing
Fame and Learning. On the lower bevel of each lock-plate is engraved the name H. HADLEY, and
stamped on the inside of each plate is the letter N. Each has a safety-catch to the rear of the cock,
and is secured by two side-screws which have a squared socket cut in their heads requiring a
special screwdriver. The priming pans are lined with gold. Walnut full-stock inlaid in silver wire
with scroll-work, the bud terminals formed from engraved inlaid silver plates. Beneath the side-
plates the stocks are stamped TM. The escutcheons bear a crest (out of a ducal coronet, a griffin's
head between two wings expanded, gorged with a bar-gemel). The silver mounts are chased with
allegorical figures, classical busts, and trophies of arms dominated by the figure of Britannia. The
barrels, which were reblued in 1975, are octagonal at the breech and round at the muzzle. The
octagonal section is inlaid with gold dots, flowers, and stars, and deeply stamped and gilded in the
Spanish style with the maker's mark containing the words H HADLEY LONDON. The barrels
have gold touch-holes and fore-sights. The undersides of the barrels are stamped with London
proof-marks and the 'Foreigner's' mark.

Dimensions: Length overall, 16.25 in (41.3 cm)   Length of barrels, 10.5 in (26.7 cm)
Calibre, .54 in (29 bore)   Weight, 2 lb 1 oz (0.935 kg).

Exhibited: 'English furniture in the eighteenth century', Paris 1959.

Literature: H.L. Blackmore, 'Henry Hadley, "Foreigner", and four pairs of his pistols', *The
Connoisseur*, 1957 CXL, pp. 82–6
(XII 1645–6)

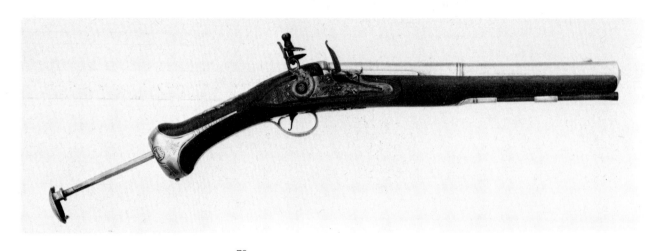

78
Air pistol
British, London, about 1770.

The air gun had one great advantage over conventional firearms, the relative silence of its discharge, and from at least the second half of the sixteenth century gunmakers were trying to produce safe, powerful, and reliable air weapons, often without complete success. This air pistol was made by the London gunmaker Edward Bate, who is recorded as working in Brounlow Street, Longacre from 1763 to 1778, and who apparently continued working until about 1800. It has an air reservoir contained within a brass sleeve surrounding the barrel, and a pump housed within the butt by which the reservoir can be pressurised. This particular form of air gun first appeared in the mid-seventeenth century, the earliest known examples being two guns from the collection of Queen Christine of Sweden made by the gunmaker Hans Köler of Kitzing in 1644 (Livrustkammaren, Stockholm, Inv. Nos. 1252, 1253). This type of airgun was probably brought to England by a German gunmaker, iron-chiseller, and engraver by the name of Johann Gottfried Kolbe. Kolbe is recorded as working in Suhl, a town in Thuringia, between 1719 and 1730, and between 1740 and 1747, but from 1730 to 1737 he is known to have been working in London. While in London he made a number of air guns of this form, and some similar repeaters with a 10-ball magazine in the fore-end of the barrel. Edward Bate was a prolific maker of various types of air guns, notably those with a ball reservoir, but he also copied both of the types made earlier in the century by Kolbe, as can be seen from this example, and the repeating magazine gun of Kolbe type by Bate in the Musée de l'Armée, Paris (No. M. 1562).

Provenance: from the collection of Clay Bedford; purchased by the Armouries in 1975.

The lock is externally of flintlock form, the flat lock-plate retaining much of its original blueing, and engraved with foliate scrolls and, before the cock, BATE. Ahead of the cock is a brass plug filling an original screw-hole. The ring-necked cock, decorated to match, cocks the internal valve-release mechanism. Full-length stock carved with a shell behind the barrel-tang. The furniture is of brass. The large side-plate is engraved with foliate and shell patterns, and the trigger-guard is engraved on the bow with floral patterns, and on the forward finial is both cast and engraved with a flowering plant. The asymmetric escutcheon is cast with a surround of a trophy of arms. The pommel, with long engraved side-spurs, is cast with the scroll and shell decoration. A spring-button on the underside of the pommel releases the engraved butt-cap, revealing the pump to pressurise the reservoirs. The butt-cap screws into the end of this cap to form a convenient handle. The brass barrel is surrounded by a round brass sleeve forming the reservoir. The sleeve has a central transverse moulding and is stamped near the breech BATE LONDON. At the muzzle is a brass-leaf fore-sight. A raised groove on the foliate-engraved barrel-tang acts as a back-sight.

Dimensions: Length overall, 20.5 in (52.1 cm)   Length of barrel, 12.25 in (31.1 cm)
Calibre, .41 in (67 bore)   Weight, 4 lb 1 oz (1.84 kg).

Exhibited: Metropolitan Museum of Art, New York, 1971, 'Early firearms of Great Britain and Ireland from the collection of Clay Bedford'

Literature: *Early firearms of Great Britain and Ireland from the collection of Clay Bedford*, New York 1971, No.161.
(XII 3833)

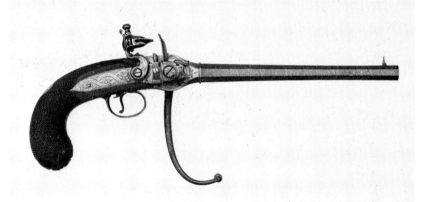

79
Cased flintlock repeating pistol
British, London, about 1800.

This pistol is a late example of a magazine repeating action which first
appeared in the late seventeenth century and which continued to be made
until the beginning of the nineteenth century. The system is usually
associated with the name of the eminent Italian gunmaker Michele Lorenzoni,
who is recorded working in Florence from 1684 to his death in 1733.
However, it now seems more probable that the system was invented by the
Bolognese gunmaker Giacomo Berselli, who was working from about 1660 to
1720. Guns of this type seem to have been first made in England by the
London gunmaker John Cookson towards the end of the seventeenth century,
and were produced occasionally throughout the next century. In the last
quarter of the eighteenth century, however, this 'Lorenzoni' system achieved
a limited but significant revival of popularity in England, the maker of this
pistol, H. W. Mortimer, being both one of the last and one of the most prolific
makers of this type of repeating gun. H. W. Mortimer (1753–1819), who traded
from a shop in Fleet Street, was appointed Gunmaker-in-Ordinary to King
George III in 1783. In about 1800 he went into partnership with his brother
Thomas, and, in about 1808 their sons joined the family business which
henceforth traded under the title of H. W. & T. MORTIMER & SONS. As this
pistol is signed by H. W. Mortimer alone, it probably dates from before 1800.
The escutcheon is engraved with the arms of the South family, and the case
bears the name CAPT SOUTH. It is probable, therefore, that the pistol was
made for Thomas South, of the 5th Hampshire Militia (Captain 1792, Major
1795) or perhaps for Samuel South of the 20th Foot, East Devon Regiment
(Lieutenant 1804, Captain 1805).

Provenance: purchased by the Armouries from a private collection in 1979 after an export licence
had been refused by the Board of Trade.

Back-action lock engraved all over with floral decoration and signed H. W. MORTIMER
LONDON GUNMAKER TO HIS MAJESTY. The action consists of a vertically revolving breech-
block which has two cavities, one for the ball, and the other for the powder. To operate it the gun is
held muzzle downwardd. A half turn of the side-lever revolves the breech-block which picks up a
ball and charge of powder from two magazines in the butt which hold enough powder and ball for
seven shots. On the reverse turn the ball is deposited in the chamber of the barrel, with the powder
charge still in the breech-block behind it. The lever also cocks the lock and causes the revolving
pan to pick up its own priming charge. The bright steel action-housing is engraved with military
trophies, and with sunbursts around the two cleaning or inspection holes drilled on the top and
bottom. The butt has a chequered grip and a silver oval escutcheon engraved with a crest (a
dragon's head ducally gorged issuing from flames of fire). The trigger-guard and lever are blued.
The browned twist barrel is of octagonal section and has a smooth bore. The top flat is engraved
H W MORTIMER LONDON GUNMAKER TO HIS MAJESTY. There is no back-sight, but the
gun is equipped with a folding fore-sight which has the form of a blade when down and of a bead on
a stalk when in the upright position. The barrel can be unscrewed with the aid of a separate wrench.
The mahogany case (not illustrated) is lined with green felt and contains the following accessories:
a red leather-covered powder-flask, a double screwdriver and pricker, a wrench, a bullet-mould
(marked 36), and a separate pricker. The folding handle in the lid is engraved CAPT. SOUTH.

Dimensions: Length overall, 19 in (48.3 cm)   Length of barrel, 10.3 in (25.7 cm)
Calibre, .515 in (34 bore)   Weight, 3 lb 15 oz (1.79 kg)   Weight complete in case, 11 lb 1 oz (5.02 kg).
(XII 4750)

80
Presentation flintlock sporting gun
French, Versailles, 1802.

This superbly decorated sporting gun formed part of a magnificent set of firearms sent as a present to Charles IV of Spain by the French government in 1802. The gift consisted of six silver-mounted guns, of which this is one, and two carbines, one double-barrelled sporting gun, and a pair of duelling pistols, all mounted in gold. Of these, four of the six silver-mounted guns and the two gold-mounted carbines are known to survive. The entire set was made at the Versailles arms factory (*see* 81) under the direction of Nicholas Noël Boutet. Boutet (1761–1833), one of the greatest names in the history of French gunmaking, became Director of the Manufacture d'Armes de Versailles in 1792. The factory produced many service arms, and also a series of highly finished and richly decorated weapons intended for presentation by the government. The design and assembly of these *armes de luxe* was almost certainly under the personal supervision of Boutet himself, but by no means all the parts were made at Versailles. For instance, the silver marks on the mounts of this gun prove that they, like the mounts of others of Boutet's luxury arms, were made in the Department of Seine-Inférieure, perhaps at Rouen, from where they could have been easily shipped up river to Versailles (*see* S. W. Pyhrr, 'Hidden marks on Boutet firearms', *Arms and armour annual*, I, Northfield, Illinois 1973). The Versailles factory was closed down in 1818, but Boutet continued in business in Paris until 1831, although he was never in high favour with the restored royalist régime. Of the six surviving pieces of this set of guns, two (this example, together with one in the Wallace Collection, London, *Cat.* No. A. 1128) bear the monogram and portrait bust of King Charles IV of Spain, while the others bear the monogram and/or arms of his successor Joseph Bonaparte. It appears, therefore, that part of the set was altered for the use of Joseph Bonaparte after his arrival in Spain in July 1808. The subsequent history of the set and its dispersal is uncertain. It is probable that the guns that have survived unaltered were taken into exile by Charles in 1808, and that, together with his other effects, they were sold after his death in Rome in 1819. At least one of the altered guns (Royal Collection, Windsor Castle, 1904 *Cat.* No.672) remained in the collection of the Bonaparte family until 1814 when it was sold in Vienna together with other items belonging to Jérôme Bonaparte. Others of the altered guns may have been captured by the British forces at the battle of Vitoria in 1813 (see A.L.F. Schaumann, *On the road with Wellington*, London 1924, p. 383). This gun was acquired by the Armouries from the collection of arms and armour at Norton Hall, which was largely assembled by Beriah Botfield between 1830 and 1840. The fox-hunting scenes on this gun, like many of those produced by Boutet, derive from the paintings of Jean-Baptiste Oudry (1686–1755).

Provenance: Norton Hall Collection; purchased in 1942 with the aid of the National Art-Collections Fund.

The lock is deeply chiselled and gilt with foxes, sporting dogs, and game birds. The edge of the lock-plate is engraved BOUTET DIRECTEUR ARTISTE MANUF^RE A VERSAILLES. The priming-pan is lined with gold. The walnut full-stock is delicately carved with foliage, and on the fore-end, with bands of ribbon ornament. Below the butt an ebony caryatid figure forms a pistol grip. The stock has been broken at the small of the butt and repaired. The silver mounts are chased with ornament on a ground of matt gold. The butt-plate is decorated with a trophy of arms and hunting scenes with figures in classical dress. The lock-screw is concealed behind a false screw-plate bearing a classical hunting scene. The trigger-guard bears a head of Medusa, a figure of Diana, and emblems of the Arts and Sciences. On the ramrod tail-pipe is a portrait-bust of Charles IV, King of Spain. All the mounts are stamped with Seine-Inférieure silver marks, and with a maker's mark, the initials J M beneath a five-pointed star and above seven pellets, all within a lozenge. The escutcheon is enamelled with the crowned initial of Charles IV. The barrel is octagonal at the breech and then round to the muzzle, with a narrow flat running as far as the fore-sight. The surface is now russet but was originally blued. The breech is inlaid with gold, engraved with a design of a garlanded obelisk, classical vases and trophies. The muzzle is similarly inlaid, the decorations here consisting of a band of pyramidal ornament and a trophy. The large, silver back-sight is secured by a band. At the breech are stamped the maker's marks, now illegible, the left side being engraved with the inscription BOUTET DIRECTEUR ARTISTE MANUF^{RE} A VERSAILLES. The barrel is secured by a false breech and sliding pins.

Dimensions: Length overall, 53.75 in (136.5 cm)   Length of barrel, 38.25 in (97.1 cm)
Calibre, .638 in (18 bore)   Weight, 5 lb, 12 oz (2.61 kg).

Literature: Sir James Mann, *Wallace Collection Catalogues; European arms and armour*, London 1962, II, pp. 532–3; A.N. Kennard, 'Un cadeau pour l'Espagne'. *Gazette des Armes*, 1975, No.29, pp. 34–9.
(XII 1278)

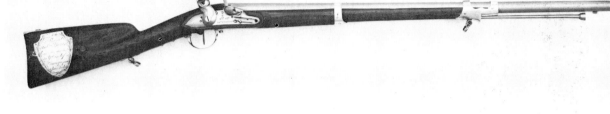

81
Presentation flintlock carbine
French, Versailles, dated 1803.

Decorations, medals, and marks of distinction were abolished at the beginning of the French Revolution, but it was soon found necessary to re-introduce some form of public recognition for distinguished services to the revolutionary cause. Between 1799 and 1804 firearms, specially made in the national arsenal at Versailles under the direction of Nicholas-Noël Boutet (*see* 80), and suitably inscribed, were presented to deserving soldiers. This example is a *mousqueton d'honneur*, a carbine of the type presented to cavalry officers. (*See* J. Boudriot, *Armes a feu françaises modèles d'ordonnance*, Cahier 16, Paris 1965, pp. 6–9). It was made for Citizen Brigadier Devin, and presented to him on 4 pluviôse an XI (23 January 1803), for his good conduct during the expedition to recover San Domingo (Haiti) in 1802, which was described in his citation as '*cette campagne difficile*' (this difficult campaign). During the campaign Devin served with the *guides* of the expedition's *capitaine-général*, General Victor-Emmanuel Leclerc who, with a large number of his men, died of disease during the campaign.

Provenance: brought from Paris in 1816; transferred to the Armouries in 1927 from the Rotunda Museum, Woolwich (1889 *Catalogue* No. VI. 214).

Flintlock of *an* IX (1800) pattern, inscribed M^{RE} N^{LE} DE VERSAILLES, and stamped with the mark of the *contrôleur* David Bouyssavey. Half-stock with silver mounts. The right side of the butt is inset with a shield-shaped plaque of silver engraved LE IER CONSUL/AU C^{EN} DEVIN/BRIG^{ER} DES GARDES/DU G^{AL} EN CHEF A/ST DOMINIQUE POUR/ACTIONS D'ECLAT. Plain round barrel inscribed at the breech ENT^{SE} BOUTET, and stamped with the initials of the *contrôleur* Pierre Bouny, and the mark of the *inspecteur* d'Audigne.

Dimensions: Length overall, 45 in (114.3 cm)   Length of barrel, 30 in (76.2 cm)
Calibre, .67 in (15 bore)   Weight, 6 lb 15 oz (3.15 kg).
(XII 1121)

82
Breech-loading, centre-fire, double-barrelled sporting gun
French, Paris, about 1815.

This type of gun, the first centre-fire, breech-loading firearm using a self-obdurating, reloadable cartridge, is rightly regarded as the ancestor of the modern gun. It was the invention of the Swiss engineer and balloonist Samuel Johannes Pauly (1766–1819?), who patented the system in Paris in 1812. Pauly worked in Paris from 1809 until its fall to the allied armies in 1814, apparently sharing a workshop with the gunmaker Prélat at 4 Rue des Trois Frères. One of the craftsmen who worked for Pauly in Paris was a journeyman lockmaker called von Dreyse, who later invented the needle-fire gun. Pauly's invention was tested by various French military authorities and was even brought to the attention of Napoleon, but it was generally considered to be impractical as a military weapon. In 1814 Pauly moved from Paris to London where he continued his interest in the design of balloons and worked on various other firearm inventions, including a system for igniting the powder-charge of a gun by means of compressed air, and an ingenious cannon-lock which was rejected as 'quite inapplicable to the Service' when submitted to the Board of Ordnance in 1818. Pauly's French patent of 1812 described two types of breeches, a drop-barrel break-action, which is represented in the Armouries by a seven-barrel volley gun (Inv. No. XII. 1761), and a lifting-block action, as on this gun. The gun is difficult to date, but was probably made by one of Pauly's successors at the workshop in the Rue de Trois Frères in Paris, the continued use of Pauly's name being explained by the patent protection which lasted until 1822. Stamped on the barrel is a mark, which is probably that of the barrel-maker A. Renette, who is known to have been working in Paris in about 1820. Two other very similar guns are known (one in a private collection, the other in the Tøjhusmuseum, Copenhagen, Cat. No. B. 1922:1), and presumably these are also the work of one of Pauly's successors. While the Tower's gun is stamped with the serial number 252 these others bear the numbers 241 and 437 respectively.

Provenance: collection of Squadron-Leader F.L. Butcher; purchased by the Armouries at Sotheby's, 7 November 1952, lot 15.

Fully enclosed action with external cocking-levers. The breech-block, containing the striking-pins, is pivoted to the rear-end of the barrel, and is opened for the insertion of a cartridge by a lever set into the small of the butt. Beneath this breech-block is housed the main-spring and cocking mechanism which is operated by the scrolling cocking-levers. The action-housing is inscribed on the left side INVENTION PAULY, and on the right BREVETÉ À PARIS, and is decorated with scrolling foliage, birds, wyverns, fruit, and flowers. The number 252 is stamped on various parts of the action, together with the letters CT, probably the initials of the finisher, and the letter M above the number 38. Wooden half-stock, chequered at the fore-end and at the small of the butt. Beneath the front of the shoulder stock is a grotesque bearded mask with a feathered head-dress. Steel furniture engraved in places with flowers, fruit, feathers, and, on the trigger-guard, with a swan. Double side-by-side barrels of browned twist steel, the breech and fore-end inlaid in gold with running vine patterns, and the breech stamped with a barrel-maker's mark. At the breech the barrels are fitted with trunnions which are secured through the sides of the action-housing by large screws. The accompanying centre-fire cartridge is similar to a modern shotgun cartridge. The base is made of turned brass with a depression in the centre to contain the detonating powder, from which a short tube leads into the cartridge. Around the base would have been glued a paper case for the charge and shot.

Dimensions: Length overall, 47.5 in (120.7 cm)   Length of barrel, 29.75 in (75.6 cm)
Calibre, .615 in (20 bore)   Weight, 6 lb 9 oz (2.98 kg).

Literature: W. Reid, 'Pauly, Gun-Designer', *Journal of the Arms and Armour Society*, 1958, II, No. 10, pp. 184–5, No. 11, pp. 206–7; H.L. Blackmore, *Guns and rifles of the world*, No. 453. (XII 1565)

83
Flintlock revolver
British, London, about 1825.

Revolvers had been produced in small numbers in the seventeenth century (*see* 67), but the first to be made in any quantity were those apparently invented by Captain Artemus Wheeler of Concord, Massachusetts, who was granted an American Patent in 1818 for a 'Gun to discharge 7 or more times'. This system was brought to Europe by Cornelius Coolidge, who patented it in France in 1819, and Elisha H. Collier, who was granted a patent for an improved version in London in 1818. Collier's revolver as patented was a single-action weapon, the cylinder being rotated automatically by a coiled spring, which had first to be wound up like a watch. Unfortunately Collier's 'improvements' resulted in a very complicated and unreliable mechanism which was rejected by the Board of Ordnance at a trial in 1819. In order to simplify the mechanism Collier omitted the automatic rotator from his later models, but even so a rotating percussion-lock rifle of this kind was again rejected by the Board of Ordnance in 1824. Following his second failure to interest the military authorities in his invention, Collier turned to the sporting market and between 1824 and 1827 (first at 54 Strand, and from 1825 at 3 North Side, Royal Exchange), Collier retailed flintlock and percussion revolving firearms, both pistols and long-guns. It appears that both the cylinders and barrels were manufactured for him by John Evans, an engine, lathe, and tool-maker who worked at 114 Wardour Street, Soho. Subsequently Collier gave up his interest in the design and manufacture of revolvers and returned to his original profession as an engineer. In 1851, however, he claimed that during his years in the gun trade, he had sold over £10,000 worth of rifles, shotguns, and pistols, mainly for the Indian market. This pistol is a typical example of the simplified version of his system retailed by Collier between 1824 and 1827. The fact that it is numbered 25 suggests an early rather than a late date of manufacture. A very similar Collier revolver, numbered 14, is in the Victoria and Albert Museum (Reg. No. M.6–1927).

Provenance: sold at Christie's, 14 December 1976; purchased by the Armouries in 1977.

Back-action lock with a loop-necked cock, the top jaw a replacement. The flat lock-plate is engraved with foliate scrolls and a trophy of arms, and is signed E H COLLIER 25 PATENT. The hand-rotated cylinder has five chambers and is equipped at the front with a flash-guard. The forward end of each chamber is counter-sunk, and the breech of the barrel is chamfered to form a gas-tight seal, the cylinder being pressed forward against the barrel by a helical spring at the rear. Attached to the top-strap above the cylinder is the frizzle which incorporates a linked, automatic priming magazine. Chequered walnut half-stock with no cap to the flat butt, the left side inlaid with a silver star showing traces of gilding. Rectangular silver escutcheon. Blued mounts engraved with martial trophies. Brass-mounted ramrod, the rear-end to take a screw-jag. The octagonal, smooth-bore barrel is engraved on the top flat with a trophy of arms and E H COLLIER 25 LONDON. It is equipped with a small silver leaf fore-sight, and a notched-block back-sight.

Dimensions: Length overall 26.25 in (66.7 cm)   Length of barrel, 6.25 in (15.9 cm)
Calibre, .473 in (44 bore)   Weight, 2 lb 2 oz (0.964 kg).
(XII 4000)

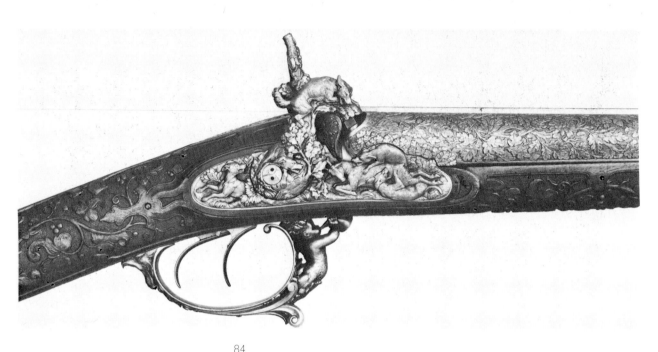

84
Double-barrelled percussion shotgun
French, Paris, 1860.

This superbly decorated gun is a magnificent example of the lavishly ornamented firearms produced in the mid-nineteenth century by the best European makers as both presentation and exhibition pieces. It was made in 1860 by the Parisian gunmaker Lepage-Moutier, and was one of a number of guns exhibited by him in the International Exhibition held at South Kensington in 1862 at which he was awarded a medal 'for the quality and beauty of his workmanship in his guns and pistols'. Lepage-Moutier is recorded working at 8 Rue de Richelieu, Paris, between 1842 and 1868. His services were sought after by many wealthy patrons including, before 1848, the French royal family. Another very similar gun by the same maker, also dated 1860, was presented in 1879 to Don Manuel Gonzales, President of Mexico, by M. Paul Jules Grevy, President of France. The decoration of both guns is copied closely from designs in Charles Claesen's *Recueil d'ornements et de sujets pour être appliqués a l'ornementation des armes*, Liege 1857. As in the seventeenth-century, weapons of this quality were in reality the result of the combined skills of many craftsmen, and it is therefore difficult to tell how much of the gun was made or decorated by the gunmaker himself. The superb decoration on all the steel parts is obviously the work of a highly skilled chiseller, and the beautiful carving of the stock is possibly the work of a master wood-carver. The barrel is signed by the Paris barrel-maker Leopold Bernard, who was active between about 1832 and 1870. The result of all these combined talents is one of the most important and beautiful examples of nineteenth-century art in the Armouries.

Provenance: purchased by the Armouries from a private collection in 1979, with the aid of the National Art-Collections Fund, after the Board of Trade had refused on export licence.

Bright steel percussion locks heavily chiselled with hunting scenes of dogs attacking a roe deer and a boar. The lock-plate is stamped on the inside with the number 1895. The half-stock of walnut is deeply carved with floral scrolls. The bright steel butt-plate is cast and chased with Diana surrounded by naked female attendants, the trigger-guard with a cherub blowing a hunting horn, and the fore-end cap with a stag's head. The butt-cap is secured by an ingenious extension of the lower sling-swivel. The double side-by-side barrels are of bright steel, the breeches and muzzles chiselled with a pattern of oak leaves, and the central rib signed LE PAGE MOUTIER ARQ^{ER} BREVETE A PARIS. The barrels are stamped underneath with the barrel-maker's name LEOPOLD BERNARD CANNIONIER A PARIS; his marks (LB under a crown and over a star); the Légion d'Honneur; the serial numbers of the barrel and of the gun, 13061 and 1895 respectively, and the date, 1860.

Dimensions: Length overall, 46.5 in (118.2 cm)   Length of barrel, 30 in (76.2 cm)
Calibre, .65 in (16 bore)   Weight, 7 lb 6 oz (3.35 kg).

Exhibited: International Exhibition, South Kensington, 1862.

Literature: J.B. Waring, *Masterpieces of industrial art and sculpture at the International Exhibition. I. 1862*, London 1863; anon. *The Burlington Magazine*, Vol. CXXIII, No.937, 1981, p. 269. (XII 4751)

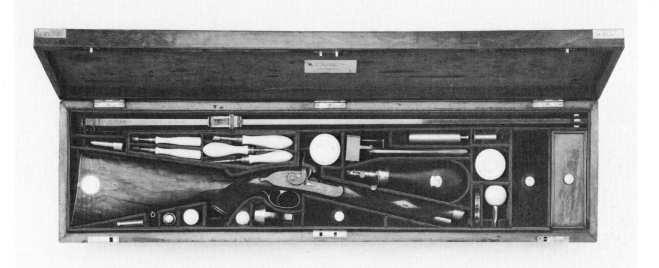

85
Cased presentation percussion target rifle
British, Edinburgh, 1861.

The adoption of the Enfield rifle as the standard weapon of all British infantry in 1853 created widespread interest in military marksmanship, and this was further stimulated in the late 1850s by the rapid expansion of the Volunteer movement which received official sanction in 1859. Late in 1859 various leaders of this movement met to discuss ways both to foster the movement and to improve the standard of British marksmanship, and on 16 November the National Rifle Association was established. The first National Prize Meeting of the Association was held on Wimbledon Common in 1860, Queen Victoria firing the first shot from a fixed Whitworth rifle, and, not surprisingly, scoring a bulls-eye. The Queen was genuinely enthusiastic about the Association and the Volunteer movement and gave an annual prize of £250 for a competition among the Volunteers. The first Queen's Prize shoot was won by the young Scottish marksman E.C.R. Ross (later Lord Ross of Halkhead), who scored 24 ex 60, 3 points higher than the runner-up Lord Feilding. This cased rifle was presented to him by a 'number of his fellow countrymen, now resident in Australia' in commemoration of this success. It is typical of many similar all-purpose target rifles produced in the 1860s, with fully adjustable but simple sighting which contrasted with the far more intricate aperture sights found on contemporary Match rifles, which were designed exclusively for competitive shooting at very long ranges. It was made in 1861 by the Edinburgh gunmaker Joseph Harkom, who was active between 1840 and 1875, and who worked at 32 Princes Street, the address on this gun, from 1856.

Provenance: purchased by the Armouries at Christie's, 18 July 1973, lot 208.

Flat lock-plate with a safety-catch ahead of the cock, decorated with scroll engraving and signed HARKOM. Half-stock of figured walnut with chequered pistol-grip and fore-end. Silver mounts decorated with scroll engraving and bearing the Edinburgh hallmark and the date letter for 1861. The escutcheon and circular patch-box lid are of gold, the latter engraved with an inscription (*see illus.*). The octagonal browned twist barrel is engraved with scroll-work at the muzzle and the breech, and is rifled with seven-groove rifling, the lands being not flat but convex. The barrel bears London commercial proof-marks, and, in several places, the number 700, and is signed JOSEPH HARKOM, 32 PRINCES ST, EDINBURGH. There is an engraved platinum vent plug. The fore-sight is hooded and is laterally adjustable for windage. The elevating back-sight is graduated up to 1000 yards. The rosewood case is lined in red velvet and contains ivory-mounted accessories, a powder-flask of the type patented by Thomas Sykes in 1814, a trade label, and the original leather outer cover. The outside of the box has plate-silver fittings and a central escutcheon bearing the crest and motto of Lord Ross of Halkhead, a hawk's head erased with beneath the words THINK ON.

Dimensions: Length overall, 52.75 in (134 cm) Length of barrel, 36.12 in (91.8 cm)
Calibre, .465 in (46 bore) Weight, 9 lb 2 oz (4.17 kg)
Weight of box, gun, and accessories, 30 lb 3 oz (13.69 kg).
(XII 3528)

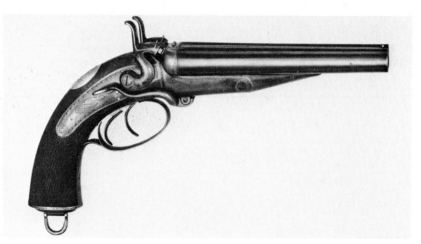

86
Cased centre-fire howdah pistol
British, London, 1875.

In India, dangerous game, such as tiger, was often hunted from the back of an elephant, the hunter firing from the shelter of a howdah. One of the dangers of this form of hunting was that the tiger might spring onto the elephant and attack the occupants of the howdah, and for this reason when, in the nineteenth century, British officers and officials took up this type of hunting, a special type of pistol was developed, powerful enough to knock down a tiger with one shot. These pistols are today known as 'howdah' pistols although there is no evidence that this term was ever used in the nineteenth century. Howdah pistols, which were produced from the era of the flintlock to that of centre-fire ignition, are generally double-barrelled, the barrels being of at least half-inch bore and strong enough to take a very heavy powder charge. This example is one of twenty centre-fire howdah pistols supplied in 1875 by Wilkinson & Sons to the Prince of Wales (later King Edward VII) for presentation by him both to members of his entourage and to Indian dignitaries on his tour to India during 1875 and 1876. Each pistol bore the Prince of Wales' crest and was supplied in a case complete with accessories. Seven of these twenty pistols, which were numbered between 6552 and 6571, have so far been identified, and some, although not this example, include among the accessories a pair of percussion nipples and a bag of caps which suggests that these pistols were capable of being fired by percussion ignition if the centre-fire ammunition ran out. The ammunition the pistols were designed to fire under normal circumstances was the .577 inch short Boxer cartridge which was very popular for such howdah pistols. The Boxer cartridge, which was adopted by the British military authorities for use with the Snider rifle, was patented in 1866 by Colonel Edward Mounier Boxer, Superintendent of the Royal Laboratory, but was in fact largely copied from the cartridge invented in the late 1850s by François Eugéne Schneider. The London gun, and sword-making firm of Wilkinson & Sons, known since 1890 as Wilkinson Sword Co. Ltd, was a prolific supplier of howdah pistols in the late nineteenth century, production continuing until 1909.

Provenance: purchased from Puttick and Simpson's in 1953.

Back-lock side-lever action, with drop-down breech, ejectors, and rebounding firing pins. Both locks and action have a mottled, case-hardened finish. The locks are inscribed WILKINSON PALL MALL LONDON and are engraved with a rosette at the rear and with a border decorated with spiral scroll-work. Chequered wooden pistol grip, with a large gold escutcheon bearing in relief the Prince of Wales' crest surrounded by the Garter and the collar of the Order of the Star of India. The steel butt-plate has a lanyard ring. Double side-by-side barrels rifled with five grooves and engraved: on the top rib, WILKINSON & SON GUN MAKERS TO HER MAJESTY AND THE PRINCE OF WALES; and on the underside with Birmingham proof-marks, the serial number 6564, and the bore number 25. Complete in a mahogany case (not illustrated) lined with red baize, the lid set on the outside with a circular brass disc engraved with the Prince of Wales' badge and motto and bearing on the inside a maker's trade label. The accessories consist of cleaning-rod and jag, a striker key, two screwdrivers, bullet-mould, wad-rammer, and a powder-measure for loading cartridges.

Dimensions: Length overall, 12.87 in (32.7 cm)   Length of barrels, 6.5 in (16.5 cm)
Calibre, .577 in (24 bore)   Weight, 2 lb 14 oz (1.3 kg).

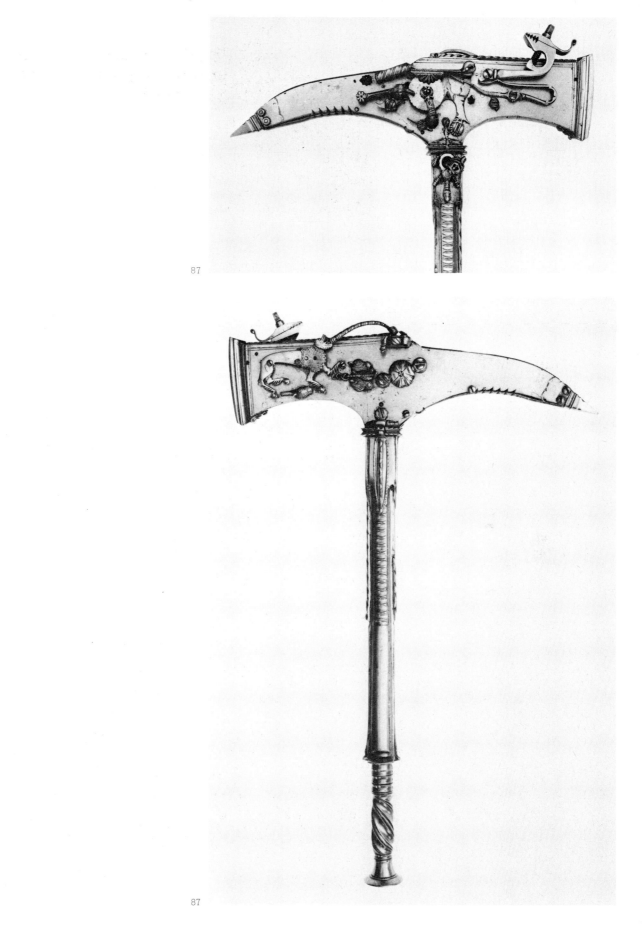

Literature: R.J. Wilkinson 'Double centre-fire presentation pistols', *Guns Review*, IX, No.12, 1969, pp. 494–5; anon. 'Royal Howdah Pistol', *Antique Arms and Militaria*, I, No.4, 1979, pp. 21–3.
(XII 1579)

87
Axe-pistol
Possibly Iberian or German, early seventeenth century.

During the sixteenth and early seventeenth centuries, when the gun was still regarded by some as an unreliable novelty, there was a considerable vogue for 'combination' weapons, in which a gun was combined with an edged weapon or sometimes even another projectile weapon such as a crossbow. Among the most popular, and certainly the most practical, of these combined weapons were maces, hammers, and axes, the hafts of which formed the barrel of a pistol. Many combined weapons, however, seem to have been produced more as curiosities than as practical weapons, and this axe-pistol with its six barrels and two locks can certainly be classed as one of these impractical curiosities. Because of the excessive weight of the head it would have been almost impossible to use either as an axe or as a gun, and, because the six barrels are fired one by a wheel-lock, one by a matchlock, and four by a hand-held match it would have been no easy matter to remember how to fire any one barrel, a problem aggravated by the fact that the axis of one of the barrels is set at right angles to the five others.

Provenance: purchased by the Armouries at Messrs Brooks, Old Bond Street, 2 April 1825, in the sale of a collection 'sent from a Nobleman's Castle in Bavaria'.

The hollow steel axe-head contains five barrels, the muzzles of which are concealed by a hinged cover forming the edge of the axe-blade. The upper barrel is ignited by a matchlock fitted on one side, the mechanism being concealed by a brass plate cut-out and engraved in the form of a lion. The second barrel is ignited by a wheel-lock, bearing traces of blueing, which occupies most of the surface of the axe-head on the opposite side to the matchlock. There is a tubular extension to the pan of the wheel-lock, intended to hold a length of match which would be ignited by the flash of the priming and then withdrawn to ignite the remaining barrels. The axe-head is balanced by a large down-curved fluke made in one with it. The steel haft contains a sixth barrel, also ignited by the hand-held match. Attached to one side of the haft is a belt-hook. The integral steel handle has a writhen grip.

Dimensions: Length overall, 21.8 in (55.4 cm)   Length of head, 15 in (38.1 cm)
Calibre, .31 in (150 bore)   Weight, 6 lb 8 oz (2.95 kg).

Literature: C. Blair, *European and American arms*, London 1962, p. 73.
(XIV 6)

88
Cartridge-box
German, probably Brunswick, about 1575.

By the middle of the sixteenth century it was becoming quite common in Germany to make up powder charges for military long guns and pistols into paper cartridges, and these cartridges were often carried in cartridge-boxes which are usually known today, perhaps incorrectly, as patrons. These boxes appear to have been normally suspended from the belt on a leather flap secured by a strap around the thigh. This example is one of two in the Armouries which are decorated with rather coarse embossing, involving mounted warriors, of a type characteristic of a group of cartridge-boxes apparently made in Brunswick. This group includes several in the family armoury of the Dukes of Brunswick which bear dates between 1572 and 1578, two of which were exhibited in the Armouries in 1953 as part of an exhibition of the collection of H.R.H. The Duke of Brunswick and Luneburg (*see Cat. Nos. 188–9*).

Provenance: collection of Ralph Bernal; purchased by the Armouries at the sale of his collection at Christie's, 5 March 1855, lot 2361.

Of wood, cased in iron, the box is semi-cylindrical and tapers slightly from the large splayed base to the sprung lid which is hinged at the rear. The casing is coarsely embossed with rosettes, lion's masks, and two mounted warriors, and the lid with a lion's mask. The wooden interior is drilled with five holes for the cartridge, and is reinforced by an iron cover-plate, similarly pierced.

Dimensions: Length, 5 in (12.7 cm)   Weight, 12 oz (0.34 kg).

Literature: C. Blair, *The James A. de Rothschild collection at Waddesdon Manor, Arms, armour and base-metalwork*, Fribourg 1974, p. 360.
(XIII 37)

89 (pl. XIV)
Powder-flask
Italian, possibly Florence, late sixteenth century.

Powder-flasks of this form were made in the late sixteenth and early seventeenth centuries for use with matchlock muskets and calivers, plain ones to accompany plain military muskets, and decorated ones to match the highly decorated muskets specially made for the ceremonial guards of kings, princes, and nobles. This example bears the arms of the Medici family, who were virtual rulers of Florence from 1530, and L. Boccia (*see* Literature) has suggested that it was made in Florence about 1565. The most popular motif for the decoration of such flasks were classical or biblical scenes, and this example is pierced and chiselled with a scene of Delilah cutting off the hair of Samson. Soon after its acquisition by the Armouries, in the middle of the nineteenth century, this flask was put on display in the Horse Armoury.

Provenance: collection of Ralph Bernal; purchased by the Armouries at the sale of his collection at Christie's, 5 March 1855, lot 2519.

Of approximately triangular shape, with concave sides, and a flattened top on which there is a steel cap and nozzle, equipped with a sprung cut-off, which are possibly of early nineteenth-century date. The body of the flask is of wood, covered with red velvet, now much faded, possibly a later replacement. On the outside, the body is covered by a steel plate, pierced, chiselled, and embossed with guilloche and strapwork involving human and monstrous masks; the Medici arms, with supporters in the form of a beast with the head and wings of an eagle and a serpent's tail; and a scene showing Delilah cutting the hair of the sleeping Samson and handing it to a warrior with a rope who waits to secure him.

Dimensions: Length, 9.4 in (23.9 cm)   Weight, 1 lb 2 oz (0.510 kg).

Exhibited: Palazzo Vecchio, Florence, 'Firenze e la Toscana de Medici nell' Europa del cinquecento', 1980.

Literature: L. Boccia in *Firenze e la Toscana de Medici nell' Europa del cinquecento, Palazzo Vecchio: Comitenza e collezionismo Medicei*. Florence 1980, appendix, p. 402. (XIII 10)

90
Powder-flask
English, late sixteenth century.

A musketeer's powder-flask, intended for use, like the last, with a matchlock musket. This example bears the arms which were granted to the Goldsmiths' Company of London in 1571, and it was presumably made for the use by a musketeer belonging to a body or company of men supplied by the Goldsmith's Company for the defence of London. Lists of London Trained Bands show that in 1588 the brothers Richard and John Martin, both goldsmiths, were captains of companies of soldiers, and that in 1599 Richard, who had been elected Lord Mayor in 1593, was still captain of a company of one hundred and eighty-nine men (*Journal of Army Historical Research*, 1925, IV, No.16, pp. 62–71). It has been suggested (*Catalogue*, 'Treasures of London Exhibition', 1976, No.8) that this flask might have been carried by Richard Martin himself, but there is no proof of this. There are in existence at least two muskets bearing the arms of London Companies (the Stationers and Haberdashers), but this is the only Company flask known to survive. When the flask was dismantled in 1949, it was found that the enamelled plaque bearing the arms was packed with pieces of playing cards, which Charles Beard (*see* Literature) suggested might be the earliest known examples of English-made cards.

Provenance: sold Christie's, 13 February 1913, lot 103, when it was said to have come from a 'private museum in the country' set up about 1800; collection of Sir G.F. Laking; purchased by the Armouries from Mrs Howe in 1949.

Of approximately triangular shape, with concave sides, and flattened top on which there is a gilt-brass nozzle, equipped with a spring cut-off in the form of the mythical beast the wyvern, or a similar monster. The body of the flask is of wood covered with red velvet, now much faded. The mounts are of gilt-brass held in place by three screws with lion-mask heads. The front is covered by a plate pierced with scroll-work, and is set in the centre with an oval medallion of translucent enamel bearing the arms of the Goldsmiths' Company of London. The base is covered by a plate pierced with strap-work. Two of the four suspension rings are missing as is the belt-hook at the back.

Dimensions: Length, 9.75 in (24.8 cm)   Weight, 1 lb 4 oz (0.567 kg).

Exhibited: Goldsmiths' Hall, 'Historic plate of the City of London', 1951; Fishmongers' Hall, 'City Treasures', 1970; Brussels 'City of London Plate', 1973; Smithsonian Institution Travelling Exhibition Service 'Treasures of London', 1976–7.

Literature: C.R. Beard, 'A XVI-century English powder flask', *The Connoisseur*, CXXIII, 1949, p. 25.
(XIII 149)

91
Pocket set of gunmakers tools
British, London, about 1690.

Pocket sets of tools for dismounting and repairing guns in the field were sometimes made to accompany suites of arms, and this set, which bears the badge of the Grand Duke of Tuscany and the initials F.M., appears to be part of a suite made by the London gunmaker Andrew Dolep for either Francesco Maria de Medici (1660–1711) or Ferdinando de Medici (1663–1713), sons of the Grand Duke Cosimo III de Medici. As Ferdinando is known to have been interested in military objects it is perhaps more likely that the suite was made for him. Hayward (*see* Literature) has suggested that it was probably a gift from the English Crown. A superimposed-load fowling piece by Dolep in the Armeria Reale, Turin (No.T. 105) bears the same badge and initials and is presumably part of the same suite, which was probably completed by a pair of pocket pistols in the Museo Capodimonte, Naples, and a pair of 'turn-off' holster pistols in the Clay Bedford collection (sold Sotheby's, London 15 May 1972, lot 306). Both of these pairs bear the Medici arms but not the F.M. monogram. The decoration on this suite of arms is Italianate in form and may be related to that found on guns made at about the same date in central Italy. Andrew Dolep was a Dutch gunmaker who settled in London shortly after the Restoration. In 1681 he was reported working for Sir Philip Howard at Charing Cross (*see* 71). In 1686, at the request of Lord Dartmouth, Master General of the Ordnance, for whom he was presumably working, Dolep was made a freeman of the Gunmakers' Company of London. He subsequently became gunmaker to Prince George of Denmark, and to the Board of Ordnance for which he made 'Three Pattern Guns' in 1711. He died about 1713.

Provenance: lent to the Armouries by E. Holland-Martin in 1948; purchased in 1973.

The tools are contained in a flat, rectangular steel box, with bevelled corners, engraved with military trophies and classical figures including on the back, a prisoner, and signed DOLEPI. One end has a nozzle-like opening into which some of the tools can be fitted and held by a screw; the other has a hinged lid. The nozzle-stopper is engraved with the crown and fleur-de-lis of the Grand Duke of Tuscany, and with the addorsed monogram F.M. The tools within the box consist of a spiral spring, a screw-driver cum handle, a hammer-head, three spring vices, and two prickers or drifts.

Dimensions: Length of box, 3 in (7.6 cm)   Weight of box and tools, 6 oz (0.172 kg).

Literature: J.F. Hayward, *The art of the gunmaker*, II, London 1963, pp. 61–2; H.L. Blackmore, *Guns and rifles of the world*, London 1965, No.83.
(XIII 192)

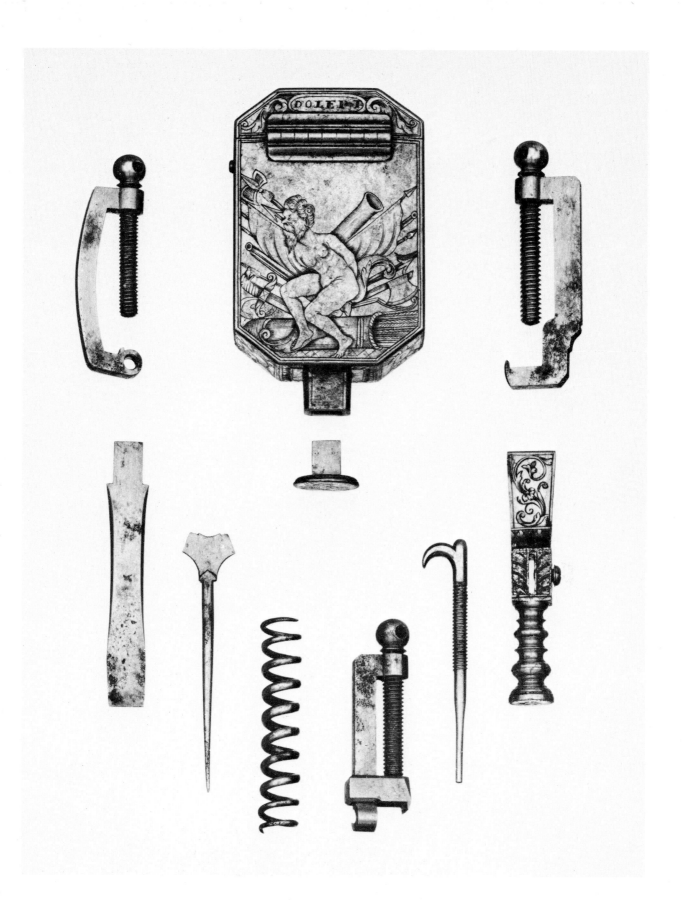

92 (pl. X)
Bronze cannon
Probably Flemish, dated 1535.

Especially in the sixteenth and seventeenth centuries the best European gun-founders sometimes produced for their noble and royal patrons lavishly decorated cannon, many of which are masterpieces of the sculptor's art. Such ornamented cannon were almost certainly intended as presentation or luxury pieces to be seen and admired rather than used in battle. This particular gun is signed by an otherwise unrecorded maker, MAISTRE DENIS, and is probably Flemish in origin. It was brought from Paris in 1816, forming part of the British share of arms 'captured' there after the battle of Waterloo. A similar but unsigned gun was in the Zeughaus, Berlin (1900 *Führer*, p. 178, No.57). The decoration of both guns includes the representation of a jew's harp. There is no obvious explanation for the presence of such musical instruments on these guns, but the German words for a jew's harp, *Maultrommel* (mouth drum) or *Brummeisen* (buzzing iron), may suggest an attempt to describe the noise of such guns in action.

Provenance: brought from Paris in 1816; transferred to the Armouries from the Rotunda Museum, Woolwich, 1930 (1864 *Cat.* No. II.3).

Of slender and elegant proportions, shaped as four staggered octagons. With the exception of the plain underside of the reinforce, the surface is richly decorated with high-relief casting, the forward part with symmetrical and formalised renaissance foliage, and the rear with gothic architectural motifs incorporating the arms of Hungary Ancient, and a jew's harp. The base ring (the raised moulding at the breech) is incised with the name of the founder MAISTRE DENIS. Just forward of this is a frieze consisting of peasant busts. The dolphins are cast in the form of the mythical beasts called wyverns, and the cascabel button as a winged mermaid. The muzzle bears the date 1535 and the number 394.

Dimensions: Length , 7 ft 10 in (238.8 cm)   Calibre, 1.7 ins (4.3 cm)   Weight, 3 cwt 3 qtr 5 lb (192.8 kg).

Literature: H.L. Blackmore, *The Armouries of the Tower of London: 1, The Ordnance*, London 1976, pp. 110–1, pls 8–9.
(XIX 166)

93
Small bronze gun and carriage
British, dated 1638, carriage mid-nineteenth century.

One of a battery of fifteen guns made for Prince Charles, later King Charles II. These guns are interesting examples of the miniature or model weapons which, in the sixteenth and seventeenth centuries, were often made for the sons of noblemen and monarchs, to interest them in the arts of war. Only ten of this set survive of which five, including this one, were cast in 1638 by the founder John Browne, and five in 1639 by the founder Thomas Pitt. John Browne, a member of a famous family of gun-founders, was appointed one of the 'King's Founders of Iron Ordnance' in 1618, and continued to supply both iron and bronze cannon to the Crown, and then the Commonwealth, until his death in 1651. Like most English founders of this period he worked in the counties south of London where the wood for the necessary charcoal furnaces was readily available. He owned a number of foundries, of which the largest, at Horsmonden in Kent, employed over 200 men.
These guns were first recorded in 1651, when they were in the Royal Armoury at St James's Palace, and were among items for the Royal collection which were put up for sale by order of Parliament. They were apparently not sold, however, for they appear in Inventories of the Tower from 1665 onwards, although by 1683 their number had been reduced to the ten which still survive. From 1750 the Tower Guide Books described them as made not for the future King Charles II but for King Charles I when a child 'to practice the Art of Gunnery with', but by 1817 the story had been corrected. The ten cannon were for many years on display in the Grand Storehouse, and in the 1841 fire one was badly damaged and all the original carriages were lost. The present carriages (not illustrated) were presumably made shortly after this disaster.

Provenance: Stuart Royal Armouries; in the Tower Armouries since 1665.

The gun has pronounced mouldings and an extended cascabel button of acorn form at the breech. On the second reinforce is cast the crown and three-feather badge of the Prince of Wales, and his motto ICH DIEN (I serve) flanked by the initials C.P. (*Carolus Princeps* – Charles Prince). Engraved on the first reinforce is the legend JOHN BROWNE MADE THIS PEACE 1638, and the weight of the gun 1–21.

Dimensions: Length, 2 ft 5.5 ins (74.9 cm)   Calibre, 1.3 in (3.3 cm)   Weight, 1 qtr 21 lb (22.2 kg).

Literature: H.L. Blackmore, *The Armouries of the Tower of London: 1, The Ordnance*. London, 1976, pp. 65–6, pl. 74.
(XIX 25)

94
Bow-stave
British, about 1545.

The longbow was used in Britain as a military weapon from the Dark Ages to the seventeenth century, and from the thirteenth century to the middle of the sixteenth century it was the major projectile weapon of the English infantry. By the time of Henry VIII the longbow was beginning to decline in popularity in favour of the gun, which, as Henry's first biographer, Lord Herbert of Cherbury, wrote, 'may be managed by the weaker sort'. Henry, however, made great efforts to prevent this decline, and the longbow was still the major projectile weapon of the English army until after the end of his reign. He sought to encourage archery both by his own considerable prowess and by strict laws and proclamations, and he imported enormous numbers of bow-staves, mainly from Venice (including 40,000 in 1510 and 30,000 in 1534), to ensure that his armies were properly supplied and his arsenals adequately stocked. This bow, together with another two in the Armouries and five others, the whereabouts of which are not known, were brought up from the wreck of Henry's warship the *Mary Rose* in 1840 by the brothers John and Charles Anthony Deane, who discovered the wreck while diving in Portsmouth Harbour in 1836. The *Mary Rose*, a ship of 700 tons, was laid down at Portsmouth in 1509 and largely re-built in 1536. On Sunday 19 July 1545, watched by Henry VIII, the *Mary Rose* rolled over and sank with almost all hands while sailing out of harbour with the rest of the English fleet to engage the French invasion forces. She carried a crew of 415 plus a contingent of soldiers, and 250 longbows are listed among her armament. Neither this bow nor its companion has at either end the notched shoes of horn, known as nocks, by which the string was attached to the bow, and ffoulkes (1916 *Cat.* II, p. 325) suggested that they were 'probably untrimmed staves, such as would be carried in store on warships'. Careful examination of the bows, however, suggests that horn nocks were at one time fitted to them, and that they were, therefore, almost certainly carried on the *Mary Rose* ready for use.

Provenance: brought up from the *Mary Rose* in 1840; sold by the Deane brothers at Portsmouth Point, 12 November 1840, together with other *Mary Rose* artefacts; acquired by the Armouries before 1845 and included in the 1845 *Guide*.

Long, straight stave of yew with a thick D-shaped section, the back (facing the target) flat, the belly (facing the archer) rounded. The stave tapers gradually towards either end. The tips are tapered to take the missing horn nocks.

Dimensions: Length, 72.75 in (184.8 cm)   Maximum girth, 4.5 in (11.4 cm)
Weight, 1 lb 10 oz (0.737 kg).

Literature: R. Hardy, *Longbow: A social and military history*, Cambridge 1976, pp. 21, 32, 54, 56.
(XI 1)

95 (pl. VIII)
Sporting crossbow
South German, early sixteenth century.

The crossbow made its first appearance in China in about the sixth century BC and has been in use in Europe since classical times. Crossbows of this type, with composite bows spanned by a cranequin (*see* 96), were produced in German-speaking lands throughout the fifteenth and sixteenth centuries and were used both for war and for sport, the military ones being very plain, those intended, like this example, for hunting, often being very richly ornamented. The composite bow, constructed of layers of wood, bone and tendon held together by animal glue, was used by the Romans and was apparently re-introduced into Europe from the East in the twelfth century. Although stronger steel bows were introduced in the fourteenth century, composite bows retained their popularity, especially for hunting weapons, well into the sixteenth century, probably because steel bows were rather liable to fracture, especially in very cold conditions. The decoration on this

crossbow is comparable to that on a similar crossbow which, in the late nineteenth century, was in the collection of Richard Zschille (see R. Forrer *Cat.*, Berlin 1893, No.1017), and which is recorded as bearing the arms of the Bavarian family of Fugger. It seems probable, therefore, that both bows are of South German origin.

Provenance: possibly the 'cross Bow, the Stock inlaid with engraved ivory', purchased by the Armouries at the sale of a collection 'sent from a Nobleman's Castle in Bavaria', held at Messrs Brook's, Old Bond Street, on 2 April 1825, lot 56; certainly recorded in the Armouries from 1859 (*see* 1859 *Cat.*, No.XI. 10).

Wooden tiller, much of the surface inlaid with carved, engraved, and stained plaques of ivory. On the side and underside of the tiller the ivory is carved with patterns of running leaf scroll-work, animals, and dragons, the ground inlaid with red, green, and black pigment: On top of the tiller the ivory is plain except for a panel of similar decoration just to the rear of the release nut, and for a heraldic shield (sable, a cross gules on a fess argent), surmounted by the letters MTS in a scroll, at the fore-end. The long, brass-covered, lever trigger operates directly upon the bone release-nut which is set into the top of the tiller and attached by a cord axle with a red leather cover.
A horn clip set longitudinally along the top of the tiller helps to retain the bolt when in position. Set through the tiller just above the front of the trigger are the steel lugs which retain the cranequin (*see* 96) with which this type of bow was spanned. The composite bow is covered with parchment tooled and gilt in patterns of moons and stars. The bow is attached to the tiller by a cord bridle which also retains the oval hanging loop of iron. Attached to the bow is the original bow string.

Dimensions: Length, 28.5 in (72.4 cm)   Span, 26.25 in (66.7 cm)   Weight, 7 lb 6 oz (3.34 kg).

Literature: G.M. Wilson, *Treasures of the Tower, Crossbows*, London 1976, pp. 6–7.
(XI 11)

96
Cranequin
German, dated 1747.

The cranequin, an early form of hand winch incorporating reduction gearing, first appeared in the second half of the fourteenth century and was used to span both military and sporting crossbows (*see* 95). Probably because it could be used easily on horseback the cranequin soon became the most popular device for spanning hunting crossbows. It operates on the rack-and-pinion principle. The cranequin rests on the top of the tiller of the crossbow and is retained by a cord loop attached to the wheel-case, which is prevented from moving forwards by lugs set on either side of the tiller. Once the cranequin is so attached, the arm can be made to move forwards or backwards along the tiller by turning the handle attached to the wheel-case, and in this manner the arm can be moved forward so that the double hook at its end engages the string of the crossbow, and then back, pulling the string with it until the bow is spanned. Once the string is held in the spanned position by the lock of the crossbow, the cranequin can be removed and carried on the crossbowman's belt by means of the belt-hook attached to the rear end of the arm. The cranequin was little used after the sixteenth century and this example is therefore especially interesting because of its late date. A very similar cranequin, dated 1727, was sold in Lucerne in 1975 (Galerie Fischer, 25 June, lot 68). Although uncommon, however, cranequins continued to be made occasionally until the first half of the nineteenth century – for instance one was made by Johann Christian Langpaur in 1824 to accompany the cased crossbow presented by the City of Augsburg to King

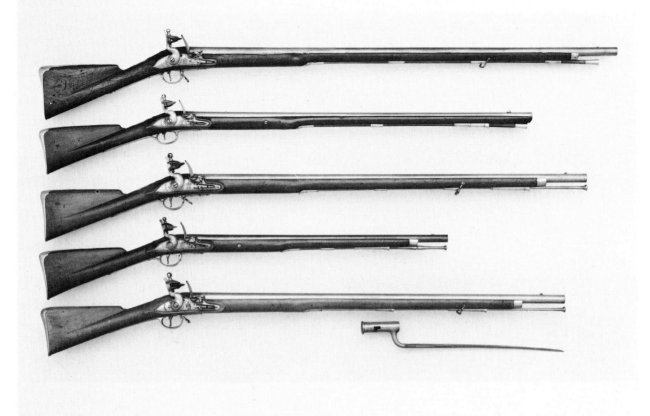

98

Maximilian I Joseph of Bavaria on the occasion of his silver jubilee
(Bayerisches Nationalmuseum, Nos. W.3102-3111).

Provenance: acquired by the Armouries before 1859 (see 1859 Cat., No. XI.19).

The toothed steel arm is etched with scrolling foliage and, near the double claws, with the letters
and date LN 1747. Between the double claws is pivoted a brass centring-plate, a later replacement.
The belt-hook has been repaired. The steel wheel-case, which contains the double-cog mechanism,
is etched round its edge with scrolling foliage, and is further decorated on either side by pierced
brass cover plates, that on the top decorated with classical deities, and that beneath with foliage and
mermaids. Attached to the underside of the wheel-case is the original cord loop for attachment to
the tiller of the crossbow. Straight steel winding lever with a wooden handle.

Dimensions: Length, 13.5 in (34.3 cm)   Weight, 5 lb 3 oz (2.35 kg).

Literature: G.M. Wilson, *Treasures of the Tower, Crossbows*, London 1976, p. 27.
(XI 24)

97–103
Weapons of the Board of Ordnance

From the sixteenth century to its disbandment in 1855, the Board of Ordnance
was responsible for the supply of arms to the British Army, Navy, and other
kindred forces, although this system of supply often came into conflict with a
parallel system which existed in the army alone, and which required the
colonels of individual regiments to procure the clothing, equipment, and
often arms of their own troops. The supply of firearms had been centralised
by the early eighteenth century, but the procurement of swords continued to
be the prerogative of individual colonels until 1788, and it was not until 1796
that the issue of standard pattern swords was centralised upon the Board of
Ordnance and its stores within the Tower. Until the beginning of the
eighteenth century, with only a few exceptions, the Board of Ordnance had
bought complete arms from contractors who were left free to arrange the
details of manufacture and of the issue of sub-contracts to the various
outworkers who supplied the different parts. While this had proved
reasonably effective, and was continued for the supply of edged weapons, it
was less successful for the supply of firearms, and together with private
procurement by individual colonels, led to the production of a plethora of
non-standard weapons with all the attendant problems of ammunition supply
and repair. Therefore, between 1706 and 1715 the Board of Ordnance
gradually adopted a new contract and supply system which was designed to
give the Board's officers far greater control over the various stages of
manufacture, thus insuring, at least in theory, far greater uniformity. Instead
of issuing contracts for complete weapons, as in the past, the Board now
issued contracts for parts only, which were then sent to the Tower for
inspection, acceptance and storage. From there the parts were distributed as
required to gunmakers working in the vicinity of the Tower for setting up as
complete firearms. In times of war and great need the Board of Ordnance still
had to buy complete weapons, often from abroad, but in general the new
system, with its obvious advantages of greater centralised control, worked
well, and was gradually improved. Most of the gun-stocks were produced by
London gunmakers, but the majority of locks and barrels were made in
Birmingham. At first Ordnance officials travelled to Birmingham occasionally
to inspect the work of these contractors, but for proper supervision a full-
time presence was required, and so from 1755 Ordnance viewers were
stationed permanently in Birmingham, and in 1796 an Ordnance proof-house
was established there. As the eighteenth century continued the number of
gunmakers employed directly by the Board of Ordnance increased and by
1750 there were about 100 gunmakers working within the Tower, cleaning,
repairing, and often assembling arms. It was only with such tight control over
the system of control over manufacture that the Board of Ordnance could
introduce the series of 'Brown Bess' flintlock firearms with which the British
army of the eighteenth and early nineteenth centuries was equipped.

97
Flintlock 'Long Land Pattern' musket
British, dated 1731.

In an attempt to increase the standardisation of the British Army's flintlock
musket, the Board of Ordnance had, since the beginning of the eighteenth
century, been attempting to discourage the private procurement of arms by

individual regiments. In 1722 the Board succeeded, and it was decreed that 'all Colonells who have any new Arms made shall be obliged to make them according to the said Pattern and proved and viewed by the Proper Officers of the Ordnance'. The first standard pattern musket, which seems to have gone into production in about 1725, was the weapon which is known today as the Long Land Pattern musket. It was not a rigid pattern, however, and underwent various alterations, for instance the change from steel to brass furniture which was ordered in 1730 (steel furniture was, however, still being issued for setting-up in 1736), and the change from wooden to steel ramrods which had been completed by 1757. Although the Long Land Pattern, with its standard 46-inch long barrel, was considered 'too long and heavy', it continued in service for a very long time. Despite the adoption of the Short Land Pattern (see 100) as the standard infantry musket in 1765, the Long Land musket continued to be made and used until the 1790s, largely because of the quantities of parts and completed weapons in store. This musket is engraved on the lock with the name of the merchant, gunmaker, and sword-blade maker Joseph Farmer, who worked in Birmingham from about 1702 until his death in 1741, and who is recorded as a gunmaker to the Board of Ordnance from 1710. When the lock of this gun was made his workship was in Old Square. At this time the manufacture of locks and barrels for the Board of Ordnance was under the control of a very few Birmingham families, which frequently inter-married and formed partnerships, and Farmer was a member of one of these families.

Provenance: Board of Ordnance; taken from store after 1916.

To the rear of the swan-neck cock the lock-plate is engraved with the name of the maker I FARMER and the date 1731, and ahead of the cock it is engraved with a crowned G R cypher and is stamped with the Board of Ordnance's crowned broad-arrow mark. The frizzle has no bridle. The plain wooden full-stock is fitted with brass furniture and steel swivels for the attachment of a sling. The escutcheon is engraved No.180, and the tang of the butt-plate No.33. The plain round barrel is stamped at the breech with Ordnance proof-marks and is attached to the stock by pins which also secure the rammer pipe. At the muzzle is a combined fore-sight and bayonet stud.

Dimensions: Length overall, 61.75 in (156.8 cm)   Length of barrel, 46 in (116.8 cm)
Calibre, .775 in (10 bore)   Weight, 9 lb 12 oz (4.42 kg).
(XII 99)

98
Flintlock cavalry pistol
British, dated 1744.

Early in the eighteenth century the Board of Ordnance produced relatively few cavalry pistols, but they gradually became more common as the century progressed. Until 1742 such cavalry pistols were produced in both carbine and pistol bore (shooting respectively 17 and 24 balls to the pound) but henceforth pistol bore became standard. Cavalry pistols were made in two sizes, with barrels both ten inches and twelve inches long. This is an example of the longer type. The lock bears the name of the Birmingham gunmaker Benjamin Willits, who received a number of Ordnance contracts in the second half of the eighteenth century. A Benjamin Willits is recorded working in Birmingham until 1817, and dying in 1824, but these late references must refer to another generation, perhaps the son of the maker of this pistol.

Provenance: Board of Ordnance; taken from store after 1916.

To the rear of the swan-neck cock the lock-plate is engraved WILLITS 1744, and ahead of the cock it is engraved with a crowned G R cypher and stamped with the Board of Ordnance's crowned broad-arrow mark. The plain wooden full-stock is fitted with brass furniture, and is stamped with a crowned 10 on the right side of the butt. The plain round barrel is stamped at the breech with Ordnance proof-marks and the number 59 over 2. It has no fore-sight.

Dimensions: Length overall, 19.5 in (49.5 cm)   Length of barrel, 12.06 in (30.6 cm)
Calibre, .6 in (24 bore)   Weight, 2 lb 4 oz (1.02 kg).
(XII 831)

99
Flintlock cavalry carbine
British, about 1770.

There is little evidence for the production of cavalry carbines by the Board of Ordnance in the first half of the eighteenth century, but in the third quarter of the century the use of the carbine seems to have dramatically increased and many patterns were developed. In 1757 it was decided that fifty thousand 'Carbines without Bayonets for Horse' should be maintained in the Tower of London, and it is possible that this carbine is an example of this pattern. It was made after 1764 when the dating of locks was abolished, but it is of exactly the same style as a number of pre-1764 carbines in the Armouries. The dating of locks was stopped because of complaints from troops that they were being issued with 'old', second-hand weapons, which were in reality weapons newly set-up from pieces that had been in store for some time. Henceforth Ordnance weapons were simply stamped, like this one, TOWER ffoulkes (1916 *Cat.*) states that this carbine bears the proof-marks of the London Gunmakers' Company but this is incorrect, the marks being normal Ordnance proof-marks. The maker's mark on the barrel of this carbine also occurs on a light dragoon carbine dated 1761 in the Armouries (Inv. No. XII. 158).

Provenance: Board of Ordnance; taken from store before 1916 (*see* 1916 *Cat.*, No. XII. 161).

To the rear of the cock the lock-plate is engraved TOWER, and in front of the cock it is engraved with a crowned GR cypher and is stamped with the Board of Ordnance's crowned broad-arrow mark and also the following marks: 3, crowned I, WH, H. The carbine is stocked to the muzzle and is not intended to take a bayonet. The furniture is of brass, and on the left side is a long straight sling-bar of iron. The wooden ramrod is the original. The plain round barrel is stamped at the breech with Ordnance proof and acceptance marks and with the maker's mark, I W beneath a star. At the muzzle is a large, domed fore-sight.

Dimensions: Length overall, 52.37 in (133 cm)   Length of barrel, 37.18 in (94.9 cm)
Calibre, .65 in (17 bore)   Weight, 7 lb 9 oz (3.43 kg).
(XII 161)

100
Flintlock 'Short Land Pattern' musket
British, about 1785.

From about 1740 there is increasing mention in the Board of Ordnance records of a musket of the same style as the Long Land Pattern, but with a shorter, forty-two-inch-long barrel, a length which had been tried as early as 1722. This musket is known today as the Short Land Pattern. At first it seems to have been intended not for the infantry but for the Heavy Dragoons, but in 1765 it was adopted as the standard musket for all British Infantry, although the Long Land Pattern (*see* 97) continued to be used until the 1790s. In 1770 the Short Land musket ceased to be used by the Heavy Dragoons who adopted instead a weapon with a forty-two inch long barrel of carbine bore. Despite the fact that steel ramrods had been in use as early as 1724, all the early Short Land muskets were equipped with wooden rammers, and even by 1757, when all Long Land muskets had been converted to steel rammers, considerable numbers of the shorter pattern still had the more fragile wooden ramrods. The Short Land Pattern musket remained the standard infantry arm of the British Army until the impact of the French Revolutionary Wars forced the adoption of the inferior India Pattern musket in 1797 (*see* 102). This particular example is a late production model which was probably made in the 1780s. It is stamped on the stock with maker's and store marks.

Provenance: Board of Ordnance; taken from store since 1945.

To the rear of the swan-neck cock the lock-plate is engraved TOWER, and ahead of the cock it is engraved with a crowned GR cypher and is stamped with the Board of Ordnance's crowned broad-arrow mark. The walnut stock is fitted with brass furniture, including an escutcheon on the small of the butt, and with two steel swivels for the attachment of a sling. The butt is stamped: on the right with the number 2; on the left with the initials FV, and SK, and with the number 52; and underneath with a crowned 6. The side-flat is twice stamped with the initials EP. The plain round barrel is stamped at the breech with Ordnance proof-marks. At the muzzle is a combined fore-sight and bayonet stud.

Dimensions: Length overall, 57.81 in (146.8 cm)   Length of barrel, 42 in (106.7 cm)
Calibre, 75 in (11 bore)   Weight, 11 lb 4 oz (5.1 kg).
(XII 3090)

101
Flintlock 'Elliot's' carbine
British, about 1785.

In 1769 a series of trials conducted by Major John La Fausille proved that the length of the barrel of a gun had very little effect upon its accuracy, and, probably as a result of his conclusions, short-barrelled carbines soon began to appear. The first of these was a carbine apparently designed for General George Augustus Elliot, which now bears his name. Elliot became Colonel of the Fifteenth, or King's Own Royal Light Dragoons in 1759, and an example of this type of carbine in the Armouries (Inv. No. XII.159) bears the inscription GEN ELLIOT'S DRAGOONS. Later examples of the carbine, like this one, were adapted to take a bayonet, and had an ingenious fitting to secure the ramrod. This improved model was approved by the King in June 1773 and was often referred to as the carbine 'with the catch in the nose cap'. Elliot's carbine proved very popular and despite the introduction of other, newer patterns, it was still in production as late as 1813. This particular example is especially interesting because, although it conforms to the dimensions and major characteristics of the standard model, it has been made up from the specially altered parts of other pattern weapons. It is possible that this was done because of the strain put on the Ordnance supply system by the American War of Independence.

Provenance: Board of Ordnance; taken from store in 1979.

The rounded lock-plate is engraved to the rear of the cock TOWER, and ahead of the cock with a crowned GR cypher. It is also stamped on the outside with the Board of Ordnance's crowned broad-arrow mark, and on the inside with the initials of the makers ID and HN, the latter probably referring to the gunmaker Henry Nock (see 102). The swan-necked cock is decorated with slight scroll engraving. The walnut stock is stamped on the butt with a storekeeper's mark, GR over 1785, and is fitted with brass furniture. The flat side-plate is of the Marine and Militia type, and the butt-plate is of the Short Land musket pattern. The trigger-guard is drilled at the front of the bow with a hole to take the sling swivel, which would not be required on this carbine which is fitted with a straight sling bar and loose ring on the left side. The steel ramrod has a button end, behind which is a swelling around which has been cut a groove or cannelure into which fits a lug on the fore-end cap. The plain round barrel is stamped underneath with the maker's initials, ID and ITH. The barrel is fitted with slots intended for retaining keys passing through the stock, but it has been converted instead for securing by means of pierced lugs and pins, presumably by the gunmaker whose initials RT are stamped by the slots.

Dimensions: Length overall, 43 in (109.2 cm)   Length of barrel, 27 in (70.7 cm)
Calibre, .65 in (17 bore)   Weight 7 lb 2 oz (3.23 kg).
(XII 4576)

102
Flintlock 'India Pattern' musket
British, about 1805.

In 1785 the Board of Ordnance, encouraged by its Master General, the Duke of Richmond, Lennox, and Aubigné, began experiments with the help of the London gunmaker Henry Nock, aimed at providing the British Infantry with a better weapon than the Short Land Pattern musket. Nock, one of the foremost gunmakers of his day, was born in 1740 and had been associated with the Board of Ordnance since 1770. By 1790 the revolutionary musket, with a screwless lock and a 13 bore barrel, had been adopted as the standard infantry weapon of the British Infantry. Unfortunately these fine muskets proved both difficult and expensive to manufacture and, to make matters worse, little or no large-scale production of the old Short Land muskets had been undertaken since the start of experiments to find a new pattern. It was against this background that Britain found herself at war with revolutionary France in 1793, and the Board of Ordnance was faced with an immediate need to obtain large quantities of muskets for British troops. The normal methods of supply were insufficient to cope with the demand, and the Board of Ordnance had to resort to more unorthodox methods. The East India Company was persuaded to hand over its stock of firearms to the Board of Ordnance, large numbers of muskets were imported from Belgium, and British gunmakers were given carte-blanche to send in as many trade and East India Company-type muskets as they could. The result was the replacement of the standard 'Brown Bess' musket by cheap arms of various shapes and sizes, and by 1797 the Board of Ordnance had decided that it must standardise production once more. With so many East India Company muskets in stock the decision was taken to base the new pattern musket upon these. The result was the 'India Pattern', with a 39 inch barrel, 3 inches shorter than that of the Short Land Pattern. It was an inferior-quality weapon, but it could be made and assembled quickly, and although standards of view and proof were lower than before they were still high enough for thousands of guns to be rejected. It was this pattern of musket which was used by the majority of the British Infantry throughout the French Wars. Between 1804 and 1815 when it was replaced by the New Land Pattern 1,603,711 India Pattern muskets were produced, and the total production figures from 1793 probably totalled nearly three million. The only significant change in design came in 1809 when the stronger ring-neck cock was substituted for the old swan-neck design. A simpler trigger, based on the New Land Pattern design, was also adopted at the same time. This example has been preserved, possibly unused, in almost perfect condition. File and vice-marks are clearly visible on the barrel and the stock retains its original light colour.

Provenance: transferred from Windsor Castle in 1972.

To the rear of the cock the lock is engraved TOWER, and ahead of the cock it is engraved with a crowned GR cypher and is stamped with the Board of Ordnance's crowned broad-arrow mark. The walnut stock is fitted with brass furniture and two steel sling swivels. It is stamped: on the underside of the butt with a crowned 6; on the right side of the butt with a government storekeeper's mark in the form of a crowned and addorsed royal cypher; and on the side-flat with a star, the letters TA beneath a crown, and the number 444. The plain round barrel is stamped at the breech with Ordnance proof-marks and a crowned 21.

Dimensions: Length overall, 55.5 in (141 cm)   Length of barrel, 39.37 in (100 cm)
Calibre, .75 in (11 bore)   Weight, 9 lb 11 oz (4.39 kg).
(XII 3507)

103
Socket bayonet
British, about 1800.

It was the development of the bayonet which, probably more than any other single factor, enabled the infantryman armed with a musket to dominate the battlefield from the late seventeenth to the early nineteenth century, for, equipped with bayonets and properly ordered, musketeers found themselves able to defeat the attacks of cavalry formations and thus were able to dispense with the unwieldy protection of massed formations of pikemen which had before been essential. The earliest bayonets were simply knives with specially tapered handles which could be fitted into the end of the barrel of the musket when required. The first recorded use of such plug bayonets in a battle dates from 1647, but by the 1660s they were in quite common use in the Low Countries by British and other armies. Later in the century bayonets were developed which fitted not into but over the muzzle of the musket, allowing the gun to be fired with the bayonet in position. The earliest bayonets of this new type had a number of different fittings, notably rings, but it was a form of bayonet with a tubular socket which was soon adopted by most European armies. It is still not known when the first socket bayonets were introduced in Britain, but they were certainly in use by about 1700. The earliest gun in the Armouries with a fixing for a socket bayonet is a musket by the London gunmaker Wooldridge (Master Furbisher to the Board of Ordnance from about 1718 to 1749), which is dated 1704 (Inv. No. XII.78). After some initial experiments, the form of the British military socket bayonet changed little until the second quarter of the nineteenth century, although the length of the blade and socket varied depending on the type of gun for which it was intended. This example is marked with the name of the sword-cutler and gunmaker Thomas Hadley, who is recorded at 47, Bull Street, Birmingham from 1781 to about 1812, and who supplied large numbers of bayonets to the Board of Ordnance. It almost certainly dates from the period of the Revolutionary and Napoleonic Wars and was probably intended, therefore, to be used with an India Pattern musket (*see* No. 102).

Provenance: Board of Ordnance; taken from store before 1916.

Made entirely of steel and consisting of a tubular socket which is cut with a longitudinal slot, forming two opposed right angles, which is intended to engage the lug on the top of the muzzle of the musket. The socket is attached to the blade by a curved shoulder of rounded section. The straight blade is of triangular section, the two outer faces being hollow ground, and the inner face flat. The socket is engraved A over 50, and the inside face of the blade is stamped at the shoulder with a crown over 29.

Dimensions: Length overall, 21.4 in (54.3 cm)   Length of blade, 16.9 in (43 cm)
Weight, 1 lb (0.453 kg).
(X 90)

104
Complete armour
North India, eighteenth century.

In the early nineteenth century the Board of Ordnance decided to turn the remains of the Royal Armoury and the National Arsenal into a comparative museum of the type just becoming fashionable. They, therefore, began to add to the collection oriental weapons and armour, of which this is an example. The East India Company gift and the purchases made at the various international exhibitions are particularly important because the place of origin of each piece is known for certain.

Provenance: acquired by the Armouries before 1859 (J. Hewitt, *Official catalogue of the Tower Armouries*, 1859, p. 107. No. XV. 306–13); lent to the British Museum in 1914 and returned in 1954.

Consisting of a shirt and trousers of fine butted mail diapered with a trellised pattern in brass with centres of copper. The shirt has a standing collar and facings of quilted black velvet studded with a pattern in small gilt nails, as well as a loose mail collar hanging in slender points over the back and shoulders.
Helmet (*top*) of hemispherical form (now lacking its applied central ornament, perhaps a spike or plume-tube), at the front is a sliding nasal-guard originally with loop, now missing, and a hook for securing it in the raised position, flanked by plume-tubes. To the lower edge of the bowl is attached a deep mail curtain of similar pattern to the shirt and trousers.
Cuirass of four octagonal plates curved to the body and joined together by straps and buckles (*char-aina*).
Arm-guards (*dastana*) of tubular form consisting of two gutter-shaped plates hinged together longitudinally, the larger one rising well under the point of the elbow, with quilted crimson velvet hand-guards studded with gilt nails.
All the plates are decorated with narrow borders of counterfeit-damascening (*koftgari*) in two colours of gold with a pattern of circles containing radiating fern leaves and tendrils. All the plates are lined with a padded peach-coloured silk brocade with flowers in fine gold orris thread and with leaves in light and dark green.
The shoes are of modern Indian workmanship.

Weight: helmet, 3 lb 3 oz (1.39 kg)   cuirass, 5 lb 14 oz (2.66 kg)   right arm-guard, 2 lb (0.907 kg)   left arm-guard, 1 lb 11 oz (0.765 kg)   mail shirt, 16 lb (7.65 kg).
(XXVI 8[A])

105
Shield (*dhal*)
Indian, Lahore, nineteenth century.

Provenance: from the Collection of Alfred, Duke of Edinburgh and of Saxe-Coburg and Gotha (1844–1900), second son of Queen Victoria, possibly acquired during the Prince's visit to India in 1869 and 1870; transferred to the Armouries from St James's Palace by Her Majesty The Queen in 1954.

Of steel, circular and slightly convex, with applied rim of semi-circular section and an inner applied border, fretted and foliate, and counterfeit-damascened in gold. There are four gilt bosses shaped like lotus flowers, through which are riveted the rings for the straps inside forming the grip. The decoration, in fine gold counterfeit-damascening (*koftgari*), consists of an outer border of scrolled foliage and flowers, four scalloped cartouches containing sprays of flowers, and a central circular ornament.
Lining of crimson velvet with remains of square leather cushion and hand-straps.

Dimensions: Diameter, 14.5 in (36.8 cm)   Weight, 3 lb 10 oz (1.64 kg).
(XXVI 22[A])

106
Sword (*tulwar*), scabbard, and baldrick
Indian, Sikh, early nineteenth century.

Provenance: presented to the Armouries by the Honourable East India Company in 1853 (J. Hewitt, *Official catalogue of the Tower Armouries*, 1859, No. XV 31); lent to the British Museum in 1914, and returned to the Tower in 1954.

The hilt which is entirely of steel has short quillons (*tholies*) the forward one supporting a recurved knuckle-guard (*paraj*) and a large saucer-like pommel (*katori*). The surface is counterfeit-damascened all over with sprays of flowers and foliage and bands of chevron pattern in rather thick gold outlined in plain steel against a gold ground.
The single-edged heavily curved blade of watered steel is of stout section, narrow at the hilt widening slightly towards the point. It has two narrow grooves (*mang*) close to the rounded spine, a short ricasso, and a bevelled cutting edge.
Scabbard of wood covered with crimson velvet with chape and upper band of gilded copper.
The baldrick or shoulder-belt is of crimson silk webbing with green borders and scrolled foliage decoration in gold orris thread. Slide-buckle of copper gilt.

Dimensions: Length overall, 34.5 in (87.8 cm)   Length of blade, 29.625 in (75.2 cm)
Weight, 2 lb 9 oz (1.16 kg).
(XXVI 138[S])

107
Matchlock gun
Indian, probably Lahore, late eighteenth century.

Generally known as *toradar*, matchlock guns of this form with straight,
slender stocks and light barrels attached by bands of wire or rawhide, were
used throughout central and northern India. The general form of these Indian
long guns appears to have been modelled upon the firearms used in Turkey.
However, a very distinctive and robust form of matchlock developed in India
which was both cheap to produce and easy to maintain and, although Indian
craftsmen also made both flintlock and percussion guns, the Indian matchlock
became so popular that it was still in use in considerable numbers until this
century. Many of these Indian guns were quite lavishly decorated. Stocks
were frequently inlaid with plaques of silver, brass, or ivory, and were also
often either lacquered or painted with flowers and animals, the favourite
colours for the ground being either gold or green. The barrels were often
inlaid with either gold or silver, usually, as here, in a form of counterfeit-
damascening known as *koftgari* work.

Provenance: first recorded in the 1859 *Catalogue* in a section of weapons 'acquired at various times
by presentation or by purchase'.

Internal matchlock of normal Indian form, the cock emerging from a slit in the stock. A holder for
the end of the match is attached to the right side of the stock beneath the pan. The wooden stock is
carved with foliage at the butt, the small, and beneath the fore-end, the carving at the butt involving,
on either side, a bird. The stock is lacquered all over in a natural wood colour, relieved by bands
and panels of floral ornament in red and green on a gold ground. The plate trigger is of recurved
form with a notched front, and is lacquered to match the stock, as is the match-holder. Attached to
the stock are two crude iron sling-swivels. The ramrod is of iron and is decorated at the top with a
band of gold *koftgari* ornament. The damascened barrel has a slightly belled muzzle and is
attached to the stock by eight cord bindings. It is decorated on raised panels at the breech and
muzzle with gold *koftgari* scroll-work. A rounded sighting rib runs the length of the barrel. There is
a bead fore-sight and a notched-block back-sight at the breech in the form of an Islamic arch. The
tang is decorated in gold *koftgari* scroll-work to match.

Dimensions: Length overall, 60.25 in (153 cm)   Length of barrel, 41 in (104.1 cm)
Calibre, .526 in (32 bore)   Weight, 6 lb 11 oz (3.03 kg).
(XXVI 119F)

108
Powder-flask (*barutdan*) and pouches
Indian, late eighteenth century.

In India a very distinctive form of powder-flask developed, shaped as a short,
broad horn, with the tip curling round in a tight curve to meet or nearly meet
one side of the flask just beneath the top. Sometimes these horn-shaped flasks
were made of horn, but often they were constructed instead of other
materials such as leather and wood. Both plain and decorated examples are
commonly found and often, as here, the decorated examples are complete
with a set of pouches, presumably intended to contain matches, wads, balls
and other accessories.

Provenance: said to have formed part of the Oriental Collection exhibited at the Great Exhibition in
1851; acquired before 1859 (*see* 1859 *Cat.*, No. XV.214).

The short, curved flask is made of horn covered with green velvet which is embroidered in gold on
the outside with herring-bone patterns within a border frieze of rosettes. At the top the flask is
pierced by a hole which is filled with a wooden plug covered with ivory carved as an onion dome.
The plug is attached to the carrying loop of the flask by a length of red cord. At the bottom of the
flask, which curves round so as to touch one side, is a horn finial carved as a lotus blossom. A
leather carrying-loop is attached to the flask by two iron staples, and by this the flask is attached to a
leather belt covered with green velvet. Also attached to the belt, each by its own loop, are three
pouches made of leather and covered in green velvet embroidered in gold on the outside. Each
pouch is closed by a strap and a buckle consisting of two gilt rings.

Dimensions: Length overall, 56 in (142.2 cm)   Height of flask, 6.5 in (16.5 cm)
Weight, 2 lb 3 oz (0.992 kg).

Exhibited: Great Exhibition, London 1851.
(XXVI 136F)

109

Turban helmet

Turkish or Egyptian, decorated in Persian style, about 1500.

Forged from a single piece of steel, conical but more steeply sloped in the lower part than in the crown. The point is slightly ogival and is topped by an ornament consisting of an inverted cone above a facetted knob. There are two arched openings in the lower edge for the eyes. Around the edge are a number of small rings for the attachment of a mail tippet to protect the sides of the face and neck. The nasal-guard is missing. The surface is heavily corroded and the helmet has been crudely repaired at some time. The decoration consists of counterfeit-damascening with fine brass wire with panels of arabesques, bands of imaginary inscriptions, and larger inscriptions in Arabic including the titles of a sultan whose name probably appeared on the part now most damaged by corrosion.

Literature: L. Kalus, 'Inscriptions arabes et persanes sur les armes musulmanes de la Tour de Londres', *Gladius*, XV, 1980, pp. 19–73, No. b. 5.

Dimensions: Height, 11.5 in (29.2 cm)   Weight, 2 lb 10.5 oz (1.20 kg).
(XXVI 125ᴬ)

110

Sword (*qilij*) and scabbard

Turkish, eighteenth century.

The jade grip is of a form until recently considered to have been purely Mughal, but it is now known that jade was also carved in this style in Turkey (R. Skelton, 'Characteristics of later Turkish jade carving', *Acts of the Fifth International Congress of Turkish Art*, Budapest 1978).

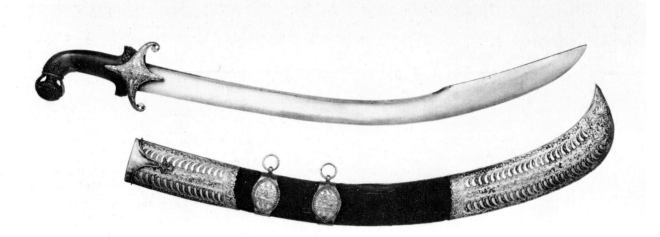

Provenance: acquired by the Armouries before 1859 (J. Hewitt, *Official catalogue of the Tower Armouries*, 1859, No. XV 622); lent to the British Museum in 1914 and returned to the Tower in 1954.

The pistol-shaped grip is of variegated green jade, the pommel carved in the form of a berry flanked by leaves. The base of the grip is recessed to take the pointed langettes at the centre of the short quillons which are tightly curled towards the blade. These are of silver-gilt engraved with stylised foliate ornament.
Broad, single-edged, curved blade of watered steel with back of T section for two thirds of its length, and with a strong chamfre for the remainder.
Scabbard of wood covered with green velvet with four heavy mounts of silver-gilt embossed and engraved to match the quillons.

Dimensions: Sword: Length overall, 33 in (83.8 cm)   Length of blade, 26.5 in (67.3 cm)
Weight, 2 lb (.907 kg).   Scabbard: Length 29.25 in (76.3 cm)   Weight 2 lb 2 oz (.964 kg).

(XXVI 101^S)

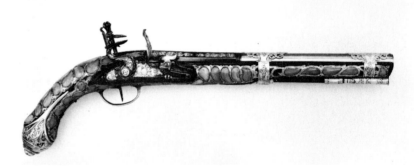

111 (pl. XIX)
Flintlock pistol
North African, probably Algerian, second half of the eighteenth century.

The great majority of pistols made in North Africa in the eighteenth and nineteenth centuries were based very closely either upon Turkish or upon European models, the former often equipped with miquelet locks and the latter either with flintlocks or snaphance locks. Such pistols were usually considerably decorated, although the ornament is not often of very high quality. The stocks were often inlaid either with wire scrolls or with larger decorative plaques, made of such materials as brass, steel and, as here, silver and coral. This pistol is of very good quality, far above the average, and, despite its very European form, it must have been the work of native craftsmen of considerable skill. Together with its pair, this gun is recorded in the armoury of George IV at Carlton House (No.3123) as having come originally from the collection of George III at Augusta Lodge, Windsor. Two miquelet-lock long guns and three pairs of pistols with identical decoration are still in the Royal Collection, together with a third gun, on which the inlays are treated in a rather different style (the long guns are currently all on loan to the Armouries). It is probable that all these guns formed parts of a number of different gifts from the Bey of Algiers to King George III and King George IV.

Provenance: collection of George III, Augusta Lodge, Windsor; Carlton House Catalogue, No.3123; Windsor Castle, North Corridor Catalogue, No.743; purchased by the Armouries at Sotheby's, 12 October, 1970, lot 34.

The lock is of conventional European form and has a flat-faced swan-necked cock and plain frizzle. The pan, although of normal proportions externally, has only a narrow internal depression, a feature common to Oriental firearms. The touch-hole does not line up correctly with the pan. The flat face of the lock-plate, the cock, the pan, and the front of the frizzle, are inlaid with plaques of silver chiselled with scroll-work. The wooden stock is inlaid with silver mounts containing polished droplet-shape plaques of coral. The facetted steel butt-cap is chiselled with scroll-work and terminates in a circular mount for a coral stud. The trigger-guard is silver as are also the two ramrod pipes and the end of the rammer. The barrel is of hexagonal section at the breech where the upper faces are inlaid with silver plaques chiselled with scroll-work. Half-way along its length the barrel becomes round, the change in section being covered by a transverse moulding. The barrel is attached to the wooden stock by a screwed breech-tang and by two silver barrel-bands, pierced and engraved with foliate scrolls.

Dimensions: Length overall, 19.25 in (48.9 cm)   Length of barrel, 12.12 in (30.8 cm)
Calibre, .615 in (20 bore)   Weight, 3 lb 5 oz (1.50 kg).

Literature: C. Blair, *Pistols of the world*, London 1968, pp. 158–9, Nos, 819–820.
(XXVI 114^{F})

Select Reading List

Introductory Books on Arms and Armour	A. Borg *Arms and Armour in Britain*, London 1979
	G.F. Laking *A Record of European Armour and Arms through Seven Centuries*, 5 vols., London 1920–1922
	H. Nickel *Arms and Armour through the Ages*, London 1971
	H.L. Peterson *Arms and Armor in Colonial America*, Harrisburg, Pa 1956
	W. Reid *The Lore of Arms*, London 1976
	G.C. Stone *A Glossary of the Construction, Decoration and Use of Arms and Armor*, New York 1934
Books on Armour	C. Blair *European Armour*, London 1958
	A.R. Dufty & W. Reid *European Armour in the Tower of London*, London 1968
General Books on Weapons	H.L. Blackmore *Hunting Weapons*, London 1971
	C. Blair *European and American Arms*, London 1962
	R.E. Oakeshott *The Archaeology of Weapons*, London 1960
Books on Edged Weapons	A.R. Dufty & A. Borg *European Swords and Daggers in the Tower of London*, London 1974
	W. May & P.G.W. Annis *Swords for Sea Service*, London 1970
	G.C. Neumann *Swords and Blades of the American Revolution*, Newton Abbot 1973
	A.V.B. Norman *The Rapier and Small-Sword 1460–1820*, London 1980
	R.E. Oakeshott *The Sword in the Age of Chivalry*, London 1964
	H.L. Peterson *Daggers and Fighting Knives of the Western World*, London 1968

B. Robson
Swords of the British Army, London 1975

J. Wallace
Scottish Swords and Dirks, London 1970

J. Watts & P. White
The Bayonet Book, 1975

Books on Bows

R. Hardy
Longbow: A Social and Military History, Cambridge 1976

E.G. Heath
Grey Goose Wing: A History of Archery, Reading 1971

R. Payne-Gallwey
The Crossbow, London 1903

Books on Firearms

J.A. Atkinson
Duelling Pistols, London 1964

D.W. Bailey
British Military Longarms 1715–1815, London 1971

D.W. Bailey
British Military Longarms 1815–1865, London 1972

H.L. Blackmore
British Military Firearms 1650–1850, London 1961

H.L. Blackmore
Guns and Rifles of the World, London 1965

C. Blair
Pistols of the World, London 1968

J.F. Hayward
The Art of the Gunmaker, two vols, London 1962 and 1963

A. Hoff
Airguns and Other Pneumatic Arms, London 1972

C.R. Riling
The Powder Flask Book, New Hope, Pa 1953

C.H. Roads
The British Soldier's Firearm 1850–1864, London 1964

A.W.F. Taylerson
Revolving Arms, London 1967

Books on Cannon

H.L. Blackmore
The Armouries of the Tower of London: I, Ordnance, London 1976
(with an excellent bibliography)

Books on Oriental Arms
and Armour

R. Elgood (ed.)
Islamic Arms and Armour, London 1979

P.S. Rawson
The Indian Sword, London 1968

H.R. Robinson
Oriental Armour, London 1967

Books on the Tower
and its Armouries

A. Borg
Heads and Horses: Two Studies in the History of the Tower Armouries,
Oxford 1976

J. Charlton (ed.)
The Tower of London: Its History and Institutions, London 1978

P. Hammond
Royal Fortress, London 1978

C. Hibbert
Tower of London, London and New York 1972

R.J. Minney
The Tower of London, London 1970

A.L. Rowse
The Tower of London in the History of the Nation, London 1972

D. Wilson
The Tower of London, London 1978

Glossary

Arms of the hilt

the 'C'-shaped guards lying in the plane of the blade and extending one from each quillon (*q.v.*) towards the edge of the blade.

Back-action lock

a lock in which the cock is set at the front of the lock-plate with all the mechanism behind it, a configuration which became popular with the invention of the percussion lock.

Back-edged

used to describe a blade sharp on one edge only.

Back-plate

a. the plate forming the rear part of the cuirass (*q.v.*)
b. the metal reinforce to the back of a sword grip usually also covering the end of the grip in place of a conventional pommel (*see* 33).

Ballock dagger

a dagger with the guard formed of two or more spheres at the base of the grip.

Basket-hilt

in the eighteenth century any hilt enclosing the hand. but today usually only applied to those resembling the Scottish claymore (*see* 28).

Basinet

relatively light helmet, often shaped like an egg or hazel-nut; fourteenth or early fifteenth century (*see* 8).

Blueing

the process of heat treatment used to give steel a deep blue colour.

Bore

the interior of a gun barrel. The diameter or calibre of a barrel is often measured as a 'bore' – 12 bore, 20 bore etc., the numbers referring to the number of solid lead balls, of the correct size to fit the barrel, which would weigh one pound.

Break-action

used to describe a breech-loading mechanism in which the barrel is moved or 'broken' from its normal position, usually by a pivoting action, to reveal the open breech.

Breath

the apertures in a helm or helmet for air.

Breech

the closed end of a gun barrel where the charge and projectile are seated before the gun is fired.

Breech-block

the moveable breech of a breech-loading gun through which the gun is loaded.

Bridle

a raised plate on the lock of a gun to secure working and moving parts.

Broad-sword

one with a straight, wide, two-edged blade.

Buff-coat

defensive coat made by buff leather thick enough to resist a sword cut (*see* 6). Buff leather is made by scraping away the outer surface of the hide.

Butt

the end of a haft or stock. For firearms the term is often used for the whole of the shoulder-stock.

Butt-box

a box, cut into the butt of a gun, with a sliding or hinged lid, to contain patches, wads, balls etc. (*see* 60).

Caliver	term used in the late sixteenth and early seventeenth centuries to describe a military long-gun, lighter than a musket, and generally used without a rest.
Cap-à-pie	head to foot.
Carbine	a light, usually short, gun of relatively small bore, intended primarily for mounted use.
Cartridge	a case to contain the propellant charge for a gun, and often including also the projectile and detonating charge.
Cascabel button	the knob at the breech end of a cannon.
Centre-fire	a cartridge detonated by percussion priming set in the centre of its base; a gun firing a centre-fire cartridge.
Chamber	the part of a barrel specially shaped to contain the charge and projectile. Sometimes the chamber is separate from the barrel and is inserted ready loaded into the breech when required. Sometimes the chamber is part of a breech-mechanism, such as the cylinder of a revolver, which is separate from the barrel.
Chamfre	the raised portion of the back edge of a sword blade towards the tip.
Chape	metal shoe protecting the tip of the scabbard.
Chasing	decoration worked on the front of the plate with a chisel, engraving tools, and variously shaped punches is said to be chased. Embossed decoration (*q.v.*) is normally finished by chasing (*see* 10).
Cheeks	the strips of iron attached on either side of the socket of a staff weapon to secure the head to the haft, and to protect the haft from cutting weapons.
Close-helmet	a helmet enclosing the whole head, and fitting closely around the neck; its front closed by a moveable visor (*see* 3).
Cock	the pivoted and sprung arm on the lock of a firearm which, on wheel-lock and flintlock guns, is equipped with jaws to hold respectively the pyrites and the flint, and on percussion guns is formed as a hammer to ignite the percussion cap (*see* p. 31). The term is also used as a verb to describe the action of preparing the lock for firing by pulling back the cock to its firing position, where it is held by a sear which can be released only by pulling the trigger.
Cod-piece	the plates protecting the genitals, fashionable in the sixteenth century (*see* 2).
Comb	the ridge, usually running fore and aft, embossed out of the skull of a helmet (*see* 3).
Corslet	a term usually applied to the armour of a pikeman (*see* 4).
Counterfeit-damascening	the process of decorating metal with patterns in gold or silver sheet and wire by hammering it onto a specially roughened surface. In true damascening (*q.v.*) the precious metal is inlaid into the surface.
Cuirass	the armour for the body, as opposed to that for the head and limbs.
Cylinder	the revolving breech-block of a revolver which is drilled longitudinally with a number of chambers to contain the propulsive charge and the projectile.
Damascened	a. steel exhibiting a 'watered' pattern produced by the structure of the metal from which it is made. b. also sometimes used to describe a 'stub-twist' barrel made by coiling a flat strip of iron around a mandril and lap-welding the edges together.

c. also sometimes used to describe metal decorated with damascening (*q.v.*).

Damascening	the process of decorating metal with inlays of a precious metal.
Dog	sometimes used to describe the cock (*q.v.*) of a wheel-lock.
Demi-hawk	a short firearm of the hackbut type, the name deriving from the hooks found on the underside of many guns of this type by which they were attached to a support.
Dolphins	the lifting handles on cannon, often shaped like dolphins or other animals.
Drift	a sharp-pointed instrument for unblocking the vent of a gun.
Drop-barrel	used to describe a breech-loading mechanism in which the barrel is lowered, usually on a pivot, to reveal the open breech.
Ejector	the mechanism for removing a spent cartridge from the barrel of a breech-loading gun.
Elbow-gauntlet	long gauntlet, usually worn on the bridle-hand, reaching to the elbow (*see* 6).
Embossing	decoration hammered up in relief from inside the plate is said to be embossed (*see* 10).
Escutcheon	the metal plate on the top of the small of the butt of a gun or on the top of the grip of a pistol, often shaped as a shield and frequently bearing the device or initials of the owner.
Etching	the removal of part of the metal by means of acid after an inhibiting agent has been applied to the parts intended to remain unaffected (*see* 3).
False breech	a piece of steel, shaped like the breech of a barrel and firmly secured to the stock, into which the real breech of a barrel is hooked. This construction allows the barrel to be removed easily when necessary.
Fence	a shield around the pan of a gun intended to prevent the powder flash, which occurs when the gun is fired, from annoying the shooter.
Field	the contemporary term applied as in 'field armour' to indicate that it was for use in battle rather than in a tournament.
Flamboyant blade	a blade of serpentine form.
Fluke	a curved point on the head of a staff weapon.
Foot-combat	a term applied as in 'armour for foot-combat' to indicate that it is for use in a friendly contest on foot.
Fore-end	that part of the stock of a gun which runs beneath the barrel forward of the lock.
Forte	the stouter part of the blade nearer to the hilt, as opposed to the faible, the more pliable part towards the point.
Fowling-piece	a shotgun used for shooting birds.
Frizzle	the pivoted and sprung 'L'-shaped plate on a flintlock which acts both as a cover to the priming pan and as a striking plate for the flint held in the cock (*q.v.*).
Full-cock	used to describe a lock which is cocked and ready to fire.
Fuller	longitudinal groove cut into a blade to lighten it without weakening it too much.

Furniture	the mounts, usually of metal, found on a gun-stock.
Gorget	the plates protecting the neck.
Gorget-plates	the plates forming the neck of some close-helmets (*see* 3).
Gilding	the application of a thin deposit of gold on the surface of the metal. In fire-gilding this is done by means of an amalgam of gold applied to the areas to be gilded, and then heated to drive off the mercury leaving the gold adhering to the surface.
Grandguard	the reinforcing plate fitting over the left shoulder, the front and left side of the helmet and part of the breast-plate, used in the tiltyard (*see* 3).
Greave	the plates protecting the shin and calf.
Haft	the wooden pole or handle of a staff weapon.
Half-cock	used to describe a lock in which the cock has been pulled away from the pan against the action of the mainspring so that the gun can be re-primed, but which, instead of being put at full-cock ready to fire, is held by a sear in an intermediary, safety position.
Hilt	the handle of a sword, consisting of grip, guards, and pommel.
Hollow-ground	a blade in which one or more sides of the cross-section are concave is said to be hollow-ground.
Jag	the notched end of a ramrod or of a special cleaning tool designed to retain a cloth for cleaning the bore of a barrel.
Jaws	the part of the cock which acts as a clamp to hold the flint or pyrites.
Knuckle-guard	a guard on a sword hilt to protect the knuckles.
Lames	the narrow articulated plates making up the parts of an armour.
Lands	the spaces between the grooves of a rifled bore.
Langette	tongue at the centre of the cross-guard of a sword-hilt in line with the main axis of the blade and placed sufficiently far from it to fit tightly over the top mount of the scabbard.
Lifting block	a breech-block which is raised for loading.
Lock	a term used to describe the mechanism by which a gun is fired. For later breech-loading guns the term 'action' is used instead.
Locket	the mid-locket is the metal mount fitted round the scabbard some way below the mouth, usually fitted with a ring so that it may be suspended from a sling on the sword-belt. The top-locket is the metal mount at the mouth of the scabbard.
Loop-neck or necked cock	similar to a ring-neck cock (*q.v.*), except that the neck is pierced not with a circular ring but with an asymmetrical loop or scroll.
Magazine	the compartment in a repeating gun designed to hold either self-contained cartridges or, separately, the propulsive charge and the projectiles.
Mail	flexible armour made of many small iron or steel rings each linked through its four neighbours. Usually the rings are closed by rivets, but occasionally in Oriental mail the ends are simply butted together (*see* 104).
Manifer (main-de-fer)	the heavy left gauntlet used in the tiltyard (*see* 3).
Match	a slow-burning taper used to ignite the priming powder of a gun. Usually a length of cord impregnated with an inflammable substance such as salt-petre.

Miquelet	a type of snaphance lock, common in countries around the Mediterranean, which is characterised by an external main-spring operating on the front, or toe, of the cock.
Muzzle	the open end of a gun barrel from which the projectile emerges when the gun is fired.
Nipple	the cylindrical seat drilled with a hole in the centre and screwed into the vent of the barrel of a percussion gun, onto which is placed the percussion cap.
Over- and under-barrels	the double barrels of a gun or pistol set one on top of each other, rather than in the more normal side by side configuration.
Pan	a depression at the outer end of the vent of a gun-barrel to contain the priming powder.
Parcel-gilt	a term used when an object is only partly covered in gilding.
Passguard	the reinforcing plate fitting over the left elbow used in the tiltyard (see 3).
Patch	a circular piece of cloth in which the ball was wrapped to make it fit firmly in to the barrel.
Patch-box	a box, cut into the butt of a gun, with a sliding or hinged lid, to contain patches, wads, balls, etc.
Pawl	a bar pivoted at one end and at the other end engaging with the teeth of a ratchet to hold it in the required position.
Pointillé	decoration made up of punched dots.
Pommel	a. the counter-weight at the opposite end of a sword from the point. b. the bulbous butt of a cavalry-type pistol.
Pricker	another term for drift (q.v.).
Priming	the small quantity of gunpowder or percussion compound which is ignited by the lock or action of a gun and which in turn ignites the main charge in the barrel or the cartridge.
Priming pan	another term for pan (q.v.).
Proof-mark	a mark indicating that a weapon has passed some form of testing for strength and quality of manufacture.
Qilij	a curved, single-edged Turkish sword (see 110).
Quillon-block	modern term for the thickened part of the cross-guard of a sword or dagger from which spring the quillons (q.v.).
Quillons	the cross-guards of a sword or dagger hilt. Hilts with knuckle-guards often have only a single rear quillon to act as a wrist-guard.
Rammer	the wooden or metal rod, usually with an expanded and reinforced tip, which is used to seat properly powder, ball and wadding in the breech of a gun barrel.
Ramrod	another term for rammer (q.v.).
Rapier	originally a sword for wear in civilian dress. Later as fencing techniques developed and the fashionable sword became a purely thrusting weapon, the name was applied specifically to swords with long, narrow thrusting blades.
Rebated	a term used of the blade or head of an edged weapon which has either been blunted or been made without a cutting edge.

Reinforce	a. additional plates to strengthen an armour are known as reinforces (*see* 3). b. the part of a cannon between trunnions and breech which is made stronger than the rest to resist the explosion of the gunpowder.
Release nut	a notched cylinder, usually of stag-horn, set into the tiller of a crossbow, which retains the spanned string until the bow is shot (*see* 95).
Repeater	a gun which can be fired more than once without re-loading.
Revolver	a repeating gun with a breech-block formed as a revolving cylinder drilled with a number of chambers.
Ricasso	the part of the blade near the hilt, usually only a few inches long, which is of rectangular cross-section.
Ring-neck or necked cock	a cock with a neck pierced just beneath the jaws with a large round hole, which combines maximum strength with minimum weight.
Round-twist	another term for a 'stub twist' barrel, made by coiling a flat strip of iron around a mandril and lap-welding the edges together.
Sabaton	plates protecting the foot.
Sabre	single-edged sword usually with a more or less curved blade.
Safety-catch	any mechanism which prevents a cocked gun from being fired until it is released.
Sallet	a helmet shaped somewhat like a sou'wester, sometimes with a visor, sometimes open-faced (*see* 9), sometimes with a vision slit cut in its front (*see* 1).
Scales	the slabs, usually of wood, of which two-part grips are made. The scales are positioned on either side of the tang (*q.v.*) and are usually secured by rivets through the tang (*see* 17).
Sear	the catch in the lock of a firearm which holds it at half-cock or full-cock.
Self-obturating	used to describe a cartridge or chamber which forms a gas-seal to prevent the backward leakage of gases from the exploding charge.
Shaffron (chamfron)	the plates protecting the head of a horse (*see* 3).
Shoulder-stock	the butt of a gun held to the shoulder for firing and shaped accordingly.
Side-plate	the metal plate on the side of a firearm opposite to the lock which acts as a washer for the transverse screws securing the lock to the stock.
Sight	a. the aperture in a helm or helmet for vision. b. mounts, generally on the barrel, by which a gun is aimed.
Single-action	used to describe that type of revolver mechanism in which the lock must be cocked by hand after each shot as opposed to a double-action mechanism in which the lock is cocked by the pull of the trigger.
Sling-bar	a metal bar attached to the left side of the stock of some firearms, notably carbines, and generally equipped with a loose ring for the attachment of a carrying strap or sling.
Sling-swivels	pivoted loops attached to the stock of a gun to which are secured the ends of the carrying strap or sling.
Small of the butt	the thin neck of a gun stock behind the barrel and in front of the shoulder stock.
Small-sword	light, thrusting sword worn in civilian dress from about 1640, and later in court uniform (*see* 23, 29, 35, 36 and 37).

Spine	the thicker section strengthening the back of some blades.
Spadroon	a cut-and-thrust sword, usually military, with a straight single-edged blade with a broad full-length fuller. (*q.v., see* 32 and 33).
Stock	the part of a firearm, usually made of wood, to which the barrel and lock are attached and by which it is carried and held.
Swan-neck or necked cock	a cock made with a solid, serpentine neck.
Tail-pipe	the ramrod pipe nearest to the butt of the gun into which the end of the ramrod fits.
Tang	a narrow extension of a part of a weapon by which it is secured to another part: a. for swords and daggers it is used for that part of the blade which lies inside the grip and which is riveted over at the pommel to attach the hilt. b. for firearms it is used both for the short tongue-like extension of the barrel at the breech by which it is attached to the stock, and for the thin strap attached to the butt-plate which runs along the top of the butt.
Target	a. a shield for use on foot (*see* 12). b. a mark to aim at in shooting practice.
Tasset	plates attached to the skirt of an armour to protect the front of the hips and thighs.
Tiller	the stock (*q.v.*) of a crossbow.
Tilt	the barrier separating the two mounted contestants in a particular form of tournament. Also the type of tournament in which this barrier is used.
Touch-hole	the small hole through a gun-barrel at the breech by which the ignition of the external priming is communicated to the main propellant charge within the barrel.
Trunnions	the large, transverse lugs by which a cannon is attached to its carriage; occasionally, smaller transverse lugs by which the barrel of a small arm is attached to a stock or a pivot mounting.
Tulwar (Talwar)	Indian sword, usually with a single-edged, curved blade (*see* 106).
Turn-over	the name used to describe a firearm with over- and under-barrels (*q.v.*) fired by one lock, the barrels being rotated to bring each in turn to the firing position.
Vamplate	plate fitted to the lance to protect the hand (*see* 1).
Vent	another term for touch-hole (*q.v.*).
Vent-plug	a plug, generally of gold or platinum, inserted into the barrel of a gun and drilled as a vent, the precious metal being resistant to corrosion from gunpowder.
Verre églomisé	a glass plaque covered on the underside with gold leaf which is then removed in places and the bare areas of glass painted with a design and varnished, the whole then being backed by a metal plate.
Vervelles	the staples fitted to the lower edge of a helmet which fit through holes in the leather edge of the mail tippet protecting the neck. A cord or wire passed through the vervelles outside the leather holds the two pieces together (*see* 8).
Visor	the moveable plate or plates, protecting the face.
Wad	a plug rammed down the barrel of a gun to keep the powder and shot in position.

DATE DUE			